The Constitution, Law,

and American Life

The Constitution,

Law, and American Life:

Critical Aspects of the

Nineteenth-Century

Experience

EDITED BY DONALD G. NIEMAN

The University of Georgia Press   *Athens & London*

© 1992 by the University of Georgia Press
Athens, Georgia 30602
All rights reserved
Set in Sabon by Tseng Information Systems, Inc.
Printed and bound by Thomson-Shore, Inc.
The paper in this book meets the guidelines for
permanence and durability of the Committee on
Production Guidelines for Book Longevity of the
Council on Library Resources.

Printed in the United States of America

96 95 94 93 92   C   5 4 3 2 1

Library of Congress Cataloging in Publication Data
The Constitution, law, and American life : critical aspects of the
    nineteenth-century experience / edited by Donald G. Nieman.
        p. cm.
    Includes bibliographical references and index.
    ISBN 0-8203-1403-X (alk. paper)
        1. United States—Constitutional history.   2. Civil rights—United States—
    History—19th century.   3. Slavery—Law and legislation—United States—
    History—19th century.   4. Sociological jurisprudence—History—19th
    century.   5. United States—History—1865–1898.   I. Nieman, Donald G.
    KF4541.C587   1992
    342.73′029—dc20
    [347.30229]   91-21385
                        CIP

British Library Cataloging in Publication Data available

FOR HAROLD,
constitutionalist, mentor,
and grandpa *par excellence*

Contents

Acknowledgments

Preparing this volume has been a labor of love, an opportunity for all the contributors to thank Harold Hyman, a man whose teaching, scholarship, loyalty, and friendship have been such an important part of our lives. Yet even in such a pleasurable endeavor there are myriad details to attend to and problems to be overcome. As editor, I have been fortunate to have the support and cooperation of many people who believed in the project and helped bring it to a successful conclusion.

The essays grew out of a symposium held at the New York University School of Law in May 1989 honoring Harold Hyman, the dean of U.S. constitutional historians. Dean John Sexton and Professor William E. Nelson of the New York University School of Law contributed immeasurably to the event's success by graciously making available the Law School's superb facilities. Allen Matusow, dean of humanities at Rice University, and Albert van Helden, then chair of the Rice history department, provided encouragement and generous financial support. Moreover, their presence in New York contributed to the symposium's success, as did the presence of numerous friends and colleagues who traveled from as far as Japan, Scotland, and England. Patricia Allen Lucie, William Wiecek, Norma Basch, Stanley Kutler, Jane Scarborough, and Kermit Hall chaired sessions and served as commentators. Although their thoughtful, witty, and often trenchant remarks do not appear in this volume, the essays are stronger because of them.

As the volume moved toward publication, the contributors made my task as editor a pleasure. They submitted polished essays, readily accepted suggested changes, made revisions promptly, and turned around the copy-edited manuscript quickly. Librarians at the Cooper Library at Clemson University and the New York University Law Library provided valuable assistance with bibliographical matters. Malcolm Call, the director of the University of Georgia Press, recognized the significance of this collection and offered wise counsel that improved the final product. Madelaine Cooke, the managing editor, moved the book through the production process smoothly and professionally. We were fortunate to have Melinda

Conner as our copy editor. She went over the manuscript with a careful and sensitive eye, pointing out a number of errors and inconsistencies and making numerous stylistic suggestions that improved the essays.

Special thanks are due to Les Benedict, a valued friend who helped at every stage of the project. Les served as co-organizer of the symposium, offering ideas on organization and format and sharing responsibility for the arrangements. Later, as I prepared the essays for publication, Les was a constant source of encouragement and good advice. Linda Nieman and Karen Benedict took time from their own busy schedules, helping with arrangements for the symposium and offering valuable suggestions as the volume moved toward publication. Ferne Hyman, a dear and valued friend for over twenty years, was a constant source of support and encouragement, offering sage advice on planning the volume and helping with arrangements for the symposium. Her warmth, enthusiasm, and intelligence have been, once again, indispensible. Finally, I must thank Harold Hyman. His warm friendship, support, wise counsel, humor, and—most important of all—his example have been an important part of my life and the lives of all who contributed to this volume. We offer these essays as a token of our appreciation and our affection.

D.G.N.

Introduction

The past twenty years have witnessed a dramatic revival of interest in U.S. constitutional and legal history. A number of major university presses now have substantial offerings in the field. *Law and History Review,* the *Georgia Journal of Southern Legal History,* and *Western Legal History* have recently joined the *American Journal of Legal History* as outlets for the work of legal historians, while law reviews and other historical journals are publishing an ever-growing number of articles on constitutional and legal history. Courses focusing on these areas have proliferated in history departments and law schools across the country, a phenomenon underscored by the growing number of textbooks available. The American Society for Legal History, the New York University School of Law's ongoing Legal History Colloquium, and numerous special symposia occasioned by the bicentennials of the Constitution and the Bill of Rights have brought together scholars from law schools and history departments, producing a remarkable cross-fertilization of ideas and approaches that has encouraged and enriched scholarship. Constitutional and legal history, moreover, is not only thriving as a specialty; its impact on the broader discipline is evidenced by the greater attention given to law and the work of constitutional and legal historians by those working in social, cultural, economic, and political history.

As interest has grown, the new practitioners have substantially redefined and significantly expanded the field. Traditionally, scholars focused their attention on formal lawmaking bodies such as legislatures and appellate courts. They were especially concerned with courts—principally the U.S. Supreme Court—and with tracing the evolution of doctrine. Even in the area of doctrine their focus generally remained quite restricted. Most stuck to constitutional issues that lay at the heart of the great political disputes, largely ignoring the development of private law and overlooking fertile fields of inquiry such as criminal, contract, tort, property, and domestic law. Few pressed beyond what was prescribed by statutes and appellate court decisions to explore how law functioned in actual practice. Although they were sensitive to the relationship between law and politics, most scholars failed to consider the social and cultural dimensions of the law.[1]

Influenced by the profession's growing interest in social and cultural history and the proliferation of interdisciplinary approaches, a new generation of scholars is asking different questions, investigating different subjects, and employing different methodologies. Recent scholarship focuses on the relationship between law and society by examining the impact of social and cultural change on the law and, conversely, the effect of law and legal institutions on society. Topics once ignored, dismissed, or considered marginal—women, the family, race, urbanization, crime—have entered the mainstream. With a growing number of practitioners formally trained in both history and law, there is increased interest in private law and a rich literature on the development of contract, tort, property, domestic, and criminal law. Although there has been a continuing concern with doctrine, scholars have not been content to equate law with the prescriptions of legislatures and courts. Increasingly they have turned to intensive studies of a single court, community, or case to explore how law is made or operates in actual practice. In the process, constitutional and legal history has begun to assess the impact of law on the lives of ordinary Americans.

The essays in this volume reflect the vitality and freshness of the new constitutional and legal history. All share a broad understanding of law. Instead of examining formal lawmaking bodies and the development of doctrine, the authors focus on law in actual practice: the social functions of law, the cultural values embodied in law, and the meaning of the Constitution and law to the powerless. The authors share a healthy skepticism of conventional wisdom and a talent for understanding the past on its own terms. Whether challenging well-entrenched views of the framers of the Constitution and slavery, arguing for the integrity of Victorian legal culture, or exploring the creativity of mugwump urban reformers, they offer tough-minded reassessments of the relationship between law and society.

The volume focuses on the nineteenth century, a period of conflict and transformation. The century witnessed the emergence and maturation of a new constitutional and political order, an urban-industrial revolution, fundamental changes in the family, the dramatic growth of the professions and their authority, the discovery and use of the asylum as a solution to domestic problems, bitter sectional conflict, civil war, and sweeping changes in the lives of women and African Americans. The essays that follow employ the unique vantage point of the law to examine these pivotal issues. They contribute to our understanding of constitutional and legal institutions and processes, but they also offer important new perspectives on American society and culture in the nineteenth century.

Two essays explore the impact of slavery—an institution that left few areas of early nineteenth-century society untouched—on the legal order. Phillip Shaw Paludan's essay offers a provocative reconsideration of slavery and the Constitution. Drawing on recent legal theory, Paludan contends that the Constitution was not designed to protect slavery and that Lincoln, in arguing for an antislavery Constitution, offered a compelling and coherent reading of the document. He also provides a way of looking at constitutional discourse that is as relevant to the late twentieth century as it is to Lincoln's day. Paul Finkelman's analysis of the South Bend fugitive slave rescue is a fascinating case study of the unbearable pressure that slavery placed on the legal process. Finkelman demonstrates that federal law offered slave owners potentially powerful remedies against escaped slaves and those who aided them and that northern federal judges often applied this law in a manner that was highly favorable to slave owners. Nevertheless, he shows that northern whites often bitterly resented the rendition of fugitives and, in the South Bend case, used the legal process to protect runaways and nullify a slave owner's legal rights.

Although frequently a tool of repression, law afforded women and African Americans the means to challenge oppression, playing a pivotal role in movements that had their genesis in the nineteenth century and would transform American life in the twentieth century—the women's rights movement and the black freedom struggle. Norma Basch reexamines *Minor* v. *Happersett,* the 1874 lawsuit that challenged the denial of suffrage to women. Skillfully blending themes from legal and social history and imaginatively connecting the debate over women's rights to Reconstruction-era reconsiderations of citizenship and republicanism, Basch offers a provocative reinterpretation of *Minor.* She shows that Virginia Minor rested her argument on broad constitutional principles, arguing that as citizens in a republican polity, women were entitled to vote. Although a unanimous Supreme Court curtly rejected this argument, Basch suggests that the case was nonetheless pivotal. Minor's argument was a conceptual breakthrough, appropriating for women the rights-oriented idiom of the constitutional order and boldly asserting that women were discrete, independent political beings.

My own contribution, "The Language of Liberation: African Americans and Equalitarian Constitutionalism, 1830–1950," also examines the influence of constitutional idiom on social discourse in the nineteenth century.

The essay shows that antebellum black leaders appropriated mainstream constitutional ideas such as citizenship, due process, and equality to challenge slavery and fight discrimination. Tracing the complex process by which these ideas spread and took root among former slaves in the South during the revolutionary upheavals of the Civil War and Reconstruction, the essay argues that blacks forged a powerful equalitarian constitutionalism that survived the end of Reconstruction, served as a potent weapon in the struggle for black rights, helped integrate blacks into American culture, and left an important imprint on the constitutional order.

Nineteenth-century constitutionalism placed significant limits on governmental interference with property but left government remarkably free to restrain personal liberty. By probing the social, cultural, intellectual, and moral underpinnings of the mid-nineteenth-century legal order, Michael Les Benedict's wide-ranging examination of Victorian moralism and civil liberty explains this paradox. Benedict refuses to dismiss or caricature nineteenth-century legal doctrines and practices that appear morally obtuse to many twentieth-century Americans: the fellow servant rule, contributory negligence, restrictive divorce laws, broad obscenity statutes, laws banning contraception and abortion, and criminal procedures that too often made a mockery of the rights of defendants. By exploring Victorian conceptions of human nature, individual responsibility, the economy, religion, the family, social reform, and the arts, he demonstrates how nineteenth-century legal culture was the product of a coherent worldview whose premises most Americans no longer accept. The result is a bold revisionist essay that integrates social and legal history to illuminate nineteenth-century legal culture.

David Courtwright's contribution explores the social and cultural forces that shaped the legal response to drug addiction, a major social problem in the decades following the Civil War. Courtwright begins with a fascinating paradox: as consumption of alcohol declined and drug use reached epidemic levels, nineteenth-century lawmakers enacted increasingly stringent sanctions against the manufacture, sale, and consumption of liquor but largely ignored the drug problem. Indeed, he notes, the nation's first "war on drugs" did not begin until after the turn of the century, when state legislatures and Congress passed tough sanctions against drug use. Courtwright finds an explanation for this long-delayed legal response in social and cultural phenomena: the demography of the addict population, the scientific and medical communities' view of narcotics, and middle-class notions of individual responsibility.

The relationship between law and society runs both ways; law is shaped by social and cultural forces, but it has a powerful impact on society and culture in turn, a phenomenon underscored by John Hughes's essay. Hughes offers an imaginative analysis of the process of involuntary commitment of the insane, using late nineteenth-century Alabama as a case study. The records of the Alabama Insane Hospital show that those incarcerated included not only persons who were clinically insane but also individuals who posed problems for their families: abusive spouses, victims of sexual abuse, alcoholics and drug addicts, aging unmarried daughters, and eccentrics. Commitment law and the asylum thus offered Alabamians new ways to deal with age-old family problems without addressing the painful underlying causes of those problems.

Law also helped shape the emerging urban landscape, as Harold Platt's essay on municipal reform in Gilded Age Chicago suggests. Traditionally, scholars have asserted that late nineteenth-century state reformers, with their antiurban bias and their hostility to active government, created restrictive constitutional provisions that prevented city governments from coping with pressing problems generated by rapid growth. Focusing on Chicago, which experienced phenomenal growth during the post–Civil War decades, Platt disputes this notion. He shows that despite restrictive provisions in the 1870 Illinois Constitution, Chicago's business elite forged political and legal institutions designed to cope with problems generated by growth. He also argues that a new style of urban politics emerged from this process. During the 1870s and 1880s, patrician reformers achieved their reform agenda by lobbying special legislation through the state legislature and by sponsoring test cases in the courts. By the 1890s, other organized interest groups began to adopt these tactics. The result, Platt contends, was a new politics of competition and coalition building among a variety of ethnic and economic interest groups—a type of politics that foreshadowed the urban progressivism of the early twentieth century.

All but two of these essays were first presented in New York in May 1989 at a conference sponsored by the New York University School of Law and Rice University to honor Harold M. Hyman, a scholar who has played a leading role in the resurgence of constitutional and legal history. Professor Hyman has written extensively on the war power and loyalty-security issues, including prize-winning studies of the nation's long and troubled experience with loyalty oaths.[2] He is perhaps best known, however, for his pioneering revisionist work on Reconstruction and his brilliant and often iconoclastic reassessments of legal-constitutional change during the Civil War and Reconstruction eras.[3]

Hyman's scholarship has helped redefine and revitalize constitutional-legal history. Early in his career he broke with the formalist, Supreme Court–centered version of constitutional history that had long dominated the field. Taking a broad, eclectic view of the constitutional order, he opened new lines of inquiry and dramatically expanded the purview of constitutional history. This is especially true of his influential studies of constitutional and legal change in the era of the Civil War and Reconstruction. Not content merely to cover well-traveled ground, Hyman went well beyond the stuff of constitutional history as traditionally defined— the amendment process, legislation, judicial interpretation, and executive action—to probe shifting attitudes toward government, law, and constitutionalism among the public and the legal profession and subtle institutional change in the executive, judicial, and legislative branches. He also explored the dramatic constitutional-legal innovation and experimentation that the war unleashed at the state, county, and municipal levels and the important role of voluntary associations in the constitutional-legal order. The result is a body of scholarship that in its breadth of vision and freshness has reshaped our understanding of nineteenth-century governmental-legal institutions and redefined the parameters of constitutional history.

In addition to his pathbreaking scholarship, Hyman has played a vital role in fostering the work of young scholars. A mentor without peer, he has produced twenty-seven Ph.D.s since his first doctoral student completed her degree at the University of California at Los Angeles in 1963. His seminars at UCLA, the University of Illinois, and Rice University have introduced a generation of graduate students to the excitement of scholarship and the rich promise of constitutional-legal history. Infused with his sharp wit and infectious enthusiasm, Hyman's seminars foster a free and sometimes furious exchange of ideas, teach neophytes to think and write clearly and to leave no source neglected, and nurture new ideas and unconventional research agendas. Like all great teachers, moreover, Hyman teaches by example. A creative scholar, a committed teacher, a generous colleague, a good citizen, and a warm, caring, and compassionate human being, he has offered his students a model for their personal and professional lives.

Hyman has also nurtured the scholarship and careers of many young scholars who did not study with him. He has critiqued their manuscripts, guided them to overlooked sources, offered encouragement and wise counsel, suggested new ways of looking at their subjects, and helped them find publishers for their work. Acknowledgment pages in dozens of books on constitutional-legal history and the history of the Civil War and Reconstruction attest to his generosity and his profound influence.

The essays in this volume were written by eight scholars whose personal and professional lives have been deeply influenced by Harold Hyman. Six of the contributors were his students, while two others (Norma Basch and Paul Finkelman) found in him a valued mentor. All of the essays are inspired by Hyman's broad view of constitutional-legal history, his insistence on treating the past on its own terms, and his disdain for conventional wisdom. They are offered as a tribute to a man whose professionalism, intellect, bold vision, and humanity have helped create the new constitutional and legal history that this volume reflects and, we trust, advances.

NOTES

1. There are, of course, important exceptions. See, for example, Richard B. Morris, *Studies in the History of American Law, with Special Reference to the Seventeenth Century* (New York: Columbia University Press, 1930); George Lee Haskins, *Law and Authority in Early Massachusetts: A Study in Tradition* (New York: Macmillan, 1960); James Willard Hurst, *The Growth of American Law: The Law Makers* (Boston: Little, Brown, 1950), and *Law and the Conditions of Freedom in the Nineteenth Century United States* (Madison: University of Wisconsin Press, 1956).

2. *The Era of the Oath: Northern Loyalty Oaths during the Civil War and Reconstruction* (Philadelphia: University of Pennsylvania Press, 1954); *To Try Men's Souls: Loyalty Tests in American History* (Berkeley: University of California Press, 1959); *Soldiers and Spruce: Origins of the Loyal Legion of Loggers and Lumbermen* (Berkeley: University of California Press, 1963); *Quiet Past and Stormy Present? The War Power in American History* (Washington, D.C.: American Historical Association, 1987).

3. *Stanton: The Life and Times of Lincoln's Secretary of War* (New York: Alfred A. Knopf, 1963); *The Radical Republicans and Reconstruction, 1861–1870* (Indianapolis: Bobbs-Merrill, 1965); *New Frontiers of the American Reconstruction* (Urbana: University of Illinois Press, 1967); *A More Perfect Union: The Impact of the Civil War and Reconstruction on the Constitution* (New York: Alfred A. Knopf, 1973); *Union and Confidence: The 1860s* (New York: Crowell, 1976); *Equal Justice under Law: Constitutional Development, 1835–1875* (New York: Harper and Row, 1982).

Hercules Unbound: Lincoln, Slavery, and

the Intentions of the Framers

PHILLIP SHAW PALUDAN

Let me begin with some disclaimers.[1] My training as a historian of the nineteenth century, especially the Civil War era, my devotion to research and writing in that period, and my need for at least seven hours sleep a night all make it impossible for me to claim vast knowledge of the late eighteenth century. Hence my conclusions about the world of the framers are of necessity tentative. Whether becoming a specialist in the field would change that fact is doubtful, because scholarship on the meaning of the Constitution and the nature of its environment is not monovocal. But at least I would know better what I was being modest about.

The contribution that I can make to the discussion of the intentions of the framers vis-à-vis slavery must come from an integration of perspectives: from reading the document and its history in the context of constitutional theory, and reading both in light of Abraham Lincoln's ideas. My contribution doesn't provide deeper digging in ground already mined by experts. In fact, I shall try to demonstrate that doing the kind of thing I do might help us escape from the dangers of more narrow digging. In doing this I take refuge behind one of my favorite sayings of Mark Twain: "The work of many scholars has already thrown much darkness on the subject and it is likely that if they keep working we shall soon know nothing at all!"

THE LIMITS OF SPECIALIZATION

One of the many good things that Harold Hyman taught me was that there is, or ought to be, a difference between lawyers and historians.

Lawyers are interested in winning their cases, and historians in telling the truth. Most historians, certainly those who study constitutional history, know of this distinction and act on their knowledge. But while they recognize the problem in terms of the differing ends of the two professions, they are not equally aware, it seems to me, of the extent to which they are prisoners of the means and methods of legal scholarship.

When we want to settle a point of historical fact we act like lawyers; we narrow the question and look strictly at the relevant precedents, defining as relevant the particular words of the document relating to, in this case, slavery. In much of our legal scholarship that is a valuable technique. We want to focus attention on the specific issue in question, not to ramble over the entire meaning of truth, justice, and the American way. But "we must never forget it is a constitution we are expounding." That means we should seek the broadest relevant context for our question asking and avoid the old canard about legal thinking: "If you can think about something that is related to something, without thinking about what it is related to, you can be a lawyer."

The pressures of professionalism are strong. Canons and customs of prevailing scholarship argue for this narrowly focused approach. Legal and constitutional history as a field concentrates on the Supreme Court and the court system, where legal styles of reasoning prevail. Both Harold Hyman in constitutional history and Willard Hurst in legal history have been deploring this narrowness for years. With some notable recent exceptions, however, scholarship in the field still suggests that "the Constitution is what the Supreme Court says it is."[2] But it is well to remember that the practice of making the Court the final arbiter in constitutional interpretation did not gather momentum until after the Civil War, and after the death of Lincoln. Before that time wider views prevailed, and a wider view on slavery and the framers is what I believe we need.

THE FRAMERS' INTENT

The framers were not in Philadelphia primarily to protect slavery. They were there to create a new system of government that would overcome the failures of the Articles of Confederation. Slavery was not in danger in 1787; in fact, it was safer under the Articles than it would be under any projected national constitution. Had there been a call to organize a new national constitution in order to protect slavery, it is doubtful that anyone would have responded.[3]

With the exception of delegates from the Deep South, most of the founding fathers at Philadelphia, even those from other slave states, did not like slavery. Madison and Washington and Mason believed slavery to be an evil, as did most of the northern delegates.[4] They did not protect slavery in the document because they wanted to. They protected it because they had to, because the Deep South delegates threatened to stay out of any government that didn't protect slavery. Slavery was the price of the new constitutional union, and the total price accumulated ominously.

The framers provided slavery with disproportionate political protection in the three-fifths clause, and thereby also in the electoral college. They gave economic protection from taxes on the exports of slave-created products, a twenty-year ban on congressional termination of the slave trade, provisions for returning fugitive slaves, and general guarantees that the newly empowered national government would not act directly on slavery.[5] All these protections benefited slavery, as did the difficult process of amendment.[6]

Yet there were limits on how much protection slavery received. The word never appears in the document, reflecting the fact that many of the framers themselves detested slavery and feared that an obvious endorsement of it would doom ratification. Given a hermeneutical perspective that emphasized the words of the document itself, that omission seems especially significant. The framers carefully avoided suggesting that slavery was lawful except by the municipal law of slave states. They only temporarily accepted the importation of slaves.[7]

Whatever they did to sustain slavery protected it only at that time or in the very near future. Even in the case of the provision concerning the slave trade, the Constitution said that the importation of such persons as "any of the states *now existing* may think proper to admit" could not be stopped before 1808.[8] Here again is a sign that the future might not be as hospitable to slavery as the present. Some delegates seem to have believed that slavery and the slave trade were dying institutions. Their present demanded protection of slavery, but they may have had higher hopes for the future.[9]

The Constitution's provisions with respect to slavery were thus not unambiguous, even taken in the narrow sense. They indicate something less than a desire to make slavery an essential part of the Constitution.

As Donald Robinson notes, "Slavery had been confined to a cul-de-sac, where it would be virtually unnecessary, as it would surely be impolitic, for national politicians to handle it."[10]

The critics of slavery were not modern egalitarians. I stress this point because the modern egalitarian standard has been used as an important part of the argument that the Constitution was a proslavery document.[11] But emphasis on that criterion obscures the important ways that the Constitution as created housed potential harms, perhaps even disaster, for slavery.

Opposition to slavery is no less important or telling if it rests on the idea that slavery is not only morally bad, it is bad for you—it has bad consequences that could be manifested in its effects on masters, perhaps turning them into tyrannical brutes, as Jefferson said; or providing a political advantage for southern states; or for what it did to the possibility of free discussion and debate over goals and options. This was well known by members of the Philadelphia convention. The issue of slavery constantly threatened the convention with disruption. In this respect the convention forecast the later history of slavery and civil liberties and union. It is these dangers—not to the moral climate of the age (though a few had moral concerns) but to the constitutional and social environment—that are the most suggestive for assessing the framers' attitudes toward slavery.

Because their predominant motive was to create a more perfect constitutional system, the framers saw slavery not as an essential part of that system but as an important factor that had to be quarantined as much as possible to keep it from overthrowing the larger system. The presence of slavery was, as later events showed, profoundly dangerous to the constitutional system as a whole; not only in the sense that it would ultimately challenge the constitutional union itself, but also in the fact that it could erode so many of the elements of the Constitution that were indispensable to the functioning of the entire system.

The framers certainly knew the dangers that slavery posed. They consciously tried to create a system that would be defended from those dangers. Less consciously, perhaps, they may have also created within the structure of the constitutional system a hidden factor, something like a computer virus, that attacked as well as defended. In the end, they created a system that endangered slavery. That, at least, was the opinion held in the eleven seceding states in 1860. We also know that by 1860 the constitutional system had created a polity that gave Lincoln his electoral majority.

Within less than three generations the system created in Philadelphia had brought slavery to this jeopardy. The framers might have anticipated this result. Or did they? How far from their conscious intent was the potential for endangering the peculiar institution they had isolated in 1787?

That question is very difficult to answer; but there is another indicator of that antislavery virus. Consider the relationship between the First Amendment and free speech in the territories. If the amendment, for example, were to be applied to the territories, Congress, the ultimate lawmaking body for the territories, could not pass laws that interfered with peaceful antislavery agitation. The territories would then be unsafe for slavery. Although this idea was not considered at the time, the potential threat to slavery in the territories would surely have been recognized.[12]

Yet William Wiecek says that "slavery was an essential component of . . . the American constitutional order." On the contrary, slavery was a threat to that very order. Could it reasonably be thought that an institution that limited or killed free speech, free press, petition, assembly, and free exercise of religion was essential to the constitutional order? Was Congress better off? Could it debate, develop thoughtful policies, or make better laws with gag rules? Was the constitutional order more vital or viable when slaves could not practice their religion? Was the constitutional order more viable when the correctness, the propriety, and the costs of the most explosive issue in the polity could not be discussed in all slave and many free states, in the territories, or in Congress? I don't think so. Paul Brest has said that the ends of constitutional government are to "(1) foster democratic government; (2) protect individuals against arbitrary, unfair, and intrusive action; (3) conduce to a political order that is relatively stable but which also responds to changing conditions, values and needs; (4) not readily lend itself to arbitrary decisions or abuses; (5) be acceptable to the populace." Slavery threatened every one of these ends. Therefore, I agree with W. B. Allen's suggestion that Wiecek confuses an " 'essential' element (intrinsic to the meaning or purpose of a whole) with a 'necessary' element (that part or condition of a whole without which the whole itself cannot be realized)."[13]

This overfast overview suggests, I think, the need to reconsider the question of the framers' intent with regard to slavery. But such reconsiderations cannot rely on mere history alone. The complexity of the historical environment cannot be unravelled adequately without some help from constitutional theory as well as from Mr. Lincoln.

CONSTITUTIONAL THEORY AND
THE ORIGINAL INTENT

We need help from theory because the issue of original intent is more complex than our scholarship on slavery and the framers seems to recognize. A consensus among theorists and historians (even, presumably, those writing on slavery and the framers) argues that the search for original intent is "a misconceived quest," a "will of the wisp." [14]

The problem has many aspects, but I shall mention only the most important of them. First, who are the framers whose intent we seek: the delegates at Philadelphia or the voting majorities in Independence Hall that produced parts of the document? Which of their intentions mattered the most to them? How precise must those intentions have been in their minds to provide guidance for interpreters? Is it necessary to distinguish hopes from expectations, to assess abiding convictions as opposed to temporary opinions? How do we do that? [15]

The framers themselves seem to have thought that the real intent of the document would be derived from the understanding and interpretations of the nearly sixteen hundred men who met in the conventions to ratify the document. As if the complexity of that debate didn't obscure the meaning of the document sufficiently, they also seem to have believed that subsequent interpretations of the document would rest not so much on what they said in Philadelphia as on a reading of the plain words of the document and the purposes that document would serve for future generations. Madison, for example, spoke of the "surest and most recognized meaning of the Constitution as of a law, is furnished by the evils which were to be cured or the benefits to be obtained; and by the immediate and *long continued* application of the meaning to those ends." [16]

The framers' very understanding of the meaning of liberty and other treasured ideals further suggests the sense of the future that shaped the Philadelphia moment. John Reid and John Diggins have recently shown that the concept of liberty in the eighteenth century was believed to be present and unchanging. As Reid says, "the civil rights or political liberty of the present existed in a timeless infinity, a frozen moment isolated from historical evolution." When they talked of abiding truths, they meant them to abide and to be demonstrated by history in their pure, clear form. Liberty at its best would be manifested in the historical experience. The framers, it would seem, anticipated that posterity would be able to, and would have to, reclaim the ideals they treasured. [17]

They meant the Constitution to have a centennial, and a bicentennial, and, if we don't manage to destroy ourselves, a tricentennial. That hope suggests to me the importance of theory about what the document means so that we can have the fullest understanding of what kept the "machine" going, and hence what allowed that bicentennial to come about.[18]

We want, in short, the best interpretation of the Constitution that will describe how it operates and how it has managed to survive. I assume that providing that interpretation will provide an understanding of what the framers intended. That assumption rests on another: they wanted the document to operate in the way most likely to achieve the goals they set for it in the preamble.

To achieve the framers' intentions that their creation survive, we need a theory of interpretation—a way of looking at the nature of the Constitution—that will reveal its possibilities, thus making it the protean and vital document its creators aspired to. Just as every author demands good readers to give her or his creation its fullest and best meaning, so every living constitution requires its best interpretation to give it life. Ronald Dworkin says it this way: "legal reasoning is an exercise in constructive interpretation . . . our law consists in [providing] the best justification of our legal practices . . . it consists in the narrative story that makes of these practices the best they can be." [19]

CHARLES BLACK AND THE STRUCTURE AND
RELATIONSHIPS OF THE CONSTITUTION

One way to look at the Constitution is the structural approach recommended by Charles Black,[20] who argues that interpreters of the Constitution should not bind themselves by focusing on a narrow doctrine or specific text and the relevant precedents on that doctrine or text. Rather, they should consider how the Constitution operates as a whole and make decisions that facilitate its continuing operation. Some examples clarify how that idea works. Commerce-clause cases should rest not on the meaning of the word *among,* as in "among the several states," but on how a prospective regulation of commerce would affect the idea of this nation being, in the purview of the Constitution, one nation commercially.[21]

Similarly, as regards the Bill of Rights, a look from the perspective of the overall structure illuminates the idea. No state, Black argues, could pass a law that would interfere with the ability of people to petition Congress for redress of grievances. This is not because of the First and Fourteenth amendments, but rather because "such a state law would constitute interference with a transaction which is a part of the working of the federal government."

Another example mentioned by Black pushes us closer to the issue of slavery in the Constitution. The electoral relationship between a legislator and his or her constituents requires full and open discussion about the merits of that legislator and his or her policies.

> Is it conceivable that a state, entirely aside from the Fourteenth, or for that matter the First Amendment, could permissibly forbid public discussion of the merits of candidates for Congress, or of issues which have been raised in the congressional campaign? . . . I start with that as the hard core, because I cannot see how any one could think our national government could run, or was by anybody at the time ever expected to run, on any less openness of public communication than that.[22]

This example comes pretty close to the First Amendment kind of example that relates to slavery. Did anyone believe that the territories could have their elections without an open discussion of slavery and its merits as a part of that process? In a national election—even in South Carolina—wouldn't the issue of slavery be fair game and very dangerous to slavery itself? Black observes that "discussion of all questions which are in the broadest sense relevant to Congress's work is, quite strictly, a part of the working of the national government. If it is not, what is our mechanism for accommodating national political action to the needs and desires of the people? And if it is, does it not reasonably follow that a state may not interfere with it?" Wouldn't the oath taken by state officials to support the Constitution, along with the supremacy clause, made especially forceful under this structural viewpoint, require that slavery be discussed?[23]

Using inference from relation and structure opens the Constitution to a wider meaning than narrow, text-focused means to analysis. It clearly recognizes that the founders created not a list of individual texts but "a Constitution." Looking at the document as a whole to discover meaning would accord with sentiments of the 1780s. As one of the delegates to the North Carolina ratification convention put it, "Is it not a maxim of universal jurisprudence, of reason and common sense that an instrument or deed of writing shall be so construed as to give validity to all parts of it?" Or, as Madison told the delegates in Philadelphia, "the only way to make a Government answer all the ends of its institution was to collect the wisdom of its several parts in aid of each other." [24]

Black's interpretation, called by Philip Bobbitt "the most potent and potentially satisfying recent development in constitutional argument," shows us what kind of Constitution would best fulfill the framers' hopes. It would be one that considered the whole, not just the parts; the essential elements of the system they created, not the dangerous elements they had to include. This suggests the truth in Frederick Douglass's observation: "Abolish slavery tomorrow, and not a sentence or syllable of the Constitution need be altered. . . . If in its origin slavery had any relation to the government, it was only as scaffolding to the magnificent structure, to be removed as soon as the building was completed." [25]

RONALD DWORKIN AND THE CONSTITUTION

Ronald Dworkin also argues for a Constitution seen as a system, not a series of unconnected texts: "We reach opinions in hard cases by asking which decision flows from the best interpretation we can give of the legal process as a whole." [26] Dworkin, however, adds a dimension to this theorizing about how to read the Constitution by introducing the idea of law as integrity. Law as integrity urges us to read the Constitution in a way that allows that document to achieve its underlying principles and goals most completely. Hercules, the name Dworkin gives to judges who follow law as integrity, seeks a solution that gives coherence between present and past. He looks into the past for a pattern of ideas about justice and fairness that he can then incorporate into the decision he will make about what the law ought to be. Precedent matters, but it is predominantly a precedent of principle and ideal. Hercules decides cases on the grounds that "follow from the principles of justice, fairness, and procedural due process that provide the best constructive interpretation of the community's legal practice." Judges who believe in integrity "decide hard cases by trying to find, in some coherent set of principles about people's rights and duties, the best constructive interpretation of the political structure and legal doctrine of their community." [27]

Hercules writes his part of a sort of chain novel that will make the story of the community's law the best it can be—the greatest fulfillment of its ideas as seen in the most coherent patterns of its law and society. And that integrity, Dworkin says, "makes no sense except among people who want fairness and justice as well [as integrity]." [28]

Law as integrity moves Dworkin's argument away from the pragmatist position that a judge ought to "think instrumentally about the best rules for the future" and make the best decision he can irrespective of what precedent or practice might suggest (an approach that makes judges, not law, supreme). Law as integrity also rejects what Dworkin calls "the backward-looking factual reports of conventionalism." Conventionalists are guided by the idea that their task is to find "what decisions have been made by institutions conventionally recognized to have legislative [that is, lawmaking] power." Practitioners of law as integrity look to the past to discover the abiding principles of the community as they point to the best outcomes for the future.

Yet Dworkin's theory stops short of securing the best imaginable outcome for the 1787 Republic. For Dworkin's theory, and Black's too, are theories of *judging*. Despite the fact that they open the Constitution to a broader vision, they still are centered in the judicial role, and that means they are restrained by the position the Constitution assigns to judges: to decide cases and controversies. In doing this, judges are limited by a tradition of legislative supremacy and a due process tradition that respects precedent. [29]

Dworkin's Hercules is bound by the fact that he is *Judge* Hercules. He cannot order Congress or state legislatures to enact his conceptions of justice. Fairness, "the structure that distributes influence over political decisions in the right way," means that he must allow popular opinion in a government "of the people" to have its say even though that may not accord with Hercules' ideas of law and integrity. He must also respect precedents because these "encourage citizens to rely on doctrines and assumptions that it would be wrong to betray in judging them after the fact." [30] Some constitutional vision outside chambers would seem to be required if the Constitution is to fulfill the founders' hopes.

ABRAHAM LINCOLN, SLAVERY, AND THE FRAMERS

When Lincoln began interpreting the Constitution, the framers' best hopes were in disrepair. First, slavery had escaped from its cul-de-sac. It was repeating in the larger constitutional system its Philadelphia performance—threatening to destroy the system unless its claims were met. Proslavery congressmen required new protections against congressional discussion of petitions. Proslavery mobs were attacking antislavery speakers—not in Dixie's "crowded theater" but in Utica, New York City, Boston, and Alton, Illinois. In addition, the nature of slavery's defense had changed. No longer was slavery a necessary evil, it was a positive good. Not only that, but the potential existed for a slave code for the territories under which speaking against slavery could be a criminal offense. In this kind of imposed silence was the making of the true "covenant with death." In 1787 slavery was protected where it existed; by 1860 slavery's reach included places where it could hardly have been imagined years before. Slavery wasn't a dying institution; though threatened, it was alive and vital, woven into states and territories, freed from congressional discussion and political debate.[31]

Public opinion also contained ominous elements for equal liberty. Jacksonian democracy was increasingly constricted to apply only to white men. Blacks, free and slave, and Native Americans saw their rights contracted. Foreign-born Americans were under attack. And the legislatures of the land were leading and turning that public opinion into law. Furthermore, the Supreme Court was stringing together a series of precedents that expanded the influence of slavery in the nation. And Stephen Douglas was endorsing most of this as legitimate in light of the long-standing tradition of consent of the governed, on the one hand, and insisting, on the other, that "it is the fundamental principle of the judiciary, that its decisions are final."[32]

Here was a crisis in constitutional integrity that Judge Hercules might not have been legitimately able to decide. When Lincoln came on the scene, precedent and legislative supremacy might have required even Judge Hercules to back away from law as pure integrity. But Lincoln was not a twentieth-century judge. He was not shackled by the tradition that speaks of the Supreme Court as our "Forum of Principle."[33] He had a larger forum in mind, one in which pure integrity might have its day, or at least have room to fight. He was going to try to save the best constitutional union from the judges and from a corrupted form of legislative supremacy.

Lincoln took two interconnected approaches. First, he moved outside narrow legal precedent and judicial supremacy by developing an alternative to the view that the Supreme Court was the final authority in deciding what the Constitution means. Second, he moved outside the specific and obvious legal text of the Constitution and integrated the Declaration of Independence within it.

Lincoln adopted a position on judicial review that the modern world has generally rejected. He denied that the Court was the sole and final interpreter of the meaning of the Constitution. He agreed that the Court's decisions were final for the parties to the particular case decided; and he agreed that the Court might provide a final statement of what the Constitution meant, but only after the whole polity had considered the matter at length. If the principle at issue accorded with "the steady practice of the departments throughout our history" and had been "before the court more than once and affirmed and re-affirmed through a course of years, it then might be, perhaps would be, factious, nay even revolutionary, not to acquiesce in it as a precedent." But the other branches of government retained the obligation to discuss and shape constitutional meanings. Quoting Andrew Jackson (and probably former attorney general Roger Taney), Lincoln said, "The Congress, the executive and the court must each itself be guided by its own opinion of the Constitution. Each public officer, who takes an oath to support the Constitution, swears that he will support it as he understands it, and not as understood by others." [34]

Thus Lincoln insisted Dred Scott's case decided only the fate of Dred Scott. The duty of congressmen was to continue to argue and to vote that slavery should not be allowed in the territories. Letting the Supreme Court have the final voice, and thus the power to end discussion of vital and contested issues, would mean that "the people will have ceased to be their own rulers, having to that extent resigned their government into the hands of that eminent tribunal." [35] On vital constitutional issues all branches of government, and the people themselves, were to determine the meaning of the Constitution.

Lincoln also challenged the interpretive claims of the Taney Court. Note that Taney was engaged in the most narrow form of conventionalism. He said that the Constitution never changed and that he was reading it directly, without interpretation, as though he had been present at its creation. The document, Taney said, "is not only the same in words, but the same in meaning . . . and intent with which it spoke when it came from the hands of its framers, and was voted on and adopted by the American people." [36] Taney also engaged in the kind of legalistic sophistry that defied common sense and broader interpretive meaning. His opinion reads at times like an effort to disconnect things that are inherently connected, lawyerly thinking with a vengeance. Thus he confined the territorial clause to territory owned by the United States in 1787; the territory subsequently added in the Louisiana Purchase, he said, was governed by a separate authority. He also manufactured a distinction between state and federal citizenship, denied the existence of black state citizens in 1787 (when they clearly did exist), and manufactured a substantive due process right to hold slaves. Taney even managed to turn the Declaration of Independence into evidence for proslavery sentiments of the framers.[37]

Lincoln probably did not have a conscious theory of interpretation. He instinctively knew the conventionalist game and he played it well. It is doubtful that the historical record has ever been mined so successfully as in his Cooper Union address to show the antislavery actions of the framers. But he also believed that the current experience might require moving beyond the framers if there was "evidence so conclusive and argument so clear that even their great authority, fairly considered and weighed, cannot stand."[38]

But Lincoln was not persuaded that their authority could not stand, for he understood that the framers' view of the Constitution encompassed a future for the nation, not just a past. To secure that future he knew that the voice of the Court had to be transcended, balanced with a wider discussion; including legislators, the president, and the people was vital.

Expanding the number of voices was only part of Lincoln's task. What the voices said was also crucial, for they might simply decide to speak for slavery in the name of popular sovereignty or democracy. Indispensable to a vital Constitution was the job of reintroducing into the political and constitutional discourse the ideal of equal liberty that came from the Declaration of Independence.[39]

Insisting that "I have never had a feeling politically that did not spring from the sentiments embodied in the Declaration of Independence," he argued to keep the equal liberty concept of that document alive in the constitutional conversation of the age. By twentieth-century standards, of course, Lincoln's support for equality was qualified. In the debates with Stephen Douglas, for example, he denied that he intended "to introduce political and social equality between the white and the black races." Nevertheless, he adamantly refused to limit the declaration's guarantees to whites. "There is no reason in the world why the negro is not entitled to all the natural rights enumerated in the Declaration of Independence," he asserted during the Ottawa debate. "I hold that he is as much entitled to these as the white man." Indeed, Lincoln was profoundly disturbed by the ways in which the "self-evident truth" that "all men are created equal" had become, in the minds of such leading Americans as Roger Taney, Stephen Douglas, John Calhoun, and their associates "a self-evident lie." "Near eighty years ago, we began by declaring that all men are created equal; but now from that beginning we have run down to the other declaration that for SOME men to enslave OTHERS is a sacred right of self government."[40]

Some historians and legal scholars have seen Lincoln's concern for the declaration as a move away from the Constitution, dividing the ideals of the former from the institutions of the latter.[41] That kind of separation can endorse the view that between 1776 and 1787 the promises of equality were withdrawn. It can support an argument that Lincoln was a mere pragmatist, ignoring historical practice and legal precedent in order to advocate his personal philosophy. But Lincoln's integration had merit. The framers had lived in the world the American Revolution created. They had debated the Constitution using the declaration as a yardstick. Morton White concludes that "[Publius's] ideology . . . was fundamentally the same as the philosophy we find in the Declaration of Independence."[42]

Lincoln therefore legitimately linked the declaration with the Constitution. He never separated the two documents and consistently referred to the founders as men of both 1776 and 1787. His celebrated Gettysburg address points to the founding of the nation in 1776 but concludes by resolving that *government* of, by, and for the people "shall not perish from the earth." He was certainly a devotee of the ideals of the declaration, but he was not choosing it over the Constitution. He was insisting that the ideals of the declaration infused the Constitution and the system founded by the framers. His critique of slavery targeted not just the rejection of equality; it was replete with criticism that slavery had expanded to corrupt the political dialogue that the Constitution established. What made this intrusion dangerous was that it interfered with the maturing of the ideals of the declaration, ideals on which the Constitution rested.[43]

Equality was not a static concept to Lincoln. For example, his own ideas about equality evolved between 1858, when he opposed negro voting, and 1864, when he supported it. Like the Constitution, equality would attain its fullest meaning over time. Lincoln said that the framers

> meant simply to declare the *right* [to equal liberty], so that enforcement of it might follow as fast as circumstances should permit. They meant to set up a standard maxim for a free society, which should be familiar to all, and reviewed by all: constantly looked to, constantly labored for, and even though never perfectly attained, constantly approximated, and therefore constantly spreading and deepening its in-

fluence, and augmenting the happiness and value of life to all people and all colors everywhere.[44]

But the realization of the goal demanded a healthy and open constitutional system in which the meanings of equality might be debated, voted on, chosen, and tested. And just as it had in Philadelphia in 1787, slavery threatened that open discussion, stifled that testing. Lincoln therefore spoke not only for equality; he spoke for an open constitutional system. He condemned the South for stopping advocates of republicanism from speaking in Dixie. He challenged *Dred Scott* as shutting down discussion of equality as a political principle. He worried about a string of precedents that might shut down discussion of slavery even in the free states. And, of course, ultimately he denied to Dixie the right to abandon the electoral process in service of the peculiar institution.[45]

As an adult, Lincoln had two callings: lawyer and politician. Both occupations made him profoundly committed to the rule of law and the Constitution. From his 1838 Lyceum address to his decision in 1861 to accept war to preserve the political system established by the Constitution, Lincoln demonstrated that commitment. But he also recognized that the system had an ideological heritage born in the late eighteenth century—the idea of equal liberty under law. He understood that the two were not alternatives. He knew that the presence of slavery in the Constitution need not corrupt the ideals of the Declaration of Independence. He was aware that judges might read the Constitution to protect slavery, and that legislators might forget equality, but he was not a mere judge or an ordinary legislator. He was, fortunately for the Constitution, Hercules unbound.

NOTES

1. I acknowledge the help of Professors Philip Kissam, University of Kansas School of Law; Rex Martin, University of Kansas Department of Philosophy; William Wiecek, Syracuse University School of Law; and John Hood, Ph.D. candidate in medieval history, University of Kansas. They are not responsible if I have strayed from their good advice, or taken their bad.

2. Leonard Levy, *Original Intent and the Framers' Constitution* (New York: Macmillan, 1988), focuses almost entirely on Supreme Court activity despite the late blooming of judicial supremacy in constitutional interpretation.

3. I follow Donald Robinson, *Slavery in the Structure of American Politics, 1765–1820* (New York: Macmillan, 1971), in describing what the framers did about slavery, but I believe that in writing about the subject of slavery in the con-

stitutional system he has naturally enough overemphasized the role of slavery at Philadelphia in 1787.

4. See William Freehling, "The Founding Fathers and Slavery," *American Historical Review* 77 (1972): 81–93; Don E. Fehrenbacher, "Slavery, the Framers and the Living Constitution," Herbert J. Storing, "Slavery and the Moral Foundations of the American Republic," and W. B. Allen, "A New Birth of Freedom: Fulfillment or Derailment," all in *Slavery and Its Consequences*, ed. Robert A. Goldwin and Art Kaufman (Washington, D.C.: American Enterprise Institute, 1988), 1–22, 45–63, 64–92, for the most recent views of the antislavery intentions of the framers. None of these authors considers the perspectives of recent constitutional theory.

5. William Wiecek and Paul Finkelman both point to the two clauses in the Constitution that promised military support to put down domestic violence and suppress insurrections as being designed to protect slavery. See Finkelman, "Making a Covenant with Death," in *Beyond Confederation: Origins of the Constitution and American National Identity,* ed. Richard Beeman et al. (Chapel Hill: University of North Carolina Press, 1987), 191–92; Wiecek, *The Sources of Antislavery Constitutionalism in America, 1760–1848* (Ithaca, N.Y.: Cornell University Press, 1977), 62–63. Robinson argues that slavery's supporters felt able to put down their own uprisings and would have worried about allowing Massachusetts militia into Dixie even for this purpose. Indeed, he notes that southern delegates usually wanted to limit the extent of these provisions; Robinson, *Slavery in the Structure of American Politics,* 218.

6. Ibid., 225.

7. Storing, "Slavery and the Moral Foundations," 53–54.

8. Fehrenbacher, "Slavery, the Framers and the Living Constitution," 9–10 (emphasis added).

9. Robinson, *Slavery in the Structure of American Politics,* 227–28.

10. Ibid., 244.

11. See William M. Wiecek, " 'The Blessings of Liberty': Slavery in the American Constitutional Order," in Goldwin and Kaufman, eds., *Slavery and Its Consequences,* 24–29; Finkelman, "Making a Covenant with Death," 223–24.

12. I asked members of a panel at the 1988 Southern Historical Association meeting (Peter Onuf, Robert Weir, John Murrin, and Richard Beeman) if they had knowledge of contemporary discussions of applying the Bill of Rights to the territories; they said that they had no such information.

13. Allen, "A New Birth of Freedom," 89–90, n. 3; Paul Brest, "The Misconceived Quest for the Original Understanding," *Boston University Law Review* 60 (1980): 226.

14. See Brest, "Misconceived Quest"; Levy, *Original Intent.*

15. See Ronald Dworkin, *Law's Empire* (Cambridge, Mass.: Harvard University Press, 1987), 317–54.

16. As quoted in Marvin Meyers, ed., *The Mind of the Founder: Sources of the*

Political Thought of James Madison (Indianapolis, Ind.: Bobbs-Merrill, 1973), 491 (emphasis added). Dworkin believes that this search for the historical intent requires the same type of interpretation that is required of the text of the Constitution itself: "seeking to understand the text in light of the principles that provide the best justification for it," in Kenneth Henley's words. See Henley, "Constitutional Integrity and Compromise," in *Philosophical Dimensions of the Constitution*, ed. Diana Meyers and Kenneth Kipnis (Boulder, Colo.: Westview, 1988), 134–51; Dworkin, *Law's Empire*, 361–63.

On the original understanding of the framers' intent see two articles: H. Jefferson Powell, "The Original Understanding of Original Intent," *Harvard Law Review* 98 (March 1985): 885–948; and Charles A. Lofgren, "The Original Understanding of Original Intent?" *Constitutional Commentary* 5 (Winter 1988): 77–113. Powell argues that the framers did not want their words at Philadelphia to control subsequent interpretations. Lofgren provides evidence to show that some of the framers did want that result. My feeling is that both interpretive traditions were operative. But what seems indisputable is that the framers wanted their handiwork to last into the future, and they knew that would require later interpretation. One of the strongest reasons for believing in their futuristic orientation derives from the framers' search for fame, not just immediate popularity or temporary approval, so that future generations would respect their accomplishments. See Douglas Adair, *Fame and the Founding Fathers* (New York: Norton, 1974).

17. John Phillip Reid, "Liberty and the Original Understanding," in *Essays in the History of Liberty: Seaver Institute Lectures at the Huntington Library*, ed. Martin Ridge (San Marino, Calif.: Henry Huntington Library, 1988), 5–6. See also John Diggins, *The Lost Soul of American Politics: Virtue, Self-Interest, and the Foundations of Liberalism* (Chicago: University of Chicago Press, 1984), 364 and passim. Reid points out that slavery and ideas of liberty were compatible in the late eighteenth century. But he cites only one example, a South Carolinian who used the rhetoric of liberty to deny the right of others to take away his slaves. Reid does not mention any other person of the founders' age who had proslavery views, and he does not mention the framers who did have such views. See Reid, "Liberty and the Original Understanding," 8.

18. For an interesting discussion of the state of modern constitutional theory see Stephen M. Griffin, "What Is Constitutional Theory? The Newer Theory and the Decline of the Learned Tradition," *Southern California Law Review* 62 (January 1989): 493–538.

19. Dworkin, *Law's Empire*, vi. Chapter 2 elaborates Dworkin's theory of interpretation. For a discussion of hermeneutics and Lincoln scholarship see Paludan, "Toward a Lincoln Conversation," *Reviews in American History* 16 (1988): 35–42; Paludan, "Lincoln and the Rhetoric of Politics," in *A Crisis of Republicanism: American Politics during the Civil War Era*, ed. Lloyd Ambrosius (Lincoln: University of Nebraska Press, 1990).

20. Charles Black, *Structure and Relationship in Constitutional Law* (Baton Rouge: Louisiana State University Press, 1969). This structural approach is analyzed in Philip Bobbitt, *Constitutional Fate: Theory of the Constitution* (New York: Oxford University Press, 1982), 74–92.

21. Black, *Structure and Relationship*, 23, 26–27.

22. Ibid., 40–43.

23. Ibid., 90–91. Justice Brennan's 1980 remarks on the First Amendment make the point: "The First Amendment embodies more than a commitment to free expression and conscience for their own sakes; it has a *structural* role to play in securing and fostering our system of government. . . . The structural model links the First Amendment to the process of communication necessary for a democracy to survive, and this entails solicitousness not only for communication itself but for the indispensable conditions of meaningful communication" (*Richmond Newspapers* v. *Virginia*, 448 U.S. 553). On reading parts of the Constitution in terms of overall structure and purpose, see Sotirios Barber, *On What the Constitution Means* (Baltimore, Md.: Johns Hopkins University Press, 1984); Alexander Meiklejohn, *Free Speech and Its Relation to Self Government* (1948), cited by Black, *Structure and Relationship*, 51; Mark A. DeWolfe Howe, "Religion and the Free Society: The Constitutional Question," in *Selected Essays on Constitutional Law*, ed. Edward L. Barrett, Jr. (St. Paul, Minn.: West Publishing Company, 1963); William F. Harris, "Bonding Word and Polity: The Logic of American Constitutionalism," *American Political Science Review* 76 (1982): 34–45.

24. As quoted in Charles Lofgren, "The Original Understanding of Original Intent?" 90. Madison, speech of June 4, 1787, in *Records of the Federal Convention of 1787*, 4 vols., ed. Max Farrand (New Haven, Conn.: Yale University Press, 1966), 1:110. See John Agresto, "The Limits of Judicial Supremacy: A Proposal for 'Checked Activism,'" *Georgia Law Review* 14 (1980): 471–95. My understanding of Madison's hermeneutics has profited from reading John Hood, "James Madison's Constitutional Hermeneutic" (Unpublished paper, University of Kansas, May 1989). The structure and relationship method is no less precise than the narrower option. As Black put it, "Precision of textual explication is nothing but specious in the areas that matter. . . . The question is not whether the text shall be respected, but rather how one goes about respecting a text of that high generality and consequent ambiguity which marks so many crucial constitutional texts." According to Black, *McCulloch* v. *Maryland*, which uses the reasoning from structure and relation, "has just as satisfying a legal quality" as *Fletcher* v. *Peck*, where the dominant textual method is used. See Black, *Structure and Relationship*, 30–31.

25. Bobbitt, *Constitutional Fate*, 78; "Address for the Promotion of Colored Enlistments," July 6, 1863, as quoted by Storing, "Slavery and the Moral Foundations," 51.

26. Dworkin, *Law's Empire*, 106, 363. Dworkin adopts Black's structural approach in discussing the Civil War amendments. Describing the duty of those

seeking the intent of the framers, he says that it is not enough for the historian to look directly at the intent of the framers with regard to segregation, for example. One must "retrieve their more abstract convictions by asking what conception of treating people as equals they are best understood as having laid down." In doing so, one "would do better to look directly to the overall structure of the post–Civil War amendments they created together, seen as a part of the more general constitutional system they left in place and ask what principles of equality are necessary to justify that structure."

27. Dworkin, *Law's Empire*, 255–56. Dworkin argues for a legal interpretation in which respect for the intentions of the lawgivers plays a contingent role. He is not satisfied with what he calls conventionalism, which would best express, I think, a historian's viewpoint; that is, our job is to find out what lawmakers in the past said and to remain faithful to it. Dworkin is talking about judicial decision making and rejecting the claim that the best judging follows the intent of the lawgiver and hence requires that the judge function as a historian to find out what that intent was and then follow the precedent. For Dworkin, the goal is not a fully faithful rendering of the past; it is deciding a case in a way that respects the integrity of the past but also the ideals then held by the community. He wants to get the case justly and fairly decided today. That might mean rejecting as precedent past cases that got it wrong (wrong in the sense of providing an argument from principles of integrity). Dworkin asks of the judges more than that they follow the past precedent. He wants them also to be able to justify any attention to precedent. I will not argue the value of history at this point. Suffice it to say that Dworkin's argument doesn't depend on whether history plays a contingent role. In fact, Dworkin himself makes a strong argument that judges need to know and understand history with the same degree of accuracy that historians do.

28. Dworkin distinguishes two kinds of interpretation: conversational and constructive. Conversational interpretation seeks to discover what meaning the speaker intends when he speaks or writes. Constructive interpretation "is a matter of imposing purpose on an object or practice in order to make of it the best possible example of the form or genre to which it is taken to belong." You as interpreter cannot make anything you want to of the object. History "constrains the available interpretations . . . though the character of that constraint needs careful accounting" (*Law's Empire*, 52).

The chain novel metaphor is presented in Ronald Dworkin, "Law and Interpretation," *Texas Law Review* 60 (March 1982): 527–50, and in *Law's Empire*, 228–38. It is criticized by Stanley Fish in "Working on a Chain Gang: Interpretation in Law and Literature," *Texas Law Review* 60 (March 1982): 551–67. Dworkin replies in W. J. T. Mitchell, ed., *The Politics of Interpretation* (Chicago: University of Chicago Press, 1983), chaps. 6 and 7.

29. Dworkin, despite his court-centered theory, does point the way to a larger view. "Law's empire," he says, "is defined by attitude, not territory or power or

process . . . it must be persuasive in our ordinary lives if it is to serve us well even in court" (*Law's Empire*, 413).

30. Ibid., 400–407.

31. Fehrenbacher, "Slavery, the Framers and the Living Constitution," 1–22.

32. William M. Wiecek, "Slavery and Abolition before the United States Supreme Court," *Journal of American History* 65 (1978): 34–59; Edward S. Corwin, "The Dred Scott Decision in the Light of Contemporary Legal Doctrines," *American Historical Review* 17 (1911): 52–69; Harry Jaffa, *Crisis of the House Divided* (Seattle: University of Washington Press, 1959); Douglas, in *Collected Works of Abraham Lincoln*, 9 vols., ed. Roy P. Basler (New Brunswick, N.J.: Rutgers University Press, 1953), 3:142–43, 243. Wiecek comments that "if war is too serious to be entrusted to the military, at times the American Constitution is too serious to be entrusted to the judges." He makes the comment to suggest the disastrous effects of judicial constitution making in *Dred Scott*. It is the burden of the present article to show how one might entrust the Constitution to extrajudicial arenas. See Wiecek, "Slavery and Abolition," 59.

33. Ronald Dworkin, "The Forum of Principle," *New York University Law Review* 56 (1981): 469–518.

34. *Collected Works*, 2:400–403. I follow two excellent essays on Lincoln's ideas of judicial review: John Agresto, "The Limits of Judicial Supremacy"; and Gary Jacobsohn, "Abraham Lincoln 'On This Question of Judicial Authority': The Theory of Constitutional Aspiration," *Western Political Quarterly* 36 (1983): 52–70. Madison's views on interpreting the Constitution were similar. He believed that where the meaning of the Constitution was unclear, it would take time and the ongoing constitutional process to provide a clear meaning. In Federalist 37 he wrote, "All new laws, though penned with the greatest technical skill and passed on the fullest and most mature deliberation, are considered more or less obscure and equivocal, until their meaning be liquidated and ascertained by a series of particular discussions and adjudications." Jacob E. Cooke, ed., *The Federalist* (Middletown, Conn.: Wesleyan University Press, 1961), 236.

35. *Collected Works*, 2:495, 4:268.

36. As quoted in Stanley Kutler, ed., *The Dred Scott Decision: Law or Politics?* (Boston: Houghton Mifflin, 1967), 15.

37. Storing, "Slavery and the Moral Foundations," challenges the *Dred Scott* decision as bad history in light of the intentions of the framers. Don E. Fehrenbacher, *The Dred Scott Case* (New York: Oxford University Press, 1978), chaps. 15 and 16, analyzes the opinion.

38. *Collected Works*, 3:535. Lincoln thus weighed the authority of the framers against competing arguments to determine if their perspective should be respected. Yet he clearly believed that they marked slavery "as an evil not to be extended but to be tolerated and protected only because of and *so far as its actual presence among us makes that toleration and protection a necessity* [emphasis added]. Let

all the guarantees those fathers gave it, be, not grudgingly, but fully and fairly maintained."

Lincoln respected the constitutional protection for slavery, which confined it to the states. He even tolerated the fugitive slave act. He remained enough bound by his legal instincts to accept what the framers allowed. But he was willing to believe that an open system would place slavery on the course to ultimate extinction. How? Perhaps by bringing to office increasing numbers of men unwilling to allow slavery to expand, and unwilling to permit slavery's influence to expand beyond the slave states. The existence of slavery was important to keeping the slave states within the union, and the union stood as the foundation and the instrument of government the Constitution had created. It was therefore necessary to compromise to keep the constitutional union together. But should the compromise ever endanger union and the constitutional order the union protected, then slavery would have to go. I think Lincoln's discussion of the dangers of slavery to the larger system suggests that he believed that a restoration of an open system could end slavery in the long run—"place it in the course of ultimate extinction."

39. Jaffa, *Crisis of the House Divided*, chap. 17, notes the contradiction inherent in affirming popular consent while denying equality. The concept of consent rests on the belief that government derives its authority from equal individuals whose opinions must be consulted. The escape used by the Court and Douglas was, of course, to deny that blacks and whites could be equal and to insist that all white men, but not black, were created equal, hence providing the necessary consent to government.

40. *Collected Works*, 2:275, 3:16.

41. Phillip Paludan, "Lincoln, the Rule of Law, and the American Revolution," *Journal of the Illinois State Historical Society* 70 (1977): 10–18; Paludan, "Lincoln and the Rhetoric of Politics." Mark Neely summarizes the historical view that Lincoln was a proponent of the declaration "rather than" the Constitution in *The Abraham Lincoln Encyclopedia* (New York: DaCapo, 1982), 70. Harry Jaffa contrasts Douglas's position on the side of the Constitution with Lincoln's defense of the declaration. See *Crisis of the House Divided*, chap. 15. Although Gary Jacobsohn argues that Lincoln had an aspirational view of the Constitution, he still seems to separate the declaration from the Constitution by neglecting to demonstrate the interaction between the two documents; see "Abraham Lincoln 'On This Question of Judicial Authority.' "

42. Morton White, *Philosophy, "The Federalist," and the Constitution* (New York: Oxford University Press, 1987), 226. Frederick R. Black, "The American Revolution as 'Yardstick' in the Debates on the Constitution, 1787–1788," *Proceedings of the American Philosophical Society* 117 (1973): 162–85, describes the many ways in which the meaning of the Constitution of 1787 was connected to the events and experiences of 1776. See also Martin Diamond, "The Declaration and the Constitution: Liberty, Democracy and the Founders," *Public Interest* 41

(1975): 39–55. Leonard Levy observes that "one has only to read the state recommendations for a bill of rights to know that the natural rights philosophy seized the minds of the Framers as it had the minds of the rebellious patriots of 1776" (Levy, *Original Intent*, 279).

43. *Collected Works*, 4:240; W. B. Allen, "A New Birth of Freedom," p. 66.

44. *Collected Works*, 2:406. For Lincoln's evolving views on equality, compare his speech at Charleston, Illinois, September 18, 1858, with his letter to Michael Hahn, March 13, 1864, in *Collected Works*, 3:145–46, 7:243. W. B. Allen refers to this point in a similar way: "The dynamics of democracy, more than any direct provisions of the Constitution, were the source of the antislavery implications of the founding. In that way the political accomplishment of the Constitution of 1787 was to deepen the influence and authority of the Declaration of Independence." He does not, however, explore the idea very deeply. See Allen, "A New Birth of Freedom," 66.

45. *Collected Works*, 3:535–50. Lincoln claimed that the *Dred Scott* decision would be followed by a decision protecting the rights of slave owners in the states. Historians have discovered a pending case in New York that might have done just that. See *Lemmon v. People*, 20 N.Y. 562 (1860); Paul Finkelman, "The Nationalization of Slavery: A Counterfactual Approach to the 1860s," *Louisiana Studies* 14 (1975): 213–40; Hyman and Wiecek, *Equal Justice under Law*, 192–96. The latter authors provide much evidence undercutting their claim that Lincoln's assertion that the Supreme Court might protect slavery even within free states deserved to be taken seriously. For example, the New York courts rejected the argument of counsel for slave owners that the privileges and immunities clause of the Constitution protected sojourning slave owners in New York. The New York State legislature wrote a resolution declaring that "this state will not allow slavery within her borders, in any form, under any pretence, or for any time however short." Massachusetts, Ohio, Maine, Vermont, and Pennsylvania all passed similar laws. In the aftermath of the reaction to *Dred Scott,* would Taney's Court have been that bold again? See Fehrenbacher, *Dred Scott Case*, 432–35. I mention the *Lemmon* case to admit the logic of Lincoln's views, expressed at Galesburg, that the Constitution as shaped by the logic of the Taney position might house expanded protections for slavery. See *Collected Works*, 3:230–34 (October 7, 1858). Note the difference in time here. Lincoln made his observation more than a year and a half before the *Lemmon* case.

"The Law, and Not Conscience,

Constitutes the Rule of Action":

The South Bend Fugitive Slave Case

and the Value of "Justice Delayed"

PAUL FINKELMAN

The South Bend fugitive slave case is an unusual example of northern resistance to the return of fugitive slaves. Unlike nearly all other cases, the alleged fugitive slaves were peacefully released by a state judge after two hearings into their status. The claimant then successfully sued a number of whites in South Bend, including the lawyer for the blacks and the sheriff who served the initial writ of habeas corpus. After five years of litigation the claimant finally obtained some compensation for his loss. In this lawsuit, *Norris* v. *Newton* (1850), Justice John McLean ruled that neither a valid writ of habeas corpus nor a decree by a state judge that the blacks were free barred the claimant from suing those who helped his slaves win their freedom.

This case lacked the excitement of a rescue, like those in Syracuse (1851), Racine, Wisconsin (1854), and Wellington, Ohio (1858); or the thrill of lethal violence, as in Christiana, Pennsylvania, in 1851. While South Bend was preoccupied with the case for a few days, this was not the drama of a major city virtually paralyzed by a fugitive slave hearing, like Boston during the Latimer case (1843) and the Burns case (1854). The South Bend litigation even lacked a poor and sympathetic defendant, an element found in many other criminal cases and civil suits stemming from the release of a fugitive slave.[1] The defendants in this case were reasonably well-off landowners. Indeed, the most important defendant, Edwin B. Crocker, was a wealthy banker and property owner. Equally unusual, the participants in the case did not appeal to antislavery advocates around the nation for financial help.[2] These circumstances may explain why the South Bend case has been neglected by most historians and why it was virtually ignored at the time.[3]

Despite the lack of contemporary and scholarly attention, the South Bend case provides a useful framework for examining a variety of antebellum legal and social issues. The capture of the Powell family—the fugitive slaves involved in the case—is a textbook example of the moral and practical difficulties posed by seizing fugitive slaves in the North. The initial legal maneuvering to win the Powells' release illustrates the difficulty of enforcing the 1793 fugitive slave law in an age when local lawyers and judges had limited access to federal decisions and an imperfect understanding of Supreme Court rulings. The activities by whites in Indiana and Michigan to save the Powells from slavery suggest that the common view of antebellum northern whites as overwhelmingly hostile to blacks must be reinterpreted in light of the financial and personal risks whites such as those in South Bend were willing to take on behalf of blacks.[4] The very visible presence in South Bend of numerous blacks from Michigan and Indiana during the hearings over the status of the fugitives illustrates the solidarity of midwestern black communities on the issue of fugitive slave rendition. The response of the South Bend citizens also shows how antislavery northerners used—and misused—the legal system to protest slavery. The failure of the Powells' owner to regain his slaves and the seven years it took for him to collect his judgment in the civil lawsuits illustrate the inadequacy of the Fugitive Slave Law of 1793 for masters hunting runaway slaves or seeking compensation when their slaves were released or rescued. Finally, the case underscores the historical problem of understanding jurists like Justice John McLean, who personally found slavery abhorrent but nevertheless enforced the fugitive slave laws with rulings that today seem unnecessarily harsh.

THE ESCAPE AND THE SEIZURE

David and Lucy Powell and their four sons were slaves owned by John Norris of Boone County, Kentucky. Norris was apparently an indulgent master who allowed the Powells to grow produce and take it to Indiana to sell. He once took David and Lucy and their eldest son, Lewis, to a circus in nearby Lawrenceburgh, Indiana.[5] In October 1847 the Powell family escaped into Indiana and eventually made their way to Cass County, Michigan, where they lived for about two years. The Powells were described as "quiet industrious persons" who never gave "any intimation that they were slaves." During this period they acquired land and "were laboring hard to pay for it."[6]

On Thursday, September 27, 1849, nine Kentuckians led by John Norris forcibly entered the Powell house, near Cassopolis, Michigan, where they found Lucy Powell and three of her sons. Norris and his men seized the Powells and informed them that they were taking them back to Kentucky. Norris later claimed that Mrs. Powell and two of her sons were willing to return with him, although he acknowledged that she expressed some concern about being separated from her husband. He also admitted that Lewis Powell, the oldest of the children, resisted, but (according to Norris) only because he had married a Michigan woman. Norris offered to take Lewis Powell's wife back to Kentucky and promised to treat her well, but, not surprisingly, she declined his offer. Norris admitted that he was forced to tie up Lewis to prevent him from escaping.

Lucy Powell offered a different story. While suing Norris for kidnapping she swore that Norris and his compatriots "broke into the house . . . while" she "was sleeping in her bed, & with threatening language & a violent & forcible manner dragged [her] . . . from [her] bed, after drawing their pistols & bowie knives & threatening to shoot" anyone who stopped them. They then "bound" Lucy "with cords" and forced her into a wagon.[7]

Whichever version of these events is correct, both sides agreed that Norris then placed Lucy and three of her sons in a wagon for the trip back to Kentucky. Some of Norris's party remained to prevent the other people in the house, including Lewis Powell's wife, some black men, and a visiting white neighbor, from seeking help.[8]

The seizure of the Powells illustrates why fugitive slave rendition was such a powerful moral, ideological, and political issue for northerners. The Powells were not recent runaways from the South. They had lived in Cass County long enough to acquire land, establish roots, and become part of the community. Their eldest son, Lewis, had married a woman from the community. Taking them back to slavery meant breaking up families, depriving mortgage holders of the opportunity to receive full payment for their loan, and destroying the continuity and harmony of a community.[9] The methods of the seizure also infringed on the rights of nonfugitives.

Norris violated the privacy of a number of blacks who shared the house with the Powells. These people, as well as a white farmer visiting the house, were threatened and held at gunpoint while the Powells were seized. Lewis Powell's wife and others in the house were held hostage by some of the Norris party while the rest of the group left for Indiana. All of this was done to vindicate Norris's property rights.

INITIAL COURT HEARINGS AND THE RELEASE

The guard left at the Powell house was either ineffective or did not remain there long enough, because by noon the next day Wright Maudlin, a white friend of the Powell family, caught up with Norris and his party at South Bend, Indiana. Maudlin swore an affidavit on behalf of the Powells, attesting that he knew them to be free residents of Michigan.[10] On the basis of this affidavit South Bend attorney Edwin B. Crocker secured a writ of habeas corpus, and the deputy sheriff, aided by a large contingent of South Bend citizens, stopped Norris about a mile south of the city. After heated words and threats of violence, Norris and his party agreed to return to South Bend, where their claim to the Powells would be decided.

In South Bend, Norris placed his alleged slaves in the custody of the sheriff while he sought counsel. Within a few hours Norris had retained Jonathan A. Liston to represent him. Through Liston, Norris answered the writ of habeas corpus, asserting that he held the Powells as slaves under Kentucky law and was returning to his home state "with the within-named persons as my own slaves and property, as such fugitives from labor." Although Norris's return did not specify that he was acting under the fugitive slave clause of the Constitution or under the federal law of 1793 adopted to implement that clause, his use of the phrase "fugitives from labor" suggests he understood that he was vindicating his federal right by seizing the slaves in Michigan and taking them back to Kentucky.[11]

In what later proved to be a catastrophic error, Edwin B. Crocker, representing the Powells, did not dispute the facts set forth in Norris's return. He did not, in other words, deny that the Powells were fugitive slaves belonging to Norris. Rather, he simply asserted that "the matters set forth in the foregoing return are not sufficient in law to authorize said Norris to restrain them in their liberty."[12]

There are three possible explanations for Crocker's action. First, the Powells may have admitted privately that they were Norris's slaves and

Crocker did not want to put himself in jeopardy by denying what he knew to be true. Second, Crocker may have believed that Norris could only remove fugitive slaves if he had a certificate of removal, as specified under the 1793 federal act. Because Norris did not have such a certificate, Crocker may have felt his answer was legally sufficient to get the Powells released without having to raise the substantive question of their actual status as slaves or free people. Finally, Crocker may have believed that this answer was sufficient because Norris failed to provide any kind of documentary proof, certified before a Kentucky judge, as set out in the Fugitive Slave Law of 1793.[13]

Because the attorneys had only about an hour to prepare their cases, neither side was able to present wholly correct arguments on the nature of the Fugitive Slave Law of 1793. Crocker argued that Norris had not complied with the law because he did not have a certificate of removal from a judge. Liston replied that "a claimant had a right to arrest any person whom he might claim as his slave, wherever he could find him, take him wherever he pleased, without any proof, certificate, warrant or process whatever, and if anyone interfered or questioned the claim, they did it at their peril." Liston offered "no authority whatever . . . to sustain this position."[14]

Both sides were only partially correct in these arguments. The leading case on this subject, *Prigg* v. *Pennsylvania,*[15] acknowledged that the fugitive slave clause of the Constitution protected the common-law right of recaption. Thus a slave owner could capture runaway slaves without first going to a magistrate or obtaining a certificate of removal. On this issue Liston was correct; Crocker was clearly wrong in asserting that Norris could not proceed under the federal law because he did not have a certificate of removal from a magistrate.

That Crocker was wrong is not surprising, since he did not have a copy of the opinion in *Prigg*. On the day of the hearing Crocker wired an attorney in Niles, Michigan, "requesting him to send up Peter's Reports containing a decision of a Pennsylvania case as there was a trial pending." The telegraph operator could not recall the name of the case, but doubtless it was *Prigg*.[16]

Liston, who also argued without the benefit of any cases or much preparation, also misunderstood the federal law, the Constitution, and the precedent in *Prigg*. While Justice Joseph Story held that a master was "clothed with entire authority, in every state in the Union, to seize and recapture his slave" without first going to a magistrate for a certificate of removal, he found that this right was limited to situations where the owner "can do it without any breach of the peace, or any illegal violence."[17] Since Norris had breached the peace in Michigan and conducted illegal violence by holding hostage the free people (black and white) in the Powell house, his taking of the Powells certainly seemed subject to judicial scrutiny.

On Friday night, after extensive argument over the requirements of the federal law of 1793, Probate Judge Elisha Egbert ruled against Norris and released the Powells. Egbert's decision apparently rested on his belief that the 1793 law required Norris to obtain a certificate of removal before taking the Powells back to Kentucky. Egbert believed that under the law of 1793 "the master had no right to arrest the fugitives to take them out of the state where the arrest was made, but for the purpose only of taking them before some judicial officer of the state, or of the United States."[18] Egbert may have also believed that Norris could not comply with the evidentiary requirements of the 1793 law because he lacked sufficient proof that the Powells were his slaves. The 1793 act provided that a claimant be given a certificate of removal "upon proof to the satisfaction of such judge or magistrate, either by oral testimony or affidavit taken before and certified by a magistrate" of the state from which the fugitive had fled.[19] But there is no indication that Norris had such a certified affidavit with him.

With Judge Egbert still on the bench, Norris and his compatriots "seized the captives with one hand, brandishing their weapons with the other, threatening to shoot the first man that interfered." Attorney Liston urged his clients to protect their property and "blow through" anyone who attempted to help the blacks escape. Both sides shouted threats and a riot almost began.[20]

When calm was finally restored, Norris produced a new warrant he had obtained for the arrest of his slaves. (He subsequently claimed that "he was but serving this writ when he drew his weapons upon the people.") Norris's writ was based on an Indiana statute of 1824 that allowed alleged fugitive slaves to be seized under a state warrant and committed "to the jail of the county, there to be kept at the expense of the applicant" for up to sixty days while awaiting a jury trial on their status.[21] After the warrant was produced and examined, the Powells were taken to the county jail.

With order restored and the Powells safely in jail, attorneys for both sides retired for the weekend, no doubt to prepare for the trial on Monday. For the first time since Norris had arrived in South Bend, the lawyers and judge involved in the case would have the time to carefully examine the statutes and cases relating to the rendition of fugitive slaves.

Legal maneuvering did not stop with the weekend. On Saturday friends of the Powells swore out warrants against Norris and his friends for assault and riot "predicated upon their violent proceedings in the court-house." In addition, the Powells initiated trespass and false-imprisonment suits against Norris. Norris's lawyer had to post a $2,000 bond guaranteeing the slave catchers would appear in this case. Meanwhile, Wright Maudlin returned to Michigan to swear out a complaint against Norris for kidnapping. He then "made affidavit before a justice of the peace in South Bend, that Norris and his party had been guilty of kidnapping in Michigan," and under this affidavit the justice issued an arrest warrant for Norris. This warrant was based on an Indiana law that allowed for the temporary incarceration of a suspected fugitive from justice upon probable cause, pending the requisition of the governor of the state in which the crime had occurred. The constable, in compliance with Crocker's wishes, refused to act on the warrant, but held it in reserve in case Norris should attempt to flee.[22]

While papers and writs were being filed from all sides, some two hundred residents of Cass County, many of them armed, arrived in South Bend in response to a telegram sent by two South Bend blacks urging a black in Niles, Michigan, to "bring his force" to South Bend.[23] The contingent from Cass County was integrated but predominantly black. In addition, blacks from other parts of northern Indiana arrived in South Bend. They were supported by the white community of that town, which was increasingly hostile toward Norris.

On Monday the Powells were once again brought before Judge Egbert on yet another writ of habeas corpus. Neither Norris nor his lawyer appeared to contest the writ. Nor did they try to enforce their right, under Indiana law, to hold the fugitive slaves. Norris's change in tactics was apparently motivated by a realistic assessment of the social situation in South Bend and an unrealistic assessment of the legal situation by his attorney, Liston.

Over the weekend Norris and Liston had concluded that it would be impossible to safely remove the Powells from South Bend, even if they should win the legal right to do so. By this time hundreds of blacks were in South Bend, armed and ready to stop Norris, and local whites seemed completely in sympathy with them. Wisely, Norris abandoned his slaves.[24]

Norris's assessment of the situation further revealed the inadequacy of the 1793 law. Just as the law failed to protect free blacks from arbitrary seizure and illegal violence, so too it failed to protect slave owners who seized their slaves. There is little doubt that the Powells were Norris's slaves. And although he may have breached the peace in seizing them, once they were in his possession he had a constitutional right to bring them back to Kentucky. While the 1793 statute provided a *procedure* for implementing that right, it did not provide any *mechanism* for actually enforcing the right against a hostile populace. Under the circumstances, Norris felt it was imprudent to attempt to vindicate his right under the law of Kentucky and the U.S. Constitution.

Norris could have called on local or state officials to enforce the Indiana act of 1824, under which the Powells were being held by the sheriff. But attorney Liston seems to have doubted the constitutionality of this act allowing for the incarceration of fugitive slaves. According to Crocker's account, Liston admitted that Norris held the blacks "by a writ issued under a *State law,* which the U.S. Supreme Court had decided to be unconstitutional and void."[25] This erroneous conclusion was based on yet another misreading of *Prigg* v. *Pennsylvania.*

In *Prigg,* Justice Story had found Pennsylvania's personal liberty law of 1826 unconstitutional because it placed additional burdens on a claimant, beyond the requirements of the 1793 Fugitive Slave Law. He declared that the states did not have the authority "to interfere, and, as it were, by way of complement to the legislation of Congress, to prescribe additional regulations, and what they may deem auxiliary provision for the same purpose."[26] The Indiana act of 1824, which facilitated the seizure of a fugitive slave and allowed for a summary proceeding before a state magistrate, did not clearly place additional burdens on the claimant. In this sense the law might have been held constitutional under *Prigg,* because in that decision Justice Story also affirmed that "the states, in virtue of their general police power, possess full jurisdiction to arrest and restrain runaway slaves, and remove them from their borders, and otherwise to secure themselves against their depredations and evil examples." Story believed that under such laws "the rights of the owners of fugitive slaves are in no just sense interfered with, or regulated by such a course; and in many cases, the operations of this police power, although designed generally for other purposes, for the protection, safety, and peace of the state, may essentially promote and aid the interest of the owners."[27]

The only part of the law that seemed to place additional burdens on the claimant was the appeal procedure, which allowed a fugitive slave to ask for a jury trial, provided the fugitive could pay for the costs of such a trial.[28] Because of this provision the U.S. Supreme Court might have found the 1824 law unconstitutional under the "extra burdens" test developed in *Prigg*. But the increasingly proslavery Supreme Court[29] might very well have determined that only the appeals clause of the law was unconstitutional, and that the rest of the law was simply a good-faith effort on the part of Indiana to help southerners capture runaway slaves.[30]

Attorney Liston, however, did not read *Prigg* as being helpful to his client, and he saw no reason to appear on Monday to defend the seizure of the Powells against the writ of habeas corpus. Without anyone to oppose the writ, Judge Egbert released Norris's slaves. Egbert also apparently believed that the Indiana law of 1824 was void under *Prigg*. The Powells "rode off singing the songs of freedom" with their black and white neighbors from Michigan.[31] They returned to Cass County and perhaps after that went on to Canada or some other more secure haven. In any event, their freedom secured, they disappeared from the records.

Once the Powells were free, the various legal actions pending against Norris melted away. The kidnapping charges in Michigan were never pressed, and the threatened indictment for the courthouse riot never materialized. False imprisonment charges were continued but never pursued.[32] Norris and his friends left South Bend on Monday, October 1, 1849.

THE LAWSUIT

The South Bend fugitive slave case might have ended with John Norris's return to Kentucky. His four-day trip from Kentucky to Michigan to South Bend had been wholly unproductive; indeed, it was a disaster. Rather than returning with his slaves, Norris had barely avoided jail and had been forced to spend money on legal fees. At this point some masters might have cut their losses and given up on the whole matter. But Norris's slaves were valuable property. Norris estimated that Lucy and her three sons were worth over $2,500, a substantial sum of money in 1849.

Under the Fugitive Slave Law of 1793 Norris had two potential causes of action against those who had helped free his slaves. The statute provided a $500 penalty for anyone who "knowingly and willingly obstructs or hinders" a claimant or "shall rescue such fugitive from such claimant." This could be recovered by an "action of debt, in any court proper to try the same." The action did not preclude a separate suit for the value of the slaves and other incidental expenses.[33] Because of jurisdictional requirements, Norris had to pursue these two causes of action in separate courts.[34]

U.S. district courts had jurisdiction over cases involving $500 or less, while cases involving more than $500 came within the jurisdiction of U.S. circuit courts. Consequently, Norris had to file the action for debt (which was limited to $500) in district court and the suit for the value of his lost slaves in circuit court.[35] These jurisdictional requirements would cause problems for Norris.

In December Norris initiated a suit in U.S. district court in Indianapolis against Edwin Crocker and eight others, for trespass on the case for the value of the four slaves who had been taken from his custody in September.[36] But because the value of the case was more than $500, and thus exceeded the jurisdiction of the district court, in January 1850 Norris asked for a dismissal of the case without prejudice. The district court dismissed the suit and ordered Norris to pay the defendants for their court costs and legal fees.[37] Norris might have sued in this court under the 1793 law for the $500 penalty, but, for unknown reasons, he failed to do so.[38]

Norris pressed ahead with his effort to recover the value of his lost property, though. His attorneys began deposing witnesses in February 1850 and continued taking depositions until April.[39] At the May term of the U.S. circuit court in Indianapolis, Norris again filed suit against eight men who had helped his slaves, naming Leander B. Newton as the first defendant (Newton was a particularly aggressive member of the posse that had stopped Norris outside South Bend). The others sued included Edwin Crocker, the Powells' attorney, and Lot Day, the deputy sheriff who first stopped Norris with his slaves.[40] This was the beginning of a five-year legal struggle marked by Norris's tenacity in seeking damages and the defendants' ingenuity in avoiding paying them.

On May 21 Norris asked that depositions in the case be published, and the defendants asked that the suit be dismissed "for want of sufficient security for costs" on behalf of the plaintiff. The next day the defendants moved for a stay in the proceedings until Norris paid their costs for the case that had been dismissed the previous term. Although these motions were dismissed, Norris was forced to post a security bond of $1,000 to cover the defendants' costs if he should lose the case. Arguments on various defense motions continued until June 5, when a jury was finally empaneled. The trial began on June 6 and continued until June 12, when the jury found in favor of Norris and awarded him $2,850 plus court costs.[41]

The evidence at the trial detailed the events of the previous September. While the facts of the case were not really in dispute, their meaning certainly was. Five aspects of the case made it quite different from most other fugitive slave cases. First, unlike the rescues of fugitive slaves in other places, the South Bend case was not a clear-cut rescue. In the famous cases of the 1850s—such as the Shadrach rescue in Boston (1851), the Jerry rescue in Syracuse (1851), the Racine rescue that led to the prosecution of Sherman Booth (1854), and the Oberlin-Wellington rescue (1858)— the alleged fugitives were forcibly removed from the custody of the local police or federal marshals. But in South Bend the only time the Powells were in police custody was when they were removed from the custody of the slave catchers.[42] Second, unlike other rescues, Norris's alleged slaves were not taken from him by a mob or an unlawful gathering.[43] On the contrary, they were removed from Norris's custody by lawful process and released after a formal hearing before a judge. When Norris then produced a second writ, the alleged slaves were once again incarcerated and held in jail so that a proper judicial forum could determine their status. In a very real sense there was not a rescue at all. Third, at no time did Norris, the claimant, produce any evidence that the Powells were, in fact, his slaves. Fourth, Norris himself failed to appear or send counsel when the status of the blacks was finally decided at a habeas corpus hearing. Not having contested their final release by a judge, it is difficult to see how Norris could have claimed that his slaves were rescued. Finally, because Norris had apparently allowed his slaves to go to Indiana on some occasions before they escaped, it was not unreasonable to argue that some of the Powells were already free under Indiana law and various precedents involving slave sojourn and transit in free states.[44]

JUSTICE MCLEAN'S CHARGE TO THE JURY

Given these uncertainties, the key element of *Norris v. Newton* was not the details of what happened in South Bend but rather the charge to the jury by Supreme Court Justice John McLean, who was riding circuit at the time and presided over the trial. A different charge to the jury might have led to a verdict for the defendants. McLean's charge, however, and his summary of the facts for the jury were slanted to favor the plaintiff, and they undermine his reputation as an "antislavery" judge.[45]

Under the fugitive slave clause of the Constitution, as interpreted in *Prigg*, Norris had a right to seize his fugitive slaves anywhere he could find them and return home with them without seeking any judicial process. This right of "self-help," however, was available to a master only if he could exercise it without any breach of the peace and without having to call on any state marshals, sheriffs, or judges for aid. If the master could not seize his runaways peaceably, or if he needed official help, then the master had to provide proof of ownership, as specified in the law, to a judge or magistrate, who would in turn issue a certificate of removal allowing the master to take the alleged fugitive slave back to his home state. The Fugitive Slave Law of 1793 allowed Norris to recover for the loss of his slaves if he could show that Newton, Crocker, and the other defendants did "knowingly or willingly obstruct or hinder" Norris in "seizing or arresting" the fugitives or did "rescue such fugitive from such claimant" or did "harbour or conceal such person, after notice that he or she was fugitive from labour." [46]

McLean's charge recounted the facts of the escape by the Powells and their eventual seizure by Norris. He took at face value the assertions by Norris that Lucy Powell and her two younger children were willing to return to Kentucky without protest. Although McLean noted that Lewis Powell had "his arms tied to prevent his escape," [47] he did not seem to think this constituted any breach of the peace. Nor did McLean point out that Norris had left armed guards at the Powell home after removing the four blacks.

Next McLean stressed that when the sheriff stopped Norris outside South Bend to serve him a writ of habeas corpus, the sheriff was accompanied by "one hundred and forty, or upward" citizens and that some were "armed, others had bricks, stones, or clubs." McLean pointed out that when Norris drew his own weapons, "Crocker, one of the defendants, informed the plaintiff that the sheriff had a writ of habeas corpus, and that they had no other object than to ascertain whether the negroes belonged to him." At this point, according to McLean's charge to the jury, Norris told Crocker to "ask the negroes whether they were not his slaves." Crocker told the blacks "to answer no questions." Crocker then told Norris that "resistance would be useless, as there was force enough to take the negroes back to [the] village; but if the plaintiff [Norris] would agree to return, he should have a fair trial, and would not detain him more than an hour or two." [48]

McLean's recounting of these events ignored the crucial fact that the writ of habeas corpus had been secured on the basis of an affidavit by a neighbor of the Powells who swore that they were free persons. Under these circumstances, the actions by Crocker and the other South Bend citizens seem not only legally justifiable but laudable. Responding to the call of the sheriff, citizens formed a posse comitatus to enforce a writ lawfully issued by a judge on probable cause. The fact that the threat of coercion was implicit when Norris found himself surrounded was hardly surprising. How else, McLean might have asked (but did not), could a writ of habeas corpus be served on a group of armed men suspected of kidnapping?

Next McLean recounted the events of the first hearing before Judge Egbert. Here again, the facts were undisputed but their meaning was less certain. None of the parties had access to the Supreme Court's opinion in *Prigg* v. *Pennsylvania,* the relevant precedent for interpreting the Fugitive Slave Law of 1793. The lawyers for both sides had confused notions of what *Prigg* had actually held. So too did Judge Egbert.

McLean apparently thought Judge Egbert or Norris should have been familiar with this precedent and the requirements of the 1793 law. But this was probably expecting too much. While the 1793 law gave state judges jurisdiction over such cases, the Court had ruled in *Prigg* that the Congress could not require a state judge to enforce a federal law. In fact, many state judges interpreted *Prigg* to deny them jurisdiction over fugitive slave cases.[49] Under these circumstances it seems odd that McLean should have expected a state judge to know the law, or even to have quick access to it. The person who ought to have known the law, and perhaps should have brought a copy of the 1793 statute and the *Prigg* opinion with him,[50] was Norris, since it was clearly in his best interest to be able to prove his right to the Powells. But he lacked any information about the Fugitive Slave Law. Nor did he carry any proof from Kentucky—such as a sworn affidavit before a Boone County judge—that he was the owner of the Powells. Thus it hardly seems inappropriate for Judge Egbert to have issued the writ of habeas corpus and discharged the Powells. In both Indiana and Michigan the law presumed that all persons were free. Since Norris had no evidence to prove otherwise, and since a white neighbor of the Powells swore they were free, the best evidence seemed to favor releasing them.

After Egbert ordered the Powells released, Norris seized them in the courtroom—at gunpoint—in order to serve his state writ. Crocker, according to McLean's account, had "warned the state officer not to issue the writ" on the grounds that the Indiana Supreme Court had declared the Indiana law to be unconstitutional under *Prigg*. Nevertheless, McLean admitted that a state officer did issue this writ, Norris did regain custody of the Powells, and the sheriff did consent to place the Powells in jail until the matter could be sorted out on the following Monday.[51]

McLean noted that over the weekend civil charges were pressed against

Norris for kidnapping, and criminal charges were initiated for Norris's breach of the peace in Egbert's courtroom. He also reminded the jury that "the streets of the village of South Bend were crowded with people, the greater part of whom were colored . . . [who had] entered the village in companies, some of them bearing firearms, and almost all of them had clubs." Testimony placed the number of blacks at anywhere from 150 to 400. On Monday there was yet another hearing on the status of the Powells. Although given notice of this proceeding, Norris chose to boycott it. As a result, McLean noted, "the slaves were discharged by the judge, and, surrounded by a great number of colored persons, they proceeded from the court-house to a wagon, in which they were conveyed off."[52]

Had McLean summarized all the relevant evidence in an evenhanded way, the jury might have sided with the defendants. It is true that the defendants had impeded Norris's return to Kentucky. But they did so under a legitimate writ of habeas corpus issued by a state judge. To find them liable for their actions would imperil the entire system of local justice, which to a great extent relied on the willingness of citizens to support the courts and law enforcement officers. Crocker had been more active in the case. He had sought various writs from the courts that did impede Norris's return to Kentucky. But given the uncertainty of the status of the Powells and the sworn testimony of a white neighbor from Michigan that they were free persons, a jury might have concluded that Crocker was within his rights—and perhaps his obligations as an officer of the court (as all lawyers are)—to prevent the kidnapping of four free people. Furthermore, Norris's refusal to make an appearance at the final habeas corpus hearing should have left him in a vulnerable position in the lawsuit. After all, he had not actively pursued or protected his claim when given an opportunity to do so.

In explaining the law to the jury, McLean carefully examined the roles of Crocker, Newton, and the other defendants in light of Norris's constitutional rights and the precedent in *Prigg*. He also weighed the excessive zeal of the defendants in the case. Crocker's role was especially important. McLean admitted that "so far as" Crocker's "acts were limited to the duties of counsel, he is not responsible" for the loss of the slaves. "But, if he exceeded the proper limits of a counsellor at law, he is responsible for his acts the same as any other individual."[53]

McLean began his analysis of the law with a discussion of *Prigg*. As a member of the U.S. Supreme Court he had dissented in *Prigg*. He had particularly opposed the right of "self-help" found in Justice Story's opinion, which McLean believed "was not necessary to the rights of the master, and, if practically enforced, would produce great excitement in the free states."[54] But this view was no longer relevant. In what has been called a "retreat to formalism,"[55] McLean told the jury he was as "fully bound by that decision as if I had assented to it."[56] In this apparent effort to assert the "formal obligation of the dissenter to accept the decision of the majority and to rule according to it,"[57] McLean offered what might be considered an extreme and harsh interpretation of *Prigg*.

McLean acknowledged the importance of the writ of habeas corpus. Noting that all people within a jurisdiction were "bound by its laws and subject to its jurisdiction," McLean believed the judge had a right to issue such a writ to "inquire into the cause of detention." He told the jury, "There can be no higher offence against the laws of humanity and justice, or against the dignity of a state and its laws, than to arrest a free man within its protection, with a view of making him a slave."[58]

Had the activities of Newton, Crocker, and the other South Bend defendants ended with this initial inquiry and the hearing before Judge Egbert, it is likely that McLean would have urged a verdict for the defendants. But McLean told the jury that the right to issue a writ of habeas corpus was "a special and limited jurisdiction." Once Norris made his return to the writ "being clearly within the provisions of the constitution, as decided in" *Prigg* v. *Pennsylvania,*

> and the facts of that return being admitted by the counsel for the negroes, the judge could exercise no further jurisdiction in the case. His power was at an end. The fugitives were in the legal custody of their master—a custody authorized by the constitution and sanctioned by the supreme court of the Union. If the facts, on the return of the habeas corpus, had been denied, it would have been incumbent on the master to prove them, and that would have terminated the power of the judge.[59]

In McLean's view, Norris's reply was sufficient to establish his claim to the Powells because Crocker's reply did not specifically deny that the Powells were slaves. Crocker's error lay in assuming that the form of the 1793 law had to be followed and that Norris's failure to follow the procedures set out in that law destroyed whatever claim he had. Thus McLean interpreted Crocker's failure to deny that the Powells were slaves as an admission that they were slaves. This was perhaps the most proslavery aspect of McLean's interpretation of the law and the *Prigg* precedent. It led McLean to assert that any attempt to interfere with Norris after the court hearing violated his rights. Because Norris held the Powells under a federal claim, "the discharge of the fugitives by the judge was void, and, consequently, can give no protection to those who acted under it."[60]

McLean's analysis was inherently dangerous for two reasons. First, the case undermined the liberty of free blacks living in the North. Norris had no documentary or other proof that the Powells were his slaves. He merely asserted it in an answer to the writ of habeas corpus. Under McLean's ruling, any white southerner might seize blacks, claim them as slaves, and take them to the South without any proof of their status. The fact that one of the Powells' white neighbors traveled as far as South Bend to protect their freedom indicates that there was a reasonable doubt about their status. But under McLean's ruling, a state judge investigating that status was required to take the word of the claimant without any other proof.

Second, McLean's ruling undermined the rule of law in the North. Based on his understanding of the law and the evidence presented, Judge Egbert had ruled that the Powells were free. Crocker, their lawyer, loudly repeated the judge's verdict. Sheriff Day enforced the verdict, with the help of spectators in the court. These people were not rioting or breaking the law so far as they knew. On the contrary, they were helping to enforce the law against a band of apparent kidnappers who wanted to use violence to seize the Powells in the face of Judge Egbert's ruling. Yet, according to McLean, those people who thought they were helping to enforce the law were now the lawless ones and liable for their actions.

McLean, no doubt anticipating this criticism of his opinion, declared that the "forms of law" that the defendants "assumed" could "afford no protection to any one." He asserted that once "the legal custody of the fugitives by the master" was "admitted, as stated in the return of the habeas corpus, every step taken subsequently was against law and in violation of his rights." In other words, because Crocker had not denied the assertions of Norris, McLean assumed he had admitted them. Once Crocker had admitted that the Powells were Norris's slaves, it did not matter how Norris asserted his authority over them. They were his, and he had a right to take them back to Kentucky.[61]

McLean also had an answer for those who might have said they were merely supporting the law as interpreted by Judge Egbert: "A mistake of the law cannot prejudice the rights of the plaintiff."[62] While this is sensible, McLean nevertheless placed men like Crocker, Newton, and Day in a cruel dilemma: either they could obey the courts of their own states and risk a lawsuit if the judge they obeyed was in error, or they could attempt to interpret the federal law for themselves and risk a contempt citation from a local judge and perhaps a suit, or even prosecution, for failing to protect free blacks from kidnapping.

This result was simply one more unfortunate legacy of *Prigg*. By determining that a master had a right of self-help to recover fugitive slaves, the Court had opened the door to a kind of lawless anarchy. Under *Prigg*, masters could seize their slaves and take them home as long as they did so without a "breach of the peace." No law was necessary, and no master needed to follow the procedures set out in the 1793 Fugitive Slave Law.[63] McLean, who had dissented in *Prigg*, in part because of the dangers the decision posed to free blacks and the public peace in the North, had now taken the doctrine of *Prigg* one step further by asserting that a master could disregard a local judge, and anyone who supported the local judge would be subject to a lawsuit.

Justice McLean might have avoided these issues if he had interpreted one piece of evidence in a different manner. Attorneys for the defendants argued that "the slaves were entitled to their freedom, from the privilege given to them by the plaintiff to visit Lawrenceburgh, in Indiana, on their own business, to sell articles of produce, and at other times were sent there on the business of the plaintiff."[64] This claim rested on a principle of law that, by 1850, was well established in the North and parts of the South, including Kentucky. This principle held that a slave became free when the master voluntarily took the slave to a free jurisdiction or permitted the slave to go to a free jurisdiction.[65]

This defense claim raised a question: Were the Powells actually in the North with the permission of their master? While the evidence was not conclusive on this question, the jury had heard enough testimony to have decided that Norris had allowed some of the Powells to visit free Indiana before their escape. McLean left this factual question for the jury, declaring that the "conflicting statement of witnesses will be examined and weighed carefully by the jury."[66] In summarizing the evidence, however, McLean presented it in such a way that jurors probably felt pressured to conclude that Norris had not let his slaves travel to Indiana.

Even if the jury had concluded that Norris had allowed his slaves to visit Indiana, McLean's presentation of the law was not helpful to the defendants. He told the jury that if they did find that Norris had allowed the slaves to visit Indiana, he would consider the issue "on a motion after verdict."[67] Had McLean been inclined to favor freedom in this case, he might easily have added that such a finding by the jury would have led to a verdict for the defendants.[68]

Like many northern jurists, Justice McLean was troubled by slavery. He personally opposed it, and his wife held "pronounced antislavery views." Salmon P. Chase, the nation's leading antislavery lawyer-politician, believed that McLean was "sound on slavery, politically and personally, if not judicially."[69] Indeed, Chase believed that McLean had "a kind heart and honest purposes" but had "suffered his reverence for imagined rights under the Constitution to lead him into conclusions from which" Chase would "ever shrink."[70]

This characterization of McLean raises two critical questions. How do we explain McLean's proslavery recapitulation of the facts and his instructions to the jury in *Norris* v. *Newton*? And how did McLean formally justify his course?

Robert Cover argues that McLean was personally antislavery but professionally faithful to his role as an "impartial judge." This created great inner tension for him, which he resolved by a "retreat to formalism." Cover argues that

> the legal actor did not choose between liberty and slavery. He had to choose between liberty and ordered federalism; between liberty and consistent limits on the judicial function; between liberty and fidelity to public trust; between liberty and adherence to the public corporate undertakings of nationhood; or, as some of the judges would have it, between liberty and the viability of the social compact.[71]

This approach to the law was certainly evident in the South Bend case. McLean concluded his charge to the jury by trying to separate law from morality. He acknowledged that "no earthly power has a right to interpose between a man's conscience and his Maker." But such a religious approach applied only to private issues. For public issues, "general rules have been adopted, in the form of laws, for the protection of the rights of persons and things. These laws lie at the foundation of the social compact, and their observation is essential to the maintenance of civilization. In these matters, the law, and not conscience, constitutes the rule of action."[72] McLean urged the jury to consider only the law and to ignore their consciences.

He also urged the jury to forget the fact that this case involved slavery, for "with the abstract principles of slavery we have nothing to do." The duty of the jurors was solely "found in the constitution of the Union, as construed by the supreme court." McLean reminded the jury that "the chief glory and excellence of our institutions" was found in "the supremacy of the laws." [73]

FROM VERDICT TO JUDGMENT COLLECTION

McLean thus virtually directed the jury to return a verdict for the plaintiff. He ended by telling the jurors that "every one who arrays himself against" the Fugitive Slave Law "and endeavors by open or secret means to bring it into contempt, so that it may be violated with impunity, is an enemy to the interest of his country." Not surprisingly, the jury returned a verdict of $2,850 for Norris.[74] Added to this were various costs and charges, including the cost and fees for bringing the plaintiff's witnesses to Indianapolis.[75] The Kentuckian might not have his slaves, but he had won enough money to replace them.

Winning a lawsuit, however, does not always guarantee that the judgment will be collected. Immediately after the verdict the defendants moved for a new trial and an arrest in judgment. Attorneys for both sides argued this motion before it was overruled. The defendants then tried, also unsuccessfully, to limit to no more than three the witnesses they would have to pay.[76]

Although Norris's award was large, the defendants seemed to be capable of paying it. Edwin B. Crocker, in particular, was a wealthy landowner and banker. But he was also a shrewd businessman who took care to protect his assets during the trial. With the trial winding down and defeat becoming more and more likely, Crocker began a series of collusive land transactions with his family and others in South Bend to make him appear to be without assets. Late in the trial Crocker telegraphed his father, Isaac Crocker, asking him to sell his land. On June 6, 1850, Isaac Crocker sold Edwin B. Crocker's property to Edwin's younger brother Charles for $25. The following day a deed for this land was recorded in Charles Crocker's name. On May 10, 1850, Crocker sold to his father all interests in land that he jointly owned with the State Bank of Indiana. On May 15 Charles Crocker sold some of this land to Theodore Cowles. Other defendants in the case sold their land and property to friends and relatives as well.[77] These transactions were designed solely to prevent Norris from collecting a judgment against the defendants. The beauty of it all, from Edwin Crocker's perspective, was that his brother Charles was actually in California when all these transactions took place.[78]

Norris, of course, had no idea that these transactions were taking place. He simply waited in court, won his case, and the following fall, when the court denied all of the defendants' motions, sought to collect his judgment. At this point, however, Crocker and the other defendants claimed they had no assets.

In May 1851 the U.S. marshal advertised a sale of land that had been owned by Crocker and the other defendants at the time of the trial. Just before the sale Crocker publicly read a notice indicating that for a variety of procedural and technical reasons the marshal's sale would be null and void. Crocker also claimed that the judgments had already been satisfied. Most important, Crocker asserted that none of the defendants had "any right, title interest or claim whatever in" the land being sold. This notice had its intended effect. The marshal reported to the court that he had tried to sell the property as a whole lot and as single parcels, but since no parcel got a bid equal to two-thirds of its value, the property was returned to its owners.[78]

In November 1851 the defendants told the federal court that their property had been levied against three times and they had no more property. Meanwhile, others in South Bend filed papers claiming that they owned various parcels of land that Norris claimed belonged to the defendants. One man argued that some of these lots were conveyed to him as early as 1847.[79]

These alleged sales, Crocker's various motions and claims, and the refusal of anyone to buy the land at auction in South Bend forced Norris back into federal court. This time he went before U.S. District Judge Elisha Huntington, who sat in his capacity as an equity judge in chancery court. In *Norris v. Lapier et al.*[80] Norris sought a ruling in equity to nullify fraudulent land sales made during and after the 1850 trial. Because the court only met twice a year, and often for only a short time, the case dragged on from 1851 until 1855. In May 1851 Norris brought the case into chancery court, but it was immediately continued until the next term. In each term from November 1851 until June 1854 the cases were continued.[81]

Finally, on December 19, 1854, Judge Huntington issued a decree declaring null and void the sales of the defendants' land and other property made during and immediately after the trial. He also ordered the property to be sold to raise $4,893, the amount then due in initial judgment, fees and costs, and accumulated interest.[82] By the time the sale was finally over, this figure rose to nearly $5,000.[83] This did not include any money Norris owed his lawyers or Norris's other expenses in these and related trials, however. In February 1855 U.S. Marshal John Robinson advertised various tracts of land owned by Crocker, Newton, Amable Lapier, and Solomon Palmer. By this time the other original defendants had settled with Norris for various sums ranging from $50 to $1,000. The land of the remaining four defendants was to be sold at auction on the steps of the St. Joseph County Courthouse in South Bend on March 29, 1855.[84]

At the March 29 sale the marshal offered to rent the land for up to seven years to anyone who would pay the sums due. There were no bidders. Then he offered all the land as one lot, but again no one bid on it. Finally, he offered it for sale as separate lots. At this point two men, William True and John Brownfield, bid on some of the lots, offering $1,150.[85] It is likely that these two purchasers were not hostile to the interests of Newton, Crocker, and the other defendants. William True may have purchased the land for a relative, David True, who was one of the defendants in the chancery case over the collusive sales.[86]

True and Brownfield immediately paid for the land, and the marshal divided their payment among the clerk of the court, Norris's attorney, the marshal, and the court, for distribution to pay various fees. Consequently, Norris himself walked away with only $200 of the first $1,000 collected.[87]

No one else bid on any of the other lots, probably because of community solidarity and pressure. This turn of events forced Norris to bid on the land himself[88] because that was the only way he might get some of the judgment owed to him. His purchases came to slightly more than $6,000, which was far more than the amount actually due.[89] There is no clear explanation why the marshal sold more land than was necessary or why Norris purchased more than was necessary.

Norris had bid on the land out of necessity. Until the land was sold he could not collect his judgment. After the land was paid for, the money would be divided among various parties, with most of it going back to Norris. He would then be the owner of large parcels of land in South Bend, which he hoped to sell. Whatever money he received for the land would constitute the collection of his judgment. Before this process could begin he had to pay for the land, but apparently he lacked the ready cash. Therefore, on May 29, 1855, the marshal reported to the U.S. district court that "the bids made by John Norris remain wholly unpaid."[90]

Even though the marshal had not yet been paid, Norris was already negotiating to sell the various parcels of property to people in South Bend. On April 23, 1855, Norris sold a large lot known as Crocker's Orchard to Clark W. Crocker for $2,300. This had once been owned by Edwin B.

Crocker; it now passed to his younger brother. The deed was not recorded until June 22. In the interim Norris received and recorded a deed from the marshal.[91]

In *Bleak House* Charles Dickens warned people to avoid Chancery Court, where cases could go on for generations. John Norris's litigation did not last a generation, but it may have seemed so to him. In May and November 1856 Norris won judgments in chancery to gain quiet title to land previously owned by Leander and Juliette Newton and Solomon Palmer. At the same time he won cases in ejectment against a variety of people, including the Newtons and Mark Whinnery.[92] In January 1857 Norris sold the Palmer property for $600 to Whinnery, who was apparently already living on it. In April 1857 Norris sold the Newton land back to Juliette Newton for a mere $325. This appeared to be the end of Norris's litigation and land transactions in South Bend.[93]

In the end, it appears doubtful that Norris ever got the full amount he won at the trial, much less all the accumulated interest and fees. Records of land transactions indicate that he sold the land for $3,200, far less than he bid for it. Moreover, numerous fees and other costs were taken out of his payment to the marshal. He also had to pay costs and legal fees for his abortive case before the district court in 1849 and his costs and legal fees, which included an expensive (and losing) appeal to the U.S. Supreme Court in *Norris* v. *Crocker*. After eight years of litigation and land transactions, Norris had regained some of the value of his slaves, but not what the court had awarded him. It is possible, of course, that Norris came closer to recouping all his costs and his judgment than we can ascertain. The deeds, records, and papers are incomplete, and we will never know the extent to which the parties settled out of court. But considering the aggravation, not to mention the time, money, and energy consumed by the affair, Norris might have been better off had he not started the litigation in the first place.

The abolitionists in South Bend suffered more. They were saddled with legal fees, and, of course, they did lose their land. Even if they bought it back, as Leander Newton did, it still cost them something.

Least hurt by these events were Edwin Crocker and his family. In the middle of the whole affair he sold his land and other possessions and moved to California to join his brother Charles (who was also a defendant in the chancery case). Charles ended up in the railroad business, joining Leland Stanford, Collis P. Huntington, and Mark Hopkins in building the Central Pacific Railroad. In 1861 Edwin became a director of the Central Pacific Railroad. In 1863 Governor Leland Stanford appointed him to the California Supreme Court, where he remained until 1865, when he left the bench for the far more lucrative position of general counsel of the Central Pacific Railroad. Clark Crocker, who had repurchased land from Norris, also moved to California, where he became a partner in a company that imported Chinese laborers to build the railroads his brothers owned and ran.[94]

Jonathan Liston, Norris's lawyer, probably profited the most from these events. He was in litigation for years, and it is likely that Liston made sure he received his fees no matter how much was left for Norris.

The biggest winners in the whole affair were, of course, the Powells, who returned to Michigan after their release. From there they may have headed further north to the permanent freedom guaranteed by the queen of England. In gaining anonymity, and being lost to history as a result, they gained what they had wanted most all along: the right to live their lives in peace and with some measure of self-determination.

If the Powells were the big winners, who were the losers? It seems that in the end the legal system, the federal courts, and the American union suffered the most from this case. Crocker and his fellow defendants were able to evade a judgment for over five years. In the end they lost, but Norris's victory was worth very little. Norris learned that the fugitive slave clause of the Constitution meant little to him. The South Bend abolitionists showed the value of using legal technicalities and procedures to tie up an opponent they could not otherwise defeat. They were able to ignore, bend, or break the rules with impunity. The slowness of the courts, the great distances Norris had to travel, and the shrewdness of their attorneys worked to their advantage. Although Justice McLean was unwilling to consider the morality of these actions, Crocker and his codefendants were not. In a war against slavery any tactic seemed just, no matter how outrageous. The fraudulent land sales, the constant continuances, and the filibustering tactics showed that northerners could be as contentious for the cause of human freedom as southerners could be for the cause of human property. Since the South Bend defendants believed in the justice of their cause, perhaps the moral of their story is that "justice delayed" can, on occasion, be justice acquired.

NOTES

The quotation in the title is from Justice John McLean's charge to the jury in *Norris v. Newton et al.*, 18 *Federal Cases* 322 (1850), at 326. A research grant from the Indiana Historical Society facilitated my work on this article. I also thank Rory Kugler, who served as my research assistant; Patrick Furlong for discussing the case and generously sharing his research with me; the very patient archivists and librarians at the Indiana Historical Society, the Northern Indiana Historical Society, the St. Joseph County Recorder's Office, and the National Archives Regional Archives and Records Center in Chicago; and Kathleen Stiso Mullins, Thomas Mason, and Roy Shoemaker.

1. For example, John Van Zandt, a Quaker farmer described by his lawyer as "an old man, of limited education and slender means, but distinguished by unquestioned integrity and benevolence of heart"; Salmon P. Chase, *Reclamation of Fugitives from Service: An Argument for the Defendant . . . in the Case of Wharton Jones vs. John Van Zandt* (Cincinnati, Ohio: R. P. Donough and Company, 1847), 6; reprinted in Paul Finkelman, ed., *Slavery, Race, and the American Legal System, 1700–1872: Series II, Fugitive Slaves and American Courts*, 16 vols. (New York: Garland Publishing, 1988), 1:341–448.

2. There are several possible reasons for the lack of contemporaneous interest in the case: the events at South Bend were no doubt thrilling to the participants, but they paled in comparison with other, more dramatic fugitive slave rescues; the relative remoteness of the events—in a small town in Indiana—and the fact that none of the participants were abolitionists in any formal sense and were not connected to any of the national antislavery societies also contributed; the defense attorneys were unknown and unconnected to any abolitionist societies; while the ultimate payout to Norris was high, it was not nearly as outrageous as in many other cases; those involved in the case were ultimately able to pay the judgment to Norris without suffering total financial ruin; and in late September, when the case began, the antislavery editor of the local paper, Schuyler Colfax, was out of town, and thus the release of the slaves was not reported until well after the event was over. The first newspaper report of the case was in the *St. Joseph Valley Register* of October 25, 1849, nearly a month after the initial events had occurred.

3. There is one recent secondary account of this event: Patrick J. Furlong, "The South Bend Fugitive Slave Case," in *We the People: Indiana and the United States Constitution*, ed. Indiana Historical Society (Indianapolis: Indiana Historical Society, 1987), 7–24 (hereinafter cited as Furlong, "South Bend Case"). Much of the following relies on Furlong's excellent reconstruction of the events surrounding the case. The only contemporaneous pamphlet describing the events was, unfortunately, published almost five years before the final outcome of the lawsuits that grew out of the case: [Edwin B. Crocker?], *The South Bend Fugitive Slave Case, Involving the Right to a Writ of Habeas Corpus* (New York: Anti-Slavery Office,

1851); reprinted in Finkelman, ed., *Slavery, Race, and the American Legal System,* 2:1–26 (hereinafter cited as *South Bend Fugitive Slave Case*).

4. The conventional view is presented in Eugene Berwanger, *The Frontier Against Slavery* (Urbana: University of Illinois Press, 1967); and Leon Litwack, *North of Slavery: The Negro in the Free States, 1790–1860* (Chicago: University of Chicago Press, 1961). For a different approach see Paul Finkelman, "The Antebellum Origins of Reconstruction and the Fourteenth Amendment," in *The Facts of Reconstruction,* ed. Eric Anderson and Alfred Moss (Baton Rouge: Louisiana State University Press, 1991).

5. *South Bend Fugitive Slave Case,* 7, 1.

6. Ibid., 1–2.

7. Certified copy of affidavit of Lucy Powell, September 28, 1849, in deposition of John T. Lindsey, clerk of the St. Joseph Circuit Court, February 13, 1850, in case file for *Norris* v. *Newton et al.,* located in the Papers of U.S. Circuit Court for the District of Indiana, Record Group 21, Regional Archives and Records Center, Chicago (hereinafter cited as RARC Case File).

8. *South Bend Fugitive Slave Case,* 1–2; *Norris* v. *Newton,* 322–23.

9. A similar situation occurred in the seizure of the slave that led to the case of *Prigg* v. *Pennsylvania,* 16 Peters (41 U.S.) 539 (1842). On *Prigg* see Paul Finkelman, "*Prigg* v. *Pennsylvania* and Northern State Courts: Antislavery Use of a Proslavery Decision," *Civil War History* 25 (1979): 5–35.

10. *South Bend Fugitive Slave Case,* 2.

11. Ibid., 3.

12. Ibid.

13. I exclude attorney incompetence as a fourth reasonable answer, although that may be the best reason of all.

14. *South Bend Fugitive Slave Case,* 4.

15. 16 Peters (41 U.S.) 539 (1842).

16. Deposition of Charles M. Heaton, April 12, 1850, in RARC Case File.

17. *Prigg,* 613.

18. *Norris* v. *Newton,* 323.

19. *The Statutes at Large of the United States* (Boston: Little, Brown, 1850), 1:302.

20. *South Bend Fugitive Slave Case,* 5. The near riot is discussed in some detail in Furlong, "South Bend Case," 9–10.

21. "An Act Relative to Fugitives from Labor," Act of January 22, 1824, *Indiana Laws, 1824.*

22. *South Bend Fugitive Slave Case,* 5–6; Furlong, "South Bend Case," 10–11.

23. Deposition of Charles M. Heaton, April 12, 1850, in case file for *Norris* v. *Newton et al.,* in RARC Case File. Heaton was the telegraph operator in South Bend.

24. Norris had not, however, given up on vindicating his property right. He

and Liston were already planning to sue anyone in South Bend who might even remotely be tied to the liberation of the slaves.

25. *South Bend Fugitive Slave Case*, 7.

26. *Prigg*, 618.

27. Ibid., 625.

28. "An Act Relative to Fugitives from Labor," Act of January 22, 1824, *Indiana Laws, 1824*.

29. William M. Wiecek, "Slavery and Abolition before the United States Supreme Court, 1820–1860," *Journal of American History* 65 (June 1978): 34–59.

30. In his concurring opinion in *Prigg*, Chief Justice Roger B. Taney argued for precisely this position.

31. *South Bend Fugitive Slave Case*, 7–8.

32. Furlong, "South Bend Case," 12.

33. *Statutes at Large of the United States*, 1:302.

34. Norris could have brought both actions under the federal law in the same state court, but this would have been unwise because a state judge and a state jury, even in Indiana, were much less likely to support him than a federal judge.

35. Section 11 of the Judiciary Act of 1789 gave original jurisdiction to the U.S. circuit courts for "all civil suits at common law where the matter in dispute exceeds $500.00." This jurisdiction was "concurrent with the courts of the several states" (*Statutes at Large of the United States*, 1:73).

36. "The Slave Case—Again," *St. Joseph Valley Register*, December 27, 1849.

37. *Norris* v. *Crocker*, Order Book D, Indiana Federal Court, December term, 1849, entry for January 1, 1850, p. 300, Regional Archives and Records Center, Chicago (hereinafter cited as Order Book D, RARC-Chicago).

38. At the December 1850 term of the U.S. district court Norris did begin an action for debt against Crocker, Judge Egbert, and a number of others in South Bend, trying to recover the $500 penalty from each of them. By that time the Fugitive Slave Law of 1850, which did not contain any action for debt, had been passed and signed. In *Norris* v. *Crocker*, 13 Howard (54 U.S.) 429 (1851), the Supreme Court ruled that the adoption of the Fugitive Slave Law of 1850 precluded Norris from initiating a separate action for the $500 penalty under the 1793 law. Had Norris initiated this case before the adoption of the 1850 law he probably would have been able to pursue it. This case, which was successfully argued by Salmon P. Chase, was one of the few victories for the antislavery bar before the antebellum U.S. Supreme Court. See Wiecek, "Slavery and Abolition before the United States Supreme Court, 1820–1860," 34–59.

39. The various depositions are found in the case file of the suit, in RARC Case File.

40. The other defendants were George Horton, Solomon Palmer, David Jordan, William Wilmington, and Amable M. Lapier.

41. Order Book D, RARC-Chicago, 324, 337, 352, 364, 370, 376, 381, 385, 388, 390, 392, 393 (May 21, 22, 24, 30, June 4, 5, 6, 7, 8, 10, 11, 12).

42. These cases are discussed in Paul Finkelman, ed., *Slavery in the Courtroom* (Washington, D.C.: Government Printing Office, 1985), 86–137.

43. More clearly a rescue was the mob action that freed Grandison Martin, an alleged slave seized in Iberia, Ohio, which led to the prosecution of Rev. George Gordon. See Finkelman, *Slavery in the Courtroom,* 134–37.

44. On this issue see Paul Finkelman, *An Imperfect Union: Slavery, Federalism, and Comity* (Chapel Hill: University of North Carolina Press, 1981).

45. He is so characterized in Robert Cover, *Justice Accused: Antislavery and the Judicial Process* (New Haven, Conn.: Yale University Press, 1975).

46. *Statutes at Large of the United States,* 1:303.

47. *Norris* v. *Newton,* 323.

48. Ibid., 323.

49. Finkelman, "*Prigg* v. *Pennsylvania* and Northern State Courts," *Civil War History* 25 (1979): 5–35.

50. Supreme Court reporter Richard Peters published a 142-page pamphlet edition of the opinions in this case, *Report of the Case of Edward Prigg Against the Commonwealth of Pennsylvania* (Philadelphia: L. Johnson, 1842). This pamphlet could easily have been carried by a master seeking his runaway slaves.

51. *Norris* v. *Newton,* 323.

52. Ibid., 324.

53. Ibid., 325.

54. Ibid., 324.

55. Cover, *Justice Accused,* 262.

56. *Norris* v. *Newton,* 324.

57. Cover, *Justice Accused,* 245.

58. *Norris* v. *Newton,* 324.

59. Ibid., 324–25.

60. Ibid., 325.

61. Ibid.

62. Ibid.

63. Finkelman, "*Prigg* v. *Pennsylvania* and Northern State Courts."

64. *Norris* v. *Newton,* 325.

65. For a full discussion of this issue see Finkelman, *An Imperfect Union.*

66. *Norris* v. *Newton,* 326.

67. Ibid.

68. McLean had ruled this way in a previous case, *Vaughn* v. *Williams,* 28 *Federal Cases* 1115 (1845), although in that case a previous master had brought the slaves to Illinois, where he kept them for six months. For a discussion of this case see Finkelman, *An Imperfect Union,* 248–51.

69. Cover, *Justice Accused,* 246, 247. Both quotations are Cover's words.

70. Chase to Charles Sumner, September 3, 1853, *Annual Report of the American Historical Association for the Year 1902,* 2 vols. (Washington, D.C.: Government Printing Office, 1903), 2:252.

71. Cover, *Justice Accused*, 235, 198.

72. *Norris v. Newton*, 326.

73. Ibid.

74. Ibid., 327.

75. Order Book D, RARC-Chicago, entry for *Norris v. Newton*, June 14, 1850.

76. Ibid.

77. "Exceptions to Crocker's Answers," May 10, 1852; copy of recorded deed of June 7, 1850, filed with the U.S. circuit court, May 13, 1854; deposition of Jonathan Crews, May 16, 1854, all in RARC Case File; Oscar Lewis, *The Big Four: The Story of Huntington, Stanford, Hopkins, and Crocker, and of the Building of the Central Pacific* (New York: Alfred A. Knopf, 1959), 57.

78. "Execution Sale," May 1, 1851; "Execution Sale," May 10, 1851; "Marshal's Sale," May 15, 1851, all in RARC Case File.

79. "Answer of E. B. Crocker and Isaac Crocker," November 5, 1851; "Answer of A. Lapier," November 5, 1851; "Answer of Elisha Briggs," November 18, 1851, all in RARC Case File.

80. Decree in Chancery, December 19, 1854, in RARC Case File. In addition to Amable Lapier, Norris ended up suing in chancery three of the other original defendants (Newton, Crocker, and Solomon Palmer) and six others who claimed to own the conveyed land (Charles Crocker, Isaac Crocker, Alexis Coquillard, Elikim Briggs, David True, and Almond Bugbee). The final order also allowed Norris to collect from the State Bank of Indiana. At the beginning of the chancery case Norris had also sued the other defendants in *Norris v. Newton* (Lot Day, George Horton, David Jordan, and William Wilmington), but these defendants had either settled or were dropped from the case along the way.

81. U.S. District Court for Indiana, Order Book E, RARC-Chicago, 45, 46, 47, 49, 97, 99, 235, 236, 273–75, 282, 448, 510.

82. *John Norris v. Amable M. Lapier et al.*, in chancery, December 19, 1854, copy certified by court clerk Horace Bassett, February 20, 1855, in RARC Case File (hereinafter cited as "Decree in Chancery").

83. Marshal's notations on "Decree in Chancery" and newspaper clipping "Real Estate," February 27, 1854, in RARC Case File (hereinafter cited as "Newspaper Notice of Sale"). The item is incorrectly dated; it should be 1855 rather than 1854.

84. "Newspaper Notice of Sale"; Furlong, "South Bend Case," 20.

85. Marshal's report of sales, May 29, 1855, in case of *John Norris v. Amable Lapier et al.*, attached to newspaper clipping advertising the sale, in RARC Case File (hereinafter cited as "Marshal's Report of Sale").

86. "Decree in Chancery."

87. "Marshal's Report of Sale."

88. More likely, as Furlong suggests, his attorney, Liston, bid on the land in his name; Furlong, "South Bend Case," 20.

89. "Marshal's Report of Sale."

90. "Marshal's Report of Sale."

91. John Norris deed to C. W. Crocker, Book V, St. Joseph County Recorder's Office, April 23, 1855, recorded June 22, 1855, 23–24; U.S. Marshall [sic] deed to John Norris, May 30, 1855, Book V, St. Joseph's County Recorder's Office, recorded June 11, 1855, 627–32. At the same time these deeds were being recorded, the U.S. marshal tried to levy against the property of all the original defendants for a judgment of $14.70. In August he returned the writ to the court "wholly unsatisfied, the defendants having no property in my District that I can find whereon to levy." Return of J. L. Robinson, U.S. marshal for Indiana, August 3, 1855, in RARC Case File. It seems unlikely that the defendants had no more assets at this point, but it is possible that the marshal had little stomach for pushing the issue.

92. U.S. Circuit Court for Indiana, Order Book F, RARC-Chicago, 335 (entry for May 27, 1856), and 394–96 (entry for November 19, 1856).

93. General Index of Deeds of St. Joseph County, Indiana, 1856–61, D-5, 341.

94. Lewis, The Big Four, 72. Edwin Crocker suffered a paralytic stroke in 1868 and died a few years later. Ibid., 105; Hubert Howe Bancroft, History of California, 7 vols. (San Francisco: The History Company, 1890), 7:544–46.

Reconstructing Female Citizenship:

Minor v. *Happersett*

NORMA BASCH

Over the course of American constitutional history, gender and race have periodically converged both as sources of tension and as catalysts for change. I do not mean to suggest that gender and race were or are neatly analogous categories. But in the thoughts and actions of reformers, the constitutional avenues for ameliorating sexism and racism have run along closely related lines, and perhaps nowhere more so than in the post–Civil War era. With Reconstruction, reformers inaugurated a series of rights-conscious drives for constitutional equality that they sustained in the face of crushing legal defeats.[1] In the long run, their contests with and for the Constitution suffused it with new meaning, breathing life into its inherently inert terms and expanding the scope of its fundamentally eighteenth-century horizons.

It was not until the advent of Reconstruction that a rights-centered drive for equality could be framed in formal constitutional terms.[2] Antebellum discourse on equality encompassed impassioned assertions about the inalienable rights of women and blacks, but it drew its inspiration from the Declaration of Independence. More important, its legal contours were shaped largely in state legislatures, state constitutional conventions, and state courts.[3] The Civil War, however, dramatically altered both the context and text of the discourse. The amendment process not only contributed to a sense of the Constitution's malleability; it also endowed debates about equality with a unified national focus. As black codes menaced the viability of black citizenship and promoted efforts to define and guarantee citizenship through constitutional amendments,[4] the amendments, in turn, unleashed a long and arduous struggle over the terms of female citizenship.

If the paramount legacy of Reconstruction was to reshape relations between the citizen, the state, and the federal government, it was, from the perspective of women's rights, a highly equivocal legacy. On the one hand, the Reconstruction amendments forged a new and powerful conception of national citizenship; on the other hand, they delineated sharp political distinctions between male and female citizens. The second section of the Fourteenth Amendment, which designated penalties for denying suffrage to the male inhabitants of a state, seemed to obliterate the broad potential for women in the first section and to render explicit what had been implicit about women in the so-called original understanding.[5] At issue now was the subordinate status of women in the political community, a status the Fifteenth Amendment confirmed by prohibiting denial of the right to vote on the basis of race but not on the basis of sex. Nonetheless, despite the unprecedented inclusion of the word *male* in the Constitution and the omission of the word *sex* from its provision for suffrage, the spacious terms of the first section of the Fourteenth Amendment carried a new, albeit ambiguous, promise of legal and constitutional equality. In gender-neutral language it prohibited states from denying any person equal protection of the laws or abridging the privileges and immunities of U.S. citizens. It was to these flexible, indeterminate promises that the radical wing of the women's movement committed itself, even as it contested the ratification of the amendment, jettisoning its old abolitionist ties and setting the campaigns against sexism and racism at odds with each other.[6]

In the political culture of post–Civil War America, however, elements in the two campaigns remained bound together. Controversy over black citizenship generated controversy over female citizenship and imbued the woman question, as contemporaries called it, with constitutional dimensions. Increasingly the relationship between citizenship and suffrage—indeed, the issue of whether there was a relationship—became a focal point in the controversy. As a writer for *The Nation* observed in 1874, after the war there was a change in the public mind over suffrage marked by a "superstitious reverence for the ballot *per se* and by the mistaken assumption that all that remained to be done after enfranchising a million black men was to enfranchise black and white women."[7] Heightened emphasis on the ballot was not lost on women's rights activists, who after 1865 began to refer to themselves collectively as "the woman suffrage movement";[8] and neither was the ballot's potentially constitutional character, which they located among the "privileges and immunities" of citizenship as soon as the Fourteenth Amendment passed Congress. At the Washington meeting of the National Woman Suffrage Association in January 1869, suffragists adopted a resolution declaring the disfranchisement of women in state constitutions to be an abridgement of the privileges and immunities guaranteed in the amendment.[9]

Debate over the status of women under the Fourteenth Amendment proliferated in a variety of public forums and was extended in 1873, when Myra Bradwell challenged Illinois's policy of excluding married women from the legal profession in the ultimate public forum, the U.S. Supreme Court. Commenting on the Court's narrow construction of the Fourteenth Amendment in the *Bradwell* case, the *New York World* asserted, "There is no limit to the follies which have clutched at that Amendment for support. The Women's-Rights people have claimed that it ordained female suffrage. A Chicago she-attorney claims 'that it admits her to the Bar.' "[10]

It is another "folly," Virginia Minor's test of woman suffrage before the Supreme Court, that is the focus of this essay.[11] The *Minor* case was not, of course, a folly but a meticulously planned and ingeniously argued case that probed the boundaries of the Fourteenth Amendment and merits far more attention than it has received. Admittedly, *Minor* v. *Happersett* did not dominate the headlines of the day, but neither, for that matter, did *Plessy* v. *Ferguson,* the landmark 1896 case establishing the separate-but-equal doctrine. Contemporaries evinced far greater interest in the *Civil Rights Cases* of the preceding decade.[12] Historians and jurists elevated *Plessy* to the status of a landmark retrospectively as their awareness of its significance mounted. And just as Justice John Marshall Harlan's dissent speaks presciently to us across the gulf of time, haunting us with the possibilities in the road not taken and with the consequences of not taking it, so too does the brief filed by Francis Minor on behalf of his disfranchised wife.

It is noteworthy, then, that the persistent but shifting constitutional marginality of women in the post–Civil War era occupies a marginal place in our historical perception of the Constitution that differs markedly from the place accorded to race. There are a number of reasons why this has been so, not the least of which is the androcentric bent of constitutional scholarship. This, in part, explains a tendency to trivialize the postbellum drive for suffrage—to view it as a tempest in a teapot—and to characterize it as naïve and premature.[13] But there has also been a tendency by feminist historians to devalue the commitment of nineteenth-century feminists to constitutionalism in general and to suffrage in particular.[14] Recently, moreover, the very notion of formal constitutional equality for women has been challenged by a radical feminist jurisprudence that celebrates the concept of difference and underscores the legal need to recognize that difference in order to produce equitable results for women.[15] To be sure, the drive for suffrage did not produce winning results until the ratification of the Nineteenth Amendment, and historians have documented the conservative components that went into winning.[16] With hindsight, moreover, the victory proved to be disappointing politically. And it is true that formal constitutional equality does not ensure just results. Yet the foregoing observations in no way diminish the radicalism of women's drive for suffrage in its post–Civil War context. As Ellen DuBois has argued, from the perspective of feminism as a social movement, the postbellum drive offered women "the clearest possible vision of equality with men," and that vision enabled them "to challenge the structures of American social and political life" in a way that no other could at the time.[17]

I draw on *Minor v. Happersett* because it encapsulates both the vision and the challenge to which DuBois alluded. My focus, however, is on the role the case played in the specific context of post–Civil War constitutionalism. To put it another way, I want to explore how and why reformers reconstructed female citizenship in formal constitutional terms that were bound to be rejected by the Supreme Court.

On October 15, 1872, Virginia Minor, identified in the plaintiff's brief as a "tax-paying, law-abiding citizen" of St. Louis County, Missouri, and the United States, appeared before Reese Happersett, an election registrar in the county. She requested that the oath to support the Constitution of the United States and the state of Missouri be administered to her so that she might vote in the presidential election of 1872. Happersett refused to place her name on the list of registered voters because "she was not a male citizen but a woman."[18] His distinction between male as citizen and woman as other went to the heart of the suit. In a sense the suit represented an effort to use the Constitution and its post–Civil War reforms to obliterate one of the oldest distinctions in Western political theory and jurisprudence, one that Francis Minor argued was contrary to the very principles of republican government.[19]

With her husband as coplaintiff and counsel, Virginia Minor sued Reese Happersett in the Circuit Court of St. Louis County, maintaining that the provisions of the state constitution that limited the franchise to males were in conflict with the original provisions of the federal Constitution and the recently ratified Fourteenth Amendment. Ironically, she did not sue for her political independence independently. She lost her suit in the circuit court, appealed to the Missouri Supreme Court and lost, and then appealed to the U.S. Supreme Court, where she lost yet again in a unanimous decision.

What more is there to say? One could say that the very presence of her case on the Supreme Court docket in the October 1874 term constitutes a turning point in the role of gender in the Constitution. The historical dimensions of *Minor* are misconstrued from the start if we conceive of it only as relegating women to second-class citizenship; women were second-class citizens both before and after the decision. The case's importance lies in the fact that it drew the inferiority of women's status out of the grooves of common-law assumptions and state provisions and thrust it into the maelstrom of constitutional conflict. The demands for woman suffrage did not die when the decision was rendered; they acquired a contentious national life.

The capacity of the Court to expose submerged demands was noted by Justice William Brennan, who refused to delegate the reading of certiorari petitions to clerks because he viewed selection of cases as the court's single most important task.[20] But there can be no cases, no docket, and no Constitution without people. It is people who convert their demands into formal tests and press the Supreme Court for "reconstitutions."[21] At certain junctures, the issues people choose to place before the Court for reconstitution and the willingness of the Court to hear them are as revealing as the resolutions themselves. Given the indeterminate language of the Fourteenth Amendment, the determination of a militant group of woman suffragists to test its boundaries, and the campaign these former abolitionists had waged against its ratification, *Minor* presents us with just such a juncture.

It is for precisely this reason that the *Minor* case invites speculation about the motives of the Court. The 1874 Court did not have the same caseload or the same options that it has today, but still, there were ways to delay and even to avoid hearing a case its members clearly declined to pursue.[22] *Minor* contrasts with the judicial disposition of the case of Susan B. Anthony and may, in fact, be related to it. The members of the Court could have been influenced by the recent experience of Justice Ward Hunt, who had presided over the federal circuit court in New York in which Anthony was prosecuted for voting in the election of 1872. When Hunt crushed Anthony's bid to bring her case up to the Supreme Court on appeal, public furor ensued. Insisting that there was no question of fact in the case but only one of law, he removed the issues from the jury's consideration and ordered a verdict of guilty.[23] Here was a procedure one critic found "contrary to all rules of law, and so subversive of the system of jury trials in criminal cases, that it should not be allowed to pass without an emphatic protest on the part of every public journal that values our liberties."[24] The Grant administration put the finishing touches on the Anthony affair by failing to prosecute Anthony for not paying her fine and by pardoning the three Rochester registrars who had also been indicted and tried for violating the federal election statute.[25] The outcry from friends of woman suffrage over procedural irregularities, coupled with the sheer political volatility of the *Anthony* case, may very well have pointed to the need for a clear and authoritative judicial resolution.

Other considerations undoubtedly influenced the Court as well. Although the prospect of woman suffrage still met with savage derision in the press, it was a viable reality. Women were already voting in the Wyoming and Utah territories and even serving on juries in Wyoming.[26] Elsewhere hundreds of women tested the Fourteenth Amendment by voting illegally, and others demonstrated against its alleged limits by casting symbolic ballots in bogus elections organized adjacent to official polling places.[27] If the Court deemed it advisable to interpret the citizenship of women in light of the Fourteenth Amendment, the *Minor* case presented them with a perfect opportunity to do so.

The decision in *Minor* indicates that that was precisely the Court's intention. Focusing on the relation between the Fourteenth Amendment and the constitutionality of Missouri's restriction of suffrage to males, Chief Justice Waite observed that the case could have been decided on other grounds: "The case was undoubtedly brought to this court for the sole purpose of having that question decided by us, and in view of the evident propriety there is in having it settled, so far as it can be by such a decision, we have concluded to waive all other considerations and proceed at once to its determination."[28]

Of even greater interest, however, are the motives of the litigants who sought a hearing for their demands in the Supreme Court. They exemplify the proposition that radical activists have often been ardent constitutionalists.[29] They belonged to what we might call the party of hope.[30] Their view of the Constitution was essentially prospective, and they dedicated their energy, intellect, and imagination to shaping the terms of what Hendrik Hartog has labeled "the constitution of aspiration."[31] According to the *History of Woman Suffrage*, the despair engendered by the new barriers for women in the federal Constitution was tempered by the prospect of constitutional challenges, and the legal arguments developed to pursue the challenges provided the movement with "a ray of encouragement." The barriers no longer seemed insurmountable.[32]

But what of the tangible consequences of constitutional defeat? Virginia Minor and Susan B. Anthony, along with the battery of able attorneys representing them, may have hoped for a broad reading of the Fourteenth Amendment; but in the wake of prior decisions they surely anticipated the probability of legal defeat.[33] The arguments in both cases, moreover, were substantially the same. When Anthony wrote to Francis Minor requesting his opinion on the effect of the *Bradwell* decision, he responded that it was not *necessarily* conclusive on the suffrage question.[34] His response reflects the mix of hope and realism that animated the challenge. Clearly, as woman suffragists and legal strategists, reformers saw a political advantage—win or lose—in working out their arguments through the legal process.

Anthony pressed her claim as an eloquent martyr prodding the conscience of the nation. She painstakingly staged her test as a legal melodrama taking the form of a federal criminal prosecution. By casting herself as a modern Joan of Arc confronting the full force and fury of the U.S. government, she evoked so much sympathy and press coverage that one journalist estimated it would be hard to find a jury in the state of New York willing to convict her.[35] Her chief counsel, Henry R. Selden, underscored the criminal nature of the case: "If the advocates of female suffrage had been allowed to choose the point of attack to be made upon their position, they could not have chosen it more favorably for themselves; and I am disposed to thank those who have been instrumental in this proceeding for presenting it in the form of a 'criminal prosecution.' "[36] Of course, these advocates of female suffrage had chosen the point of attack, for Anthony had cajoled the Rochester registrars into enrolling her and fourteen other women and had guaranteed that she would provide them with counsel if they were criminally prosecuted.[37]

In contrast, the Minors' campaign was less dramatic but no less well planned, and from a constitutional perspective it provided a clearer and broader challenge. Even if Anthony had succeeded in appealing her case to the Supreme Court, it hinged on the claim that she had voted in good conscience and without criminal intent, and not exclusively on the inherent constitutionality of woman suffrage. The Minors, then, confronted the Fourteenth Amendment head-on in a test of the relations between female citizenship, state suffrage provisions, and the Constitution.

In a letter published in January 1870, Francis Minor announced Virginia Minor's intention to initiate the action in the federal election of 1872 and indicated that he and his wife had presented their legal strategy as a formal resolution at the Missouri National Woman Suffrage Association, of which Virginia Minor was president. Alluding to the transforming potential in their test, he reasoned it would place the cause of woman suffrage "upon higher ground than ever before" because it would rest on citizenship secured by the U.S. government. Anticipating the distinctions made by the Court between citizenship and suffrage, Minor outlined his determination to argue that states may impose only those qualifications for suffrage that all citizens may attain sooner or later. It was a way to come to terms with qualifications such as age and to move beyond demeaning common-law classifications lumping women together with children. He averred that "to say one-half the citizens possess all the qualifications but shall never vote" was the essence of "despotism." [38]

It is evident that the Minors hoped to take advantage of the reforming spirit of Reconstruction to reshape legal constructs and social attitudes in order to legitimate a role for women in politics. As for effecting woman suffrage by judicial fiat, the state of Missouri did not take the challenge seriously enough to file a brief, leaving Happersett with a defense consisting of a three-sentence demurrer.[39] The opening of the Minors' brief, moreover, speaks to posterity, implying that they had few illusions about the immediate outcome. Comparing slavery with the disfranchisement of women, the brief predicted that just as the one injustice to which the nation had been inured had been wiped out over time, so too would the other. But the Minors acknowledged that men were not yet prepared to view the disfranchisement of women that way:

> Men accept it as a matter of fact, and take for granted it must be right. So in the days of African slavery, thousands believed it to be right— even a Divine institution. But this belief has passed away; and, in like manner, this doctrine of the right of the States to exercise unlimited and absolute control of the elective franchise of citizens of the United States, must and will give way to a truer and better understanding of the subject.
>
> The plaintiff's case is simply one of the means by which this end will ultimately be reached.[40]

The Minors launched their case to promote "a truer and better understanding of the subject." The promotion of such an understanding through a hearing before the Supreme Court depended not on hope alone but also on an innovative reading of the Constitution. By invoking for women as a class specific rights derived from and defined by the Constitution, the Minors endowed the role of gender in constitutional discourse with visibility and rhetorical coherence and transcended almost a hundred years of silence on the subject. In this ultimate constitutional forum they expressed their disagreement about one issue, woman suffrage, by appearing to agree on everything else—the only way in which disagreement can enter into formal constitutional dialogue.[41] They cast their disagreement in the common language of the Constitution. Rearranging and reinterpreting the inherited terms at hand, they forged an argument for reconstructing female citizenship.

The Minors built their case on the original silences and gender-neutral language in the Constitution, on provisions in the Bill of Rights, and even on the Thirteenth Amendment. The Fourteenth Amendment, the historical catalyst for the case, emerged as supportive of but not absolutely essential to their primary argument. Francis Minor's reading of original intent proposed that women had been empowered to vote in *federal* elections from the inception of the Constitution. The Missouri "bar of perpetual disfranchisement," and disfranchisement by other states as well, was the result of a monumental misreading of the original text. That the women of New Jersey had voted in the early republic when the founding fathers were alive and well became proof of the founders' intent. Not only did Minor argue that further enabling legislation was unnecessary, he asserted that the disfranchisement of qualified female voters was a bill of attainder, an infringement on freedom of speech, a form of involuntary servitude, and a violation of due process.[42] The Fourteenth Amendment, then, merely obliterated any remaining doubts on the subject.

Minor's emphasis on pre–Civil War constitutional provisions allowed him to thread his argument through the new provisions for males in the Fourteenth and Fifteenth amendments. He interpreted the section of the Fourteenth Amendment that reduced congressional representation to states denying males the right to vote to be a special security for the black population; however, by the terms of the Ninth Amendment, it in no way denied other rights retained by the people.[43] As for the Fifteenth Amendment—a formidable obstacle for woman suffragists because it prohibited denying anyone the right to vote on account of race but not on account of sex—it was not in his path at all. It was prohibitory and had no direct bearing on the case, except that it confirmed a right already expressed in the Fourteenth Amendment.[44]

The most provocative strand in the brief invoked the provision that "the United States shall guarantee to every state a Republican form of government."[45] Implicit here was the claim that unless public authority—in this case the Supreme Court—reconstructed female citizenship to encompass suffrage, it had no legitimacy because it reflected not a republican form of government, but rather "despotism."[46] Minor asked the members of the Court to compare the "perfect freedom" and "self-respect" of suffrage with the despotism and servitude that accompanied its denial: "We ask the Court to consider what it is to be disfranchised; not this plaintiff only, but an entire class of people, utterly deprived of all voice in this government under which they live! We say it is to her and to them, a DESPOTISM, and not a Republic."[47] Either we give up a fundamental principle of our government, he continued, drawing on the Declaration of Independence, that "governments derive their just powers from the consent of the governed," or we acknowledge the legitimacy of the plaintiff's claim.[48]

The brief concluded that "the great principle of fundamental right" for which Virginia Minor was suing embraced "the rights of millions of others, who are thus represented through her." As Minor put it, the suit rested on "those principles upon which, as upon a rock, our government is founded," for a government that disfranchises half of its citizens cannot be a republican one.[49]

It was a powerful argument, a dazzling reconstruction of law as it ought to be, and a trenchant indictment of the way it was. In a unanimous decision the Court saw it otherwise. The opinion found that woman suffrage was neither intended in the Constitution nor guaranteed in the privileges and immunities clause of the Fourteenth Amendment. Responding to the characterization of the disfranchisement of women as antirepublican, the opinion declared that inasmuch as all states except New Jersey had limited the franchise to males at the time of ratification, it was too late now to contend that such a government was not republican. Women were undoubtedly citizens and members of the political community, as were children, but suffrage was not an incident of citizenship. The opinion ventured that if the law was wrong, it ought to be changed, but it was not within the power of the Court to change it.[50] In the end, it took almost half a century and a constitutional amendment to effect the change.

The *Minor* case, however, represents more than a test of woman suffrage under the Fourteenth Amendment. The terms and timing of the Minors' challenge provide insights to the relation between the social construction of gender in Victorian America and the legal and constitutional order, and nowhere more than in their insistence on a political role for women in the American Republic. Although numerous assertions in the brief were left unaddressed by the Court, such as the equation of disfranchisement with involuntary servitude, the Minors' definition of a republican form of government provoked a response. In its decision the Court appeared to bristle at the contention that the prevailing constitutional understanding about women was fundamentally unrepublican. If eighteenth-century synonyms for *republican* had grown murky in the aggressively competitive world of the 1870s, antonyms had retained their clarity. To be unrepublican was to be despotic, selfish, uncaring, and bereft of virtue. Yet the bourgeois culture of the nineteenth century attached the caring, cooperative virtues of the republic ever more firmly to the moral superiority of its women, and not to the political capacity of its men.

This disjunction of politics and morals in the nineteenth century had profound consequences for women. Both women and men believed that women spoke "in a different voice," to use Carol Gilligan's popular phrase.[51] As historians have noted, it was a voice that afforded women considerable dignity in the domestic sphere and sufficient authority in the public sphere to participate in community reforms and quasi-political activities. But it was a voice without terms for expressing the autonomous female self. The *Minor* case provided those terms, and therein lies its constitutional significance. Without such terms, the assertion of the female self as a discrete, independent, political being became a subversive form of selfishness; and the moral superiority of women served, in the end, to buttress their legal and political inferiority.

To be sure, advocates of woman suffrage insisted that women would purify politics, but they faced the counterclaim that politics would contaminate women.[52] Only by appropriating the rights-oriented, "masculine" voice of the constitutional order, as the Minors did, was it possible to challenge directly the exclusion of women from politics. Conversely, the masculine voice of the dominant culture gave men no compass for affirming cooperative values. Thus gender both informed and obfuscated the disjunction of politics and morals in post–Civil War America.

The small capsule of historical evidence presented here may lend itself to alternative readings, but at the very least it should encourage us to affix the *Minor* case firmly and prominently in our historical image of the Constitution. It also suggests the potential of gender as an analytical tool in constitutional history and discourse. To view the opposition of masculine and feminine as contextually defined and in flux, as Virginia and

Francis Minor did, invites new readings of the constitutional past and new strategies for shaping the future.[53]

NOTES

Parts of this essay appeared in Norma Basch, "Reconstitutions: History, Gender, and the Fourteenth Amendment," in *The Constitutional Bases of Political and Social Change in the United States,* ed. Shlomo Slonim (New York: Praeger, 1990). The author wishes to thank the publisher for permission to use this material here.

1. My emphasis on right consciousness draws on Hendrik Hartog's thoughtful essay "The Constitution of Aspiration and 'The Rights That Belong to Us All,'" *Journal of American History* 74 (1987): 1013–34.

2. Ibid., 1017.

3. For a classic example of the antebellum assertion of women's inalienable rights, see Thomas Herttell, *Remarks Comprising in Substance Judge Herttell's Argument in the House of Assembly of the State of New-York in the Session of 1837 in Support of the Bill to Restore to Married Women "The Right of Property" as Guaranteed by the Constitution of This State* (New York: Henry Durell, 1839).

4. For a comprehensive history of the Reconstruction amendments see Harold M. Hyman, *A More Perfect Union: The Impact of the Civil War and Reconstruction on the Constitution* (New York: Alfred A. Knopf, 1973); Harold M. Hyman and William Wiecek, *Equal Justice under Law* (New York: Harper and Row, 1982).

5. The original text of the Constitution employs such distinctly gender-neutral terms as "Persons" and "Electors" in Article I, sections 2 and 3, and Article II, section 1. Although Article II, which deals with the executive branch, employs the pronoun "he," it uses "Person" in spelling out eligibility for the presidency.

6. On the schism, see Ellen Carol DuBois, *Feminism and Suffrage: The Emergence of an Independent Women's Movement in America, 1848–1869* (Ithaca, N.Y.: Cornell University Press, 1978), 53–125.

7. "Woman Suffrage in Michigan," *The Nation* 18 (May 1874): 312. For similar disparagement of suffrage for both women and blacks see "Vox Populi," *Galaxy* 19 (January 1875): 123–24.

8. DuBois, *Feminism and Suffrage,* 54. On the earlier development of the concept of woman suffrage, see Norma Basch, "Equity vs. Equality: Emerging Concepts of Women's Political Status in the Age of Jackson," *Journal of the Early Republic* 3 (Fall 1983): 297–318.

9. The rationale for the resolution was attributed to Francis Minor. See Elizabeth Cady Stanton, Susan B. Anthony, Matilda Joslyn Gage, and Ida Husted Harper, eds., *History of Woman Suffrage,* 6 vols. (Rochester and New York: Fowlers and Wells, 1881–1922), 4:3–4.

10. Cited in Page Smith, *The Constitution: A Documentary and Narrative History* (New York: Morrow, 1978), 459.

11. *Minor* v. *Happersett*, 88 U.S. 162 (1875).

12. Michael Kammen, *A Machine That Would Go of Itself: The Constitution in American Culture* (New York: Alfred A. Knopf, 1986), 28.

13. In particular, the time that elapsed until the ratification of the Nineteenth Amendment colors assessments of the post–Civil War drive for suffrage. Commenting on the optimism Stanton and Anthony exhibited with respect to woman suffrage, Eleanor Flexner notes, "From a historical vantage point their optimism seems unfounded, and women themselves were not interested in suffrage." But Page Smith asserts that "there was every reason in 1870 to anticipate the rapid passage of an amendment which, it was hoped, would give the franchise to women." Flexner, *Century of Struggle: The Woman's Rights Movement in the United States* (New York: Athenaeum, 1968), 145; Smith, *Daughters of the Promised Land: Women in American History* (Boston: Little, Brown, 1970), 167.

14. For conflict among historians over definitions of feminism and feminist politics, see Ellen Carol DuBois, Mary Jo Buhl, Temma Kaplan, Gerda Lerner, and Carroll Smith-Rosenberg, "Politics and Culture in Women's History: A Symposium," *Feminist Studies* 6 (1980): 26–64.

15. For an overview of this new jurisprudence, which sometimes identifies itself with "relational feminism," see Kenneth L. Karst, "Woman's Constitution," *Duke Law Journal* (1984): 447–508. Karst likens its relationship to traditional jurisprudence as that of a web to a ladder. See also "Papers from the 1986 Feminism and Legal Theory Conference," *Wisconsin Women's Law Journal* 3 (Winter 1987).

16. DuBois locates the shift toward conservatism in 1878 following the decision in the *Minor* case. See "Outgrowing the Compact of the Fathers: Equal Rights, Woman Suffrage, and the United States Constitution, 1820–1878," *Journal of American History* 74 (1987): 861–62.

17. DuBois, *Feminism and Suffrage*, 17–18.

18. Argument and Brief, *Minor* v. *Happersett*, in *Landmark Briefs and Arguments of the Supreme Court of the United States*, ed. Philip B. Kurland and Gerhard Casper, 80 vols. (Arlington, Va., 1975), 7:209–50, citation on p. 214 (hereinafter referred to as Argument and Brief, *Minor*).

19. On women's otherness in Western political theory see Susan Moller Okin, *Women in Western Political Thought* (Princeton, N.J.: Princeton University Press, 1979).

20. Interview, National Public Radio, broadcast February 5, 1987.

21. For both the term and the concept of *reconstitution* in law, I have relied on James Boyd White, *When Words Lose Their Meaning: Constitutions and Reconstitutions of Language, Character, and Community* (Chicago: University of Chicago Press, 1984).

22. In the post–Civil War period the caseload of the Court increased signifi-

cantly, and several years could elapse between the filing of a case and the time of oral argument. See Nancy T. Gilliam, "A Professional Pioneer: Myra Bradwell's Fight to Practice Law," *Law and History Review* 5 (1987): 119.

23. *An Account of the Proceedings of the Trial of Susan B. Anthony on the Charge of Illegal Voting* (Rochester: Daily Democrat and Chronicle, 1874), 78–82 (hereinafter cited as *Trial of Susan B. Anthony*).

24. John Hooker, "Judge Hunt, and the Right of Trial by Jury," in *Trial of Susan B. Anthony,* 206.

25. Stanton et al., eds., *History of Woman Suffrage,* 2:949.

26. Women on juries in Wyoming provoked considerable attention. See, for example, *Albany Law Journal* 1 (1870): 197, 210, 313; and "The Woman Suffrage Movement in Wyoming," *Galaxy* 8 (June 1872): 755–60.

27. Tests in the District of Columbia include *Spencer* v. *Board of Registration* and *Webster* v. *Superintendents of Election,* cited in *Albany Law Journal* 4 (1871): 281–82; for other tests see Stanton et al., eds., *History of Woman Suffrage,* 2: 586–600.

28. *Minor* v. *Happersett,* 88 U.S. 165.

29. On the commitment of American radicals to constitutionalism see Kammen, *A Machine That Would Go of Itself,* 398.

30. On the juxtaposition of hope and memory in American political culture see Ralph Waldo Emerson, "The Conservative: A Lecture Delivered at the Masonic Temple, Boston, December 9, 1841," in *The Collected Works of Ralph Waldo Emerson,* vol. 1, *Nature, Addresses, and Lectures,* ed. Robert E. Spiller and Alfred R. Ferguson (Cambridge, Mass.: Harvard University Press, 1971), 185–200.

31. Hartog, "The Constitution of Aspiration."

32. Stanton et al., eds., *History of Woman Suffrage,* 4:3.

33. In addition to her husband, Francis Minor, the brief filed in the Supreme Court listed John M. Krum and John B. Henderson as attorneys for the plaintiffs. Anthony was represented by Henry R. Selden and John Van Voorhis and consulted other attorneys as well from time to time.

34. Gilliam, "A Professional Pioneer," 130.

35. *New York Sun,* January 4, 1873, cited in Stanton et al., eds., *History of Woman Suffrage,* 2:937–38.

36. *Trial of Susan B. Anthony,* 17.

37. Stanton et al., eds., *History of Woman Suffrage,* 2:628.

38. "Letter from Francis Minor," *The Revolution* 5 (January 20, 1870): 38–39. Aside from the criminal nature of the *Anthony* case, the argument made by Anthony's counsel, Henry R. Selden, and by Anthony herself followed the same basic lines.

39. Argument and Brief, *Minor,* 216–17. According to the brief, Smith P. Galt had represented Happersett in the Missouri Circuit Court, but in the U.S. Supreme Court there was no opposing counsel for Happersett or the state of Missouri.

Minor v. Happersett, 88 U.S. 164. It is noteworthy that the same was true for the state of Illinois in the *Bradwell* case, the only other test of sex discrimination before the Supreme Court during the period. See Gilliam, "A Professional Pioneer," 123.

40. Argument and Brief, *Minor,* 220.

41. White, *When Words Lose Their Meaning,* 246.

42. Argument and Brief, *Minor,* 222, 224, 227, 235, 244–48.

43. Ibid., 215.

44. Ibid., 235–37.

45. Ibid., 214, citing Article IV, section 4, of the Constitution.

46. Ibid., 241.

47. Ibid.

48. Ibid.

49. Ibid., 250.

50. *Minor v. Happersett,* 162, 167, 170, 178.

51. Carol Gilligan, *In a Different Voice: Psychological Theory and Women's Development* (Cambridge, Mass.: Harvard University Press, 1982).

52. See, for example, *The Nation* 3 (December 20, 1866): 498–99, 5 (November 1867): 416–17, and 18 (May 1874): 311–13.

53. Joan W. Scott, "Gender: A Useful Category of Historical Analysis," *American Historical Review* 91 (1986): 1053–75. Scott's analysis of gender as a historical tool and her critique of Gilligan provide the foundations for this essay.

The Language of Liberation:

African Americans and Equalitarian

Constitutionalism, 1830–1950

DONALD G. NIEMAN

On January 15, 1851, 37 black men assembled in the Second Baptist Church of Columbus, Ohio, to open the annual Convention of the Colored Citizens of Ohio. Representing 26,000 black Ohioans in cities and towns across the state, the delegation included artisans, barbers, teachers, and ministers. Despite the absence of lawyers, much of the discussion was carried on in a constitutional idiom, and delegates frequently invoked constitutional principles to support their arguments. Of particular concern was the Fugitive Slave Act of 1850, a federal measure that denied alleged fugitives basic procedural rights essential to protect their freedom: the right to habeas corpus, to be represented by counsel, to testify and summon witnesses, and to trial by jury. Consequently, the law not only put runaway slaves at risk, it made free blacks vulnerable to legalized kidnapping. In leading the attack on the measure, John Mercer Langston—who later joined the bar, established the law department at Howard University, and became president of that institution—invoked the Constitution. Citing the Constitution's guarantee of trial by jury and habeas corpus, he contended that the Fugitive Slave Act was not only unjust but flagrantly unconstitutional. "This enactment," Langston charged, "possesses neither the form nor the essence of true law . . . [and] is a hideous deformity in the *garb* of law. It kills alike the true spirit of the Declaration of Independence, the Constitution, and the palladium of our liberties." [1]

Not all the delegates agreed that the Constitution was antislavery. Reflecting northern blacks' growing disillusionment with the proslavery poli-

cies of the national government, H. Ford Douglas, a nineteen-year-old
barber from Cleveland, challenged Langston's analysis. Drawing on the
Garrisonian critique of the Constitution, Douglas argued that the 1787
document was thoroughly proslavery and therefore an obstacle to black
liberation.

> I hold, sir, that the Constitution of the United States is pro-slavery,
> considered so by those who framed it. . . . It is well known that in 1787
> in the Convention that framed the Constitution, there was consider-
> able discussion on the subject of slavery. South Carolina and Georgia
> refused to come into the Union without the Convention would allow
> the continuation of the Slave Trade for twenty years. . . . the Conven-
> tion submitted to that guilty contract. . . . Here we see them engrafting
> into the Constitution a clause legalizing and protecting one of the
> vilest systems of wrong ever invented by the cupidity and avarice of
> man. . . . That instrument also provides for the return of fugitive
> slaves. And, sir, . . . the "Fugitive Law" is in accordance with that
> stipulation;—a law unequaled in the worst days of Roman despotism,
> and unparalleled in the annals of heathen jurisprudence.

Douglas concluded that blacks must reject the Constitution and refuse to
participate in a constitutional order that held millions of African Americans in chains. He therefore urged delegates to stop demanding the right
to vote, and instead to resolve that "no colored man can consistently vote
under the United States Constitution."[2]

Douglas's characterization of the Constitution did not meet with a sympathetic response. William Howard Day countered that the Constitution
was a malleable document and that, correctly understood, it could be a
force for black liberty. He charged that Douglas had confused the Constitution with the interpretation given it by proslavery judges and politicians.
"Sir, coming up as I do in the midst of three millions of men in chains, and
five hundred thousand only half-free, I consider every instrument precious
which guarantees to me liberty," Day explained. "I consider the Constitution the foundation of American liberties, and wrapping myself in the flag
of the nation, I would plant myself upon that Constitution, and using the
weapons they have given me, I would appeal to the American people for
the rights thus guaranteed." In the end, Langston and Day easily prevailed,
and Douglas's motion went down to defeat, twenty-eight to two.[3]

It is hardly surprising that so much of the discussion at Columbus—and
at dozens of other antebellum colored conventions—was carried on in con-

stitutional language, with delegates invoking constitutional principles to attack slavery and discrimination. As Harold Hyman has observed, ante-bellum Americans did not view the Constitution as the special preserve of a priesthood of judges, lawyers, and scholars: "The continuing popular commitment to keeping public law the public's law, and for mixing constitutional idiom into political argumentation, made attitudes toward and interpretations of the Constitution something higher than gamesmanship and more serious than partisanship. Wherever Americans gathered, discussion resulted of political issues cast in constitutional terms."[4]

Black Americans were no exception. In the decades preceding the Civil War, northern blacks challenged the discrimination against persons of color that existed in many of the free states, in the process articulating a powerful equalitarian constitutionalism. During the revolutionary years of the Civil War and Reconstruction, black leaders not only pressed their constitutional vision on Republican policymakers in Washington, but also took it to the South, where it found a receptive audience. Indeed, during the years following the war, southern blacks—humble freedpersons as well as the literate, property-holding free black elite—eagerly embraced doctrines of color-blind citizenship and equal rights and used them to shake the foundations of the southern social order. Moreover, the results of blacks' commitment to equalitarian constitutionalism reached far beyond Reconstruction and contained profound implications for American constitutionalism and African American culture.

The process began in earnest during the 1830s and 1840s, as northern black leaders focused attention on the problem of discrimination. In several northern states blacks were denied basic legal rights such as the right to testify in cases involving whites, and nearly everywhere they were denied the right to vote and segregated in schools and public accommodations. Black leaders realized that discriminatory law marked members of their race as inferior and thus deepened the racism that constrained black economic opportunity. "The colored people of this State are, from the non-possession of the right of the suffrage, the proscribed class," representatives of New York's black community explained. "This proscription is the fountain of Marah, from whence proceed those bitter waters that run through all the ramifications of society, connecting themselves with all our relations." Black leaders also understood that blacks could achieve self-respect only by asserting their right to equal treatment. As Michigan blacks noted in demanding political rights, "the enjoyment of those rights in a free country, is a stimulant to enterprise, a means of influence, and a source of respect; they send life, vigor and energy through the entire heart of a people."[5]

Northern blacks built their case for equal rights on the foundation of black citizenship. They argued that native-born free blacks were citizens of the state where they resided and of the United States. They pointed out that European, English, and American authorities agreed that "the strongest claim to citizenship is birthplace" and that "in whatever country or place you may be born, you are in the first and highest sense a citizen." "The claims are . . . founded in the fact that they [blacks] are citizens by birth and blood," noted Hosea Easton, a black minister, in 1837. "Complexion has never been made the legal test of citizenship in any age in the world. It has been established generally by birth and blood."[6] Because the framers of the Constitution did not define citizenship, abolitionists contended, they must be presumed to have accepted this common understanding.

The most potent argument on behalf of black citizenship, however, grew out of the historical memory of the black community. Black abolitionists reminded Americans that in many states in 1787 free blacks had been citizens with access to the ballot box, and they had shouldered the responsibilities of citizenship, serving with distinction in the American Revolution and the War of 1812. "We are Americans. We were born in no foreign clime," explained the report of the 1840 Convention of the Colored Inhabitants of New York. "We have not been brought up under the influence of other strange, aristocratic, and uncongenial political relations. In this respect, we profess to be American and republican."[7]

As citizens, blacks argued, they were entitled to full equality. The principles of republicanism and the ideas expressed in the Declaration of Independence were the animating principles of American constitutionalism and entitled all citizens to equal rights regardless of race. "That Declaration, and that Constitution . . . may be considered as more fully developing the ideas of American republicanism, than any other documents," delegates to the 1840 New York convention asserted in a petition calling for an end to the state's discriminatory suffrage laws. "In these, individuals are regarded distinctly and respectively—each and every one as men, fully capacitated by the Creator for government and progressive advancement."[8]

These ideas—widely accepted by northern blacks—served as a rallying point, encouraging them to assert their rights and challenge the caste system. In the late 1840s, fresh from a campaign of sit-ins that compelled Massachusetts railroads to end segregation, Boston blacks began litigation to end racial segregation in the city's schools. Robert Morris, a black lawyer, joined Charles Sumner in arguing that the Boston School Committee's policy violated the state constitution's guarantee of equality. "The equality declared by our fathers . . . was *Equality before the Law*," they explained. "Its object was to efface all political or civil distinctions, and to abolish all institutions founded upon *birth*."⁹ Although the Massachusetts Supreme Judicial Court rejected this argument in 1854, the legislature banned school segregation the following year. New York City blacks likewise marshaled equalitarian constitutional arguments to challenge segregation of the city's privately owned street railroads. Led by Rev. James Pennington, they staged a series of sit-ins to protest the companies' policy and organized the Legal Rights Association, which challenged the railroads in the courts. Like their counterparts in Boston, Pennington and his colleagues did not prevail in the courtroom. Nevertheless, their campaign of direct action—inspired by the belief that as citizens they were entitled to equal rights—convinced several street railroads to end segregation.¹⁰

While events of the late 1850s shook many blacks' faith in the constitutional order and strengthened the position of emigrationists, the revolutionary dynamic of the Civil War created new possibilities, rekindling northern blacks' commitment to equalitarian constitutionalism. As Republican leaders transformed the war into a struggle to extirpate slavery and recover the republican principles of the Declaration of Independence, long-ignored advocates of equal rights found politicians increasingly receptive to their arguments. And as 180,000 black men donned the uniforms of the Union army, it became more difficult to deny blacks' claims to the rights of citizenship, which, in republican terms, necessitated equality. Perhaps Representative Robert Schenck, a Republican from Ohio, best indicated the altered climate of opinion near the end of the war when, in introducing legislation creating the Freedmen's Bureau, he noted that the measure made "no discrimination according to color—a favorite phrase . . . in these days among us all."¹¹

Taking advantage of changes in the political climate, black leaders intensified their demand for equal rights. Delegates to the 1864 National Negro Convention formed a National Equal Rights League "to obtain full recognition of our rights as American citizens . . . to the attainment of equality before the law."¹² Joined by white abolitionists and Republicans, blacks won repeal of discriminatory laws in California and Illinois, convinced Massachusetts legislators to ban discrimination in public accommodations, and launched an all-out effort for the ballot. Energized by the expansive sense of national power that the war created, and buoyed by the belief that the nation would honor the debt it owed its black citizens for their wartime service, black leaders began to demand federal action to guarantee equal rights, a step that had been unthinkable five years earlier. Indeed, as Congress convened its first postwar session in December 1865, northern blacks sent a handful of lobbyists to Washington to press legislators for a federal guarantee of equality.[13]

The war broadened as well as deepened blacks' commitment to equalitarian constitutionalism, spreading its principles beyond the small community of northern free blacks to blacks throughout the South. During the months following the war, southern blacks held dozens of mass meetings and conventions. The tone of the resolutions and petitions adopted at these gatherings was moderate; indeed, at times it was almost deferential toward whites (who were, after all, in the driver's seat as a result of Andrew Johnson's program of Reconstruction). They emphasized the mutual dependence of southern whites and blacks and generally requested rather than demanded that whites grant them the basic rights of citizenship. Nevertheless, these postwar gatherings were reminiscent of the antebellum northern colored conventions in asserting, however politely, that republican principles entitled blacks to equal rights. "Personal servitude having been abolished in Virginia," Norfolk blacks explained a month after Appomattox, "it behooves us, and is demanded of us . . . to speak and act as freemen, and as such to claim and insist upon equality before the law, and equal rights of suffrage at the 'ballot box.'" Tennessee black leaders agreed, appealing directly to the Constitution: "Inasmuch as the United States Constitution guarantees to every state in the Union a republican form of government, we are at a loss to understand that [government] to be a republican . . . government that does not protect the rights of all citizens irrespective of color."[14]

These pronouncements were largely the work of literate, skilled, property-holding blacks who had been free before the war. Many of the leading figures in the South's mass meetings and conventions were northern blacks who had come south during the war as teachers, representatives of northern religious and benevolent societies, and soldiers. Bringing with them the idiom of equalitarian constitutionalism that had been articulated in the northern colored conventions, and approaching the task with missionary zeal, they were eager to mobilize former slaves to demand their rights. Southern free men also figured prominently among the leaders at the 1865 conventions. Most were literate, had long been aware of abolitionist arguments on behalf of equal rights, and realized that northern Republicans had come to define the war as a struggle to regenerate the nation by returning it to the republican principles of the founders. They were also men whose literacy, skills, pride, and force of personality would enable them to advance if they could be freed from discrimination on account of their color. Not surprisingly, they embraced the ideology of equal rights with the enthusiasm of recent converts.[15]

Concern for law and equal rights was not, however, limited to the black elite; it spread quickly to the masses of former slaves during the war and its immediate aftermath. The tens of thousands of former slaves who served in the Union army played an especially important role in this process. Although their white officers were often as arbitrary, oppressive, and unjust as their former owners had been, black soldiers quickly learned that army regulations gave them certain rights, and they eagerly invoked those rights in the face of injustice. Thus William Mayo, a Louisiana sergeant who was sentenced by a court-martial to twenty-one months at hard labor for disobedience of orders and mutinous conduct, complained that his superiors had compromised his effort to win acquittal by taking his copy of the army regulations away from him. "When I was sent to the Guard house I was deprived of My own private property," he explained. "I had the Army Regulations that I bought and paid for with my own money, and [they] charged me with reading that which a Nigar had no business to know." Nevertheless, Mayo was sufficiently familiar with the regulations to know that the court had violated his rights by limiting to two the number of witnesses summoned on his behalf, and he demanded that his conviction be reversed. Although his appeal failed, it suggests that black soldiers were cognizant of their rights and eager to use them. Ira Berlin has argued that it was through this process that "former slaves learned something about the system of government under which they lived. They came to understand that justice depended not on the favor of a single powerful individual, but on impersonal rules and regulations that governed all citizens." [16]

Black soldiers learned other civic lessons as well. Officers and chaplains of black regiments devoted considerable time to education. Although the emphasis was on practical matters such as sanitary procedures and basic literacy, there were also lessons on American history and government that introduced black soldiers to the republican principles of rights and equality. Indeed, black troops learned their lessons too well for the taste of many white officials, asserting their right to equal pay in a series of protests that rippled through black regiments during 1863 and 1864. The understanding of law and of the principle of equality that black soldiers developed during the war years shaped southern blacks' consciousness in the postwar years when veterans returned home and assumed positions of leadership in their communities.[17]

Many former slaves who did not enter the army learned about citizenship, rights, and equality from the thousands of northerners who were sent to the South by churches and benevolent societies to establish schools for the freedpeople. In recent years scholars have emphasized that these women and men took with them a profoundly conservative message. Teachers and the authors of the texts written for the freedpeople feared that the former slaves would confuse liberty with license and behave irresponsibly, thereby confirming racist charges that blacks were incapable of living in freedom. They therefore emphasized the obligations of free persons and exhorted former slaves to work hard, fulfill their contracts, honor their wedding vows, live frugally, and avoid alcohol, tobacco, and other frivolous vices. Yet there was more to the teachers' message than warmed-over Yankee notions of morality. Many of the teachers were northern blacks whose familiarity with the tradition of protest and the language of equalitarian constitutionalism fitted them for spreading the gospel of equal rights among the former slaves. Moreover, many of the white teachers and most of the authors of the textbooks used in the freedpeople's schools also had roots in the abolitionist movement. Consequently, teachers and texts taught that all persons shared common origins regardless of race and espoused republican principles of citizenship and equal rights.[18]

Consider two examples. The American Tract Society's widely used text, *The Freedmen's Third Reader,* contained a short biography of Toussaint L'Ouverture that emphasized his efforts "to establish order and discipline" among former slaves in Haiti. It also included a sketch of Frederick Douglass's life that emphasized his piety, and short essays on "Love to Enemies," "Humility," "Pride of Dress," "Labor," and, of course, "Temperance." Yet it also taught blacks that they should demand their rights. A chapter on Paul Cuffe, for example, praised the black shipbuilder for his role in the struggle for equal rights in revolutionary Massachusetts: "The young man's influence was felt beyond his own State, for other States followed the just and humane example of Massachusetts, so that the efforts of Paul and his brother affected the welfare of colored people all over the country, and are helping, this day, to solve the question of the rights of man as man." *The Freedmen's Book,* Lydia Maria Child's popular text, followed a similar course. Child offered the typical admonitions to hard work, cleanliness, chastity, temperance, and patience. But she also emphasized, "I do not mean by this that you ought to submit tamely to insult or oppression." Black men and women, she asserted, should leave employers who abused them, seek redress in the courts, and demand the equality that was their due. "A good government," she insisted, "seeks to make laws that will equally protect and restrain all men." [19]

Of course, instruction was not limited to the classroom. As the intense debate between President Andrew Johnson and congressional Republicans over Reconstruction policy came to focus on civil rights, blacks followed the arguments closely. At the Capitol, where Republican lawmakers opened the spectators' galleries to blacks, debates on civil rights legislation were regularly attended by black men and women. While most southern blacks could not view the debates firsthand, those who were literate did follow them in the press and passed on to friends and neighbors information about the civil rights revolution. A Freedmen's Bureau agent stationed at Staunton, Virginia, reported that blacks in his district were well informed on the civil rights question, noting that "news of that kind spreads through the country very quickly. I am acquainted with one colored man who takes the 'Washington Chronicle,'" he explained, "and regularly imparts the news to his color." [20]

Ironically, blacks often heard accounts of congressional civil rights legislation—accounts that sometimes wildly exaggerated its scope—from panic-stricken southern whites. "I often hear [white] men of intelligence and good sense denouncing social equality as if they were afraid of it, putting constructions on the civil rights bill so absurd that the most enthusiastic negroes would hardly entertain them," noted one bemused agent. "All these discussions fasten the impression on the white people that the blacks are seeking social equality, and feed the black man with the hope of attaining it." Although this agent may himself have exaggerated blacks' interest in social relations with whites, he correctly understood that the civil rights debate had reverberations throughout the South. It encouraged former slaves to think of themselves as citizens who possessed rights and were entitled to have their rights protected by the national government. [21]

As the war ended and the newly created Freedmen's Bureau took charge of freedmen's affairs, bureau agents played a crucial role in spreading concepts of rights and equality throughout the southern countryside. Like the northern teachers, they stressed that freedom entailed obligations and responsibilities. Diligent toil, respect for the law, and fidelity to contracts, they incessantly preached, were essential elements of the ordered liberty that would make freedom a blessing rather than a curse. But bureau officials also called attention to the rights freedom conferred and encouraged blacks to assert those rights. Agents sponsored Fourth of July celebrations at which the Declaration of Independence was read and speeches were given stressing the nation's equalitarian tradition. Moreover, circulars that agents read to gatherings of former slaves and posted in villages throughout the South also spread the doctrine of equal rights. "The freedmen," one typical bureau circular emphasized, "are not to be restrained in the exercise of their liberty by any rules or customs of the country that do not apply equally to white men." [22]

The day-to-day actions of bureau agents reinforced this message. During the years of presidential Reconstruction, as southern legislatures enacted the black codes and as white sheriffs, judges, and justices of the peace used their authority to minimize the effects of emancipation, blacks learned that state and local officials offered them only a charade of justice. It is not surprising that they went to the nearest Freedmen's Bureau agent— the local manifestation of the national government that had emancipated them—for redress when they were beaten or robbed or cheated. Indeed, freedpeople often appealed to the bureau in such large numbers that they overwhelmed the harried agents, whose largely rural jurisdictions often included several counties. "My office is so crowded . . . with freedmen coming to complain of not being settled with [by their employers] that it takes four of us from 9 o'clock in the morning to 5 o'clock in the evening doing scarcely anything else but trying to adjust cases of cheating and stealing," noted one agent in early 1867. [23]

Blacks' experience with bureau justice reinforced the notion that they were entitled to the rights enjoyed by other free men and women. An incident in Greenville, Alabama, in August 1866 illustrates the point. A freedman working on a county road to fulfill his tax obligation was assaulted by a white passerby who was offended that the freedman (who probably hoped to bag a few squirrels while fulfilling his civic obligation) had his gun at his side. The white seized the gun, smashed it, and threatened the freedman with a pistol. The freedman quickly protested to local bureau agent James McGogy, who sent him to the county prosecutor with a note demanding that the prosecutor bring charges against the offending white man. "All men has [sic] the right to the highway," McGogy forcefully concluded, "and the law should protect the person and property of all men regardless of color." Although the prosecutor and other local officials predictably ignored the agent's demand, McGogy used the threat of military intervention to prod them into making the arrest. In this case—and others like it—the agent's words and deeds not only reaffirmed the equalitarian sentiments expressed by teachers, textbooks, and orators, but gave them an immediacy and concreteness that must have deeply impressed former slaves.[24]

Bureau agents did not always—perhaps not even often—share McGogy's success. Intent on returning authority to state and local officials, President Andrew Johnson carefully circumscribed the bureau's judicial authority. Consequently, agents could hear cases brought by blacks and could order the parties to abide by their decisions, yet they lacked the authority to compel obedience. Similarly, agents could demand that local officials arrest whites who beat, murdered, or robbed blacks, and they could cajole and threaten them when they refused. But unlike McGogy, they usually lacked the military support necessary to enforce their demands. Nevertheless, the presence of a bureau agent who was willing to entertain their complaints encouraged blacks to demand their rights. And such acts, repeated thousands of times by blacks in all corners of the South, gave concrete reality to abstract concepts of law, rights, and equal protection.[25]

Former slaves not only became familiar with such previously alien concepts as law, citizenship, and equality; they also developed a passion for equal rights that equaled their desire for land. A bureau official in Virginia noted this phenomenon after completing an investigation of the state in mid-1867: "The black man feels that he has certain rights and is anxious to know what they are and how to procure, protect, and maintain the same. There is no appearance on the part of the colored people that they intend invading the rights of the white man but there is an inflexible will manifested that no white man shall trample with impunity on their own."[26]

This passion for rights was largely a response to blacks' situation. Indeed, land and equal rights were attractive for the same reason: both offered independence from white authority and therefore the autonomy that former slaves viewed as essential to freedom. As slaves, they had been subject to the personal control of owners whose arbitrary decisions had affected their family life, work, religion, and personal security. Landownership would free blacks from day-to-day supervision by white planters and overseers and deprive whites of considerable economic leverage against their former chattels. Equal rights and the rule of law complemented this. By freeing them from discriminatory vagrancy, apprenticeship, license, and contract laws, equal rights promised to shield blacks from planters' efforts to make them a semiservile work force. Moreover, by establishing a body of impersonal rules and regulations that applied to all persons and defined their rights and obligations, the rule of law offered a means to curb the arbitrary power that whites had enjoyed under slavery and showed no sign of relinquishing in the aftermath of the war.

The practical considerations that moved blacks to demand equal protection of the law are apparent in the rough eloquence of the petitions and letters that semiliterate freedmen sent to bureau officials. In November 1865 freedmen in Tuscumbia, Alabama, asked the bureau to set aside municipal ordinances that barred them from purchasing liquor, weapons, and ammunition. "Because I am Black dont make me a Rouge [sic]," the petitioners concluded. "We want Justice gennel you can send us one company [of troops] if you pleas We are treated here like dogs." Blacks in Newberry, South Carolina, voiced an even more typical concern when they complained of discriminatory law enforcement that left them without protection against white violence. "We are murdered with impunity in the streets of this place, and the murderers are walking at large and no notice taken of them," they explained. And they were quite clear about the source of the problem: "We have no law."[27]

If former slaves developed an understanding of and a passion for equal rights and the rule of law during the war and the early years of Reconstruction, it was suffrage that offered them the ability to secure those rights. Blacks understood that unless they possessed the ballot, elected officials would remain unresponsive to them and would continue to deny them justice, regardless of rights proclaimed by constitutions and statutes. Since the colored conventions of 1865, black leaders had stressed the importance of suffrage and had urged that as free men and taxpayers, black citizens were entitled to the right to vote. During the following fifteen months the demand for the ballot became more insistent and was embraced by former slaves across the South. As Congress debated the Reconstruction Act in early 1867, a bureau official in Florida reported that the interest in suffrage among the freedmen had become feverish: "The . . . discussions in Congress relating to negro suffrage are well known here, which creates much interest and causes freedmen to look forward to a revolution quite equalling the strife which brought about their freedom."[28]

Blacks not only anticipated a revolution but helped to bring it about. In the wake of the Reconstruction Act of 1867 (which gave blacks in the unrestored states of the former Confederacy the right to vote), they flocked to the Union Leagues and other political clubs that sprang up across the

South. There they learned about the process of registration and voting and debated the political issues that most directly affected their lives. Moreover, in the face of whites' use of suasion, economic coercion, and terrorism to deter them, blacks registered and voted at a high rate. In many locales it was common for 90 percent of adult black males to vote, and white newspaper editors frequently lamented that whites turned out at a far lower rate than the freedmen.

This surge of black political participation swept traditional political elites from power at the state and local level, establishing Republican regimes that were truly revolutionary. Although most Republican officials were white southerners themselves, they marked themselves as radicals in the eyes of their white neighbors by supporting legal and political equality for blacks. Indeed, most southern whites spoke of the Radical party rather than the Republican party. Moreover, black Republicans served as justices of the peace, county commissioners, sheriffs, state legislators, and members of Congress, thus bringing members of a despised caste into positions of prestige and authority over whites. And as blacks' assertiveness and political sophistication increased, they won a stronger voice in party affairs and secured a greater share of the spoils.[29]

Black political power brought the ideal of equal rights closer to reality for southern blacks and produced a significant shift in public policy that affected the ongoing struggle between whites and blacks over the meaning of emancipation. During the early years of Reconstruction, southern whites had mobilized the power of the state to reassert their dominance over the former slaves and to guarantee white planters and farmers a cheap, tractable labor supply. Republican legislatures denied whites this weapon, repealing the remnants of the black codes and giving blacks a voice in the legal process by admitting them to the jury box. They also attempted to strengthen the position of the vast majority of blacks who worked as agricultural laborers, sharecroppers, and tenant farmers. Republicans gave agricultural laborers and sharecroppers a first lien on the crops they produced and afforded tenants greater protection against landlords. Moreover, Republican homestead laws exempted small amounts of personal property (e.g., farming tools and livestock) from seizure by creditors. This afforded at least some protection to poor sharecroppers and tenants who relied on credit from planters and merchants to make their crops and who were in danger of losing what little property they had accumulated in the event of a poor harvest.[30]

Practice as well as policy changed, a fact that was brought home to blacks and whites by their day-to-day experiences. Persons attending trials in the county courthouse—an entertainment popular among both races—were struck by the presence of black jurors. Nothing conveyed the revolutionary nature of Reconstruction more graphically; jury service was a mark of respect in rural communities in the nineteenth century, and jurors made decisions that affected the well-being of the community. But the presence of blacks on juries was of more than symbolic importance. It gave blacks a voice in matters that directly affected their lives, and it broke another of the bonds of white authority that had circumscribed their lives. With blacks present, juries were more likely to seriously consider black testimony and cases initiated by the freedpeople. And they were less likely to indict or convict blacks merely because whites accused them of crimes. This made the freedpeople less vulnerable to white authority, shielded them from capricious prosecutions that threatened their liberty, and afforded them greater personal security.[31]

Even more alarming to planters, they now confronted local officials—sheriffs, district attorneys, judges, and justices of the peace—who were responsive to the freedpeople. Under Republican rule, arrests and prosecutions of blacks for vagrancy were almost unknown. This denied planters and farmers one of the tools they had relied on during the early years of Reconstruction to compel blacks to enter contracts on terms favorable to employers. Whites also found that local officials no longer automatically prosecuted black workers at the behest of their employers. When a group of planters in Greenwood, South Carolina, brought charges against blacks who salvaged discarded fence rails to use for firewood, for example, a Republican justice of the peace dismissed the case, noting that the rails "are of no use to any but to assist the poor in the way of fuel." "I believe in justice," he explained, "and if they [the planters] do not like it they can lump it." For planters accustomed to manipulating the law to discipline and control their workers, it was a devastating blow to see such men in control of local justice.[32]

Planters were also outraged when local officials proved responsive to blacks' complaints against them. Republican justices of the peace frequently fined employers who assaulted their employees, and they offered black workers redress against planters and farmers who tried to deny them the fruits of their labor. Whites expected deference from blacks and bitterly resented being called to account by the freedpeople. Unwilling to admit that the rule of law governed their relations with blacks and that their former slaves had a right to demand redress against them, they denounced

Republican officials as troublemakers who needlessly encouraged blacks to challenge their employers. "If a negro [sic] should sustain any ill feelings against a white man and can muster the slightest shadow of a case against him," seethed one wealthy South Carolinian, "he rushes off immediately to Beaufort [the county seat] and there he finds a ready and willing mill to grind the respectable portion of the community to ashes." The result of local officials' responsiveness to blacks, complained another planter, was loss of control over workers and "the disorganization of labor."[33]

As southern blacks used the ballot and concepts of citizenship and equal rights to shake the foundations of white supremacy, northern black communities continued to employ the principles of equalitarian constitutionalism in their battle for first-class citizenship. Because the Reconstruction Act extended the ballot only to blacks in the unrestored southern states, most northern blacks remained voteless in 1867 and 1868 while former slaves were reshaping the political landscape of the Confederate South. Moreover, in many parts of the North blacks continued to be denied service at hotels, theaters, and restaurants, assigned separate and unequal accommodations on trains and steamboats, and forced to attend segregated schools (or in some places were excluded from public schools altogether).

Energized by the triumph over slavery, northern blacks intensified their demands for equal suffrage and an end to discrimination in public accommodations. With memories of blacks' wartime services still vivid and support for legal and political equality for the freedpeople growing, this campaign achieved significant results. Two states (Minnesota and Iowa) gave blacks the right to vote, bringing to eight the number of northern states in which blacks possessed the ballot; Massachusetts (1865), New York (1873), and Kansas (1874) banned discrimination in public accommodations; Michigan, Connecticut, Iowa, Minnesota, Kansas, Colorado, and Illinois prohibited school segregation; and school boards in Chicago, Cleveland, and Milwaukee operated integrated schools and even employed a few black teachers in them. Nevertheless, resistance remained powerful in many states, and most northern blacks had to wait until ratification of the Fifteenth Amendment (1870) to win the ballot and did not enjoy remedies against discrimination in public accommodations until passage of the federal Civil Rights Act of 1875.[34]

The promise of Reconstruction was short-lived, of course. During the early 1870s the Democratic counterrevolution gained momentum, and by 1877 white Democrats had driven Republican regimes from power in every southern state and had begun the process of reducing blacks to

second-class citizenship. Blacks' commitment to equalitarian constitutionalism nevertheless survived the demise of Reconstruction. In 1883 the U.S.
Supreme Court ruled that Congress did not have authority to ban discrimination in public accommodations, striking down the federal Civil
Rights Act of 1875. In the face of a blow that the black press likened to the
Dred Scott case, northern blacks redoubled their efforts "to see to it that
the full and equal protection of the laws are afforded every citizen, without respect to race, color, or previous condition of servitude."[35] Although
blacks constituted only 2 percent of the northern population, they brought
intense pressure on northern legislators and won passage of state antidiscrimination measures. Between 1884 and 1887 thirteen states passed laws
prohibiting discrimination in hotels, restaurants, public transportation,
and places of amusement. During the late 1880s and the 1890s many of
these states expanded the types of establishments covered by the acts, and
four more states passed antidiscrimination measures. Moreover, in enforcing these laws, state supreme courts refused to permit affected businesses
to make any distinction on account of color. In the three states where the
issue arose, state supreme courts ruled that restaurant and theater owners
could not segregate blacks within their establishments.[36]

    In their quest to preserve equal rights, blacks resorted to litigation as
well as political action. As J. Morgan Kousser has demonstrated, throughout the nineteenth century blacks waged an impressive campaign against
segregated education. Wielding the principles of equalitarian constitutionalism, they mobilized their meager economic resources to initiate well over
fifty suits between 1830 and 1903 demanding integrated schools. Most of
this litigation was begun after the end of Reconstruction. Although they
were generally unsuccessful in using the Fourteenth Amendment to secure
relief, blacks relied on state constitutions and statutes and won a majority
of the cases they initiated. (After 1880, in fact, they were successful in 75
percent of the cases.)[37]

    Most of the education cases were brought in the North, where it was
far safer for blacks to challenge segregated schools. Nevertheless, southern blacks did not abandon the legal process in their pursuit of equality.
In 1878, when Louisiana Democrats reimposed segregation on the New
Orleans schools (which had been integrated during Reconstruction), the
city's black leaders turned to the courts, charging that segregation denied them equal protection as guaranteed by the Fourteenth Amendment.
Although they did not win, the New Orleans suit demonstrates that the
black community did not passively accept second-class citizenship and

that blacks continued to use the legal process and doctrines of equalitarian constitutionalism to demand their rights. In the late 1870s and early 1880s Kentucky blacks challenged legislation providing that taxes paid by members of each race be used to support their own schools. Aware that this formula would provide grossly unequal support for their schools, blacks resorted to a campaign combining litigation with political action to secure the law's repeal and to establish a more equitable system for funding public education.[38]

As the Kentucky example suggests, southern blacks also remained politically active during the two decades following the end of Reconstruction. In the absence of legal restrictions on suffrage (only a few southern states experimented with poll taxes and literacy tests prior to 1890), black voter turnout continued to be heavy in most southern states. Former slaves remained politically dominant in several dozen predominantly black counties scattered throughout the South, and Republicans (many of whom were black) continued to serve as local officials, state legislators, and even congressional representatives. Where there were sizable contingents of white Republicans (as in Tennessee and North Carolina) or dissident white Democrats (as in Florida, Arkansas, and Texas), blacks formed alliances that challenged Democratic hegemony at the state level. In Virginia the Readjuster movement forged a powerful alliance of dissident white farmers and former slaves that controlled state government between 1879 and 1883. The Virginia experience is, of course, the exception to the rule of continued Democratic dominance. In most states Democrats used a combination of fraud and violence to hold back their challengers and maintain their hegemony. Nevertheless, blacks' determination to vote suggests that they continued to view Reconstruction's promise of citizenship and equal rights as an important objective; indeed, it was worth risking their lives to realize.[39]

Southern blacks eloquently demonstrated the depth of their commitment to equalitarian constitutionalism in their response to the onset of legal segregation. Beginning in the late 1880s, southern legislatures adopted laws requiring railroads to provide equal but separate accommodations for black and white passengers, initiating a process that led to the rigid segregation of most areas of southern life during the next quarter century. Recognizing that Jim Crow legislation was designed to place a badge of inferiority on them by marking them as unfit for contact with whites, blacks denounced the proposed legislation and argued vigorously against its enactment. In Louisiana, for example, the newly organized American

Citizens' Equal Rights Association denounced a pending separate-coach law as "class legislation" and asserted that "citizenship is national and knows no color." And when the measure became law despite their objections, the association's leaders carefully devised the ill-fated *Plessy* suit to challenge its constitutionality.[40]

Arkansas blacks also made a determined effort to block passage of a Jim Crow railroad law in 1891, one year after Louisiana blacks had initiated their campaign. A meeting attended by some six hundred Little Rock blacks passed resolutions denouncing the proposed legislation as "caste and class legislation, which has no place in our country." On the floor of the legislature, black lawmakers carried on the fight. "We are opposed to the measure because, if not unconstitutional, which we deny . . . it is contrary to the genius of our government as expressed and as read between the lines of our State and National Constitutions," argued Representative John Gray Lucas. "Though Mr. Tillman, of South Carolina, has denied the divine truths uttered by Jefferson . . . yet we predict that these immortal truths . . . will survive the attacks of this lilliputian."[41]

Blacks' appeals to equalitarian constitutionalism did not halt the juggernaut of lynching, disfranchisement, and Jim Crow that made a lie of the promise of equality. And the U.S. Supreme Court, while paying lip service to the Reconstruction amendments, deprived them of substance and left them empty phrases that proclaimed principles belied by the reality of black experience. Faced with the gap between rhetoric and reality, many blacks abandoned the quest for equal rights under law. Some (notably Booker T. Washington and his supporters) argued that in the face of black poverty and white hatred, blacks should temporarily forgo political and legal rights and instead concentrate on obtaining the education and skills necessary for economic advancement. Others—most notably Marcus Garvey—rejected the quest for equal rights as irrelevant, urged blacks to cultivate racial pride and community solidarity, and advocated emigration as the only means of liberation.[42]

Disillusionment was particularly powerful among the black masses, whose everyday experiences suggested that law was a tool of the white man and that principles of equal rights were a smokescreen for the brutality of white racism. This was reflected by the widespread appeal of Garveyism among impoverished urban blacks who had found that the Promised Land of the North was, like the South, for whites only. It was also articulated powerfully in black popular music, most notably in the blues. After

World War I a Texas bluesman voiced this sense of disillusionment with the promise of equality:

Geo'ge Washin'ton, I hate to say you nevah tole a lie
I wish there wuz no Washin'ton, I do, I hope I die.
When I wuz a little boy some white man felt o' my haid,
Said, "Some day you may be president,"—some day I nevah see.
Somebody lie, dats sho as you born, somebody lie on me.

Even more direct was the bluesman's pungent comment on law:

White folks and nigger in great Co't house
Like a Cat down cellar wit' no-hole mouse.[43]

This sense of disillusionment, while widespread among northern and southern blacks in the first half of the twentieth century, by no means destroyed faith in the Constitution's promise of equality. Just as the ascendancy of proslavery constitutionalism in the 1850s had bent but not broken blacks' reliance on constitutional principles, the triumph of white racism in the early twentieth century failed to snuff out the flame of equalitarian constitutionalism. Among black leaders this was best reflected in the Niagara Movement launched by W. E. B. DuBois in 1905, and in the steady growth of the National Association for the Advancement of Colored People (NAACP) during the decades after its founding in 1909. Committed to ending disfranchisement and Jim Crow and winning genuine equality for blacks, the leaders of both organizations demanded that the nation return to its equalitarian roots. "Besides a day of rejoicing, Lincoln's birthday in 1909 should be one of taking stock of the nation's progress since 1865," explained the NAACP's organizers. "How far has it [the nation] gone in assuring to each and every citizen, irrespective of color, the equality of opportunity and equality before the law which underlie our American institutions and are guaranteed by the Constitution?" During the ensuing half century, NAACP attorneys in courtrooms throughout the South developed constitutional arguments that prodded the nation to return to the equalitarian promise of the Reconstruction amendments.[44]

But this faith continued to abide not only among such accomplished lawyers as Charles Hamilton Houston and Thurgood Marshall and other members of the black elite. As Richard Kluger and Mark Tushnet have demonstrated, the success that the NAACP enjoyed in its legal campaign against segregation rested on broad support in southern black communities. Local teachers' groups in Virginia and Maryland provided crucial support for the successful salary equalization suits of the 1930s and 1940s. Moreover, the direct challenge to segregated education that came before the U.S. Supreme Court in *Brown* v. *Board of Education* and *Bolling* v. *Sharp* grew out of grass-roots challenges to segregation in four states and the District of Columbia. They were not instigated by NAACP officials in New York, and the plaintiffs received strong support from their communities. Indeed, when *Briggs* v. *Elliott* (the South Carolina school segregation case) was tried in the U.S. district court in Charleston in May 1951, between two and three dozen blacks from Clarendon County (where the suit originated) made the two-hour drive to Charleston to watch. They were drawn by their commitment to equal rights and their sense that fulfillment of the Constitution's promises was imminent. "I never did get to sit down in the courtroom," recalled James Gibson, one of the black spectators, "but I never did get tired that day." [45]

The Clarendon County suit and the plaintiffs' trek to Charleston symbolized the survival of blacks' commitment to equalitarian constitutionalism. Born in the antebellum North and flowering in the South during the Civil War and Reconstruction, this commitment had significant implications for American culture and constitutionalism. Lawrence Levine has argued that after emancipation African American culture became less self-contained and absorbed more and more elements of white culture. Former slaves' adoption of concepts of citizenship, equal rights, and the rule of law during the war and its aftermath was an important part of this process. As they adopted the idiom of equalitarian constitutionalism, using it as a tool to escape arbitrary white authority, former slaves embraced a central aspect of the American myth. [46]

But adoption of equalitarian constitutionalism by blacks had another, equally significant, result; the exchange between blacks and whites was not a one-way street. By mobilizing concepts of citizenship, equal rights, and the rule of law, African Americans helped change the Constitution and left an indelible mark on American constitutionalism. Under pressure from blacks and their white allies, the Constitution was transformed from a document primarily concerned with property rights and federal relations into a charter that guaranteed equality. This guarantee, born during the Civil War and its aftermath, was snuffed out by the racism of the post-Reconstruction years and by formalistic Supreme Court rulings that left the concept of equality an empty shell. Nevertheless, faith in equalitarian constitutionalism survived in the black community. During the twentieth century blacks continued to use the idiom of equalitarian constitutionalism to demand justice. In the process they played a crucial role in prodding the nation to keep the promise of the Declaration of Independence and the Reconstruction amendments. It was a process that would fundamentally alter the constitutional order during the decades following World War II.[47]

NOTES

1. Philip S. Foner and George E. Walker, eds., *Proceedings of the Black State Conventions, 1840–1865*, 2 vols. (Philadelphia: Temple University Press, 1979), 1:259–60.

2. Ibid., 1:261.

3. Ibid., 1:262–63.

4. Harold M. Hyman, *A More Perfect Union: The Impact of the Civil War and Reconstruction on the Constitution* (New York: Alfred A. Knopf, 1973), 4–5.

5. Foner and Walker, eds., *Proceedings of the Black State Conventions*, 1:11, 195.

6. *Colored American*, May 9, 1840; Hosea Easton, *A Treatise on the Intellectual Character and Civil and Political Condition of the Colored People of the U. States* (Boston: I. Knapp, 1837), 47.

7. Foner and Walker, eds., *Proceedings of the Black State Conventions*, 1:21.

8. Ibid., 1:22.

9. Quotes are from Sumner's brief, in Leonard Levy and Douglas Jones, ed., *Jim Crow in Boston: The Origin of the Separate but Equal Doctrine* (New York: DaCapo Press, 1974), 181, 210.

10. R. J. M. Blackett, *Beating Against the Barriers: Biographical Essays in Nineteenth-Century Afro-American History* (Baton Rouge: Louisiana State University Press, 1986), 59–61; Leon Litwack, *North of Slavery: The Negro in the Free States, 1790–1860* (Chicago: University of Chicago Press, 1961), 111, 264.

11. Schenck, quoted in Herman Belz, *A New Birth of Freedom: The Republican Party and Freedmen's Rights, 1861 to 1866* (Westport, Conn.: Greenwood Press, 1976), 108.

12. "Appeal from the Executive Board of the National Equal Rights League," in *A Documentary History of the Negro People in the United States*, 2 vols., ed. Herbert Aptheker (New York: Citadel Press, 1969), 1:527.

13. Eric Foner, *Reconstruction: America's Unfinished Revolution, 1863–1877* (New York: Harper and Row, 1988), 27–28; James M. McPherson, ed., *The Negro's Civil War* (New York: Alfred A. Knopf, 1965), 245–70; *New York Times*, December 11, 1865.

14. Aptheker, ed., *Documentary History*, 1:536, 539; Leon Litwack, *Been in the*

Storm So Long: The Aftermath of Slavery (New York: Alfred A. Knopf, 1980), 502–31; Foner, *Reconstruction,* 110–19.

15. Litwack, *Been in the Storm So Long,* 507–14.

16. Ira Berlin et al., eds., *Freedom: A Documentary History of Emancipation, 1861–1867. Series II. The Black Military Experience* (Cambridge, U.K.: Cambridge University Press, 1982), 453 (first quote), 28 (second quote).

17. John Blassingame, "The Union Army as an Educational Institution for Negroes, 1862–1865," *Journal of Negro Education* 34 (1965): 152–59, esp. 157, 159; Berlin et al., eds., *Black Military Experience,* 362–405, 611–32; McPherson, *Negro's Civil War,* 197–203, 211–13.

18. McPherson, *Negro's Civil War,* 133–42; Jacqueline Jones, *Soldiers of Light and Love: Northern Teachers and Georgia Blacks, 1865–1873* (Chapel Hill: University of North Carolina Press, 1980), 17–27, 138–39; Robert C. Morris, *Reading, 'Riting, and Reconstruction: The Education of Freedmen in the South, 1861–1870* (Chicago: University of Chicago Press, 1976), 68, 70, 72, 85–130, 174–212; Joe M. Richardson, *Christian Reconstruction: The American Missionary Association and Southern Blacks, 1861–1890* (Athens: University of Georgia Press, 1986), 35–54, 161–210.

19. *The Freedman's Third Reader,* quoted in Morris, *Reading, 'Riting, and Reconstruction,* 198–200; Lydia Maria Child, *The Freedmen's Book* (Boston: Ticknor and Fields, 1865), 274–75.

20. Lieutenant George Cook to Captain R. S. Lacey, October 31, 1866, Reports on Conditions, Assistant Commissioner, Virginia, Bureau of Refugees, Freedmen, and Abandoned Lands, R.G. 105, National Archives (hereinafter cited as BRFAL).

21. Lieutenant E. Lyon to General Orlando Brown, May 31, 1866, Reports on Conditions, Assistant Commissioner, Virginia, BRFAL.

22. Charles H. Howard to O. O. Howard, July 11, 1865, Oliver Otis Howard Papers, Bowdoin College Library; Circular 35, December 12, 1865, Circulars and Orders, 1865–1868, Assistant Commissioner, Louisiana, BRFAL.

23. Captain H. Sweeney to General John Sprague, January 5, 1867, Assistant Commissioner, Arkansas, Letters Received, BRFAL; Donald G. Nieman, *To Set the Law in Motion: The Freedmen's Bureau and the Legal Rights of Blacks, 1865–1868* (Millwood, N.Y.: Kraus, 1979), passim.

24. LaWanda Cox, "James F. McGogy and the Freedmen's Bureau in Alabama" (Unpublished MS in possession of the author).

25. Nieman, *To Set the Law in Motion,* passim.

26. E. M. Webber to Lieutenant Garrick Mallery, July 24, 1867, Letters Received, Assistant Commissioner, Virginia, BRFAL.

27. Petition dated November 27, 1865, Letters Received, Assistant Commissioner, Alabama, BRFAL; G. Franklin et al. to General Daniel Sickles, August 8, 1866, Letters Received, Assistant Commissioner, South Carolina, BRFAL.

28. General John Sprague to General O. O. Howard, February 28, 1867, Letters Received by the Commissioner, BRFAL.

29. Foner, *Reconstruction*, 281–307, 346–64.

30. Ibid., 364–411; Nieman, "Black Ballots and Republican Justice: The Impact of Black Political Power on the Administration of Justice in the Reconstruction South" (Unpublished MS in possession of the author).

31. Donald G. Nieman, "Black Political Power and Criminal Justice: Washington County, Texas, 1868–1884," *Journal of Southern History* 55 (1989): 391–420; Nieman, "Black Ballots and Republican Justice."

32. James Bailey to Robert K. Scott, February 26, 1870, Governors' Papers, South Carolina Archives. On whites' use of law as a means of labor control during presidential Reconstruction and in the decades following Reconstruction, see Nieman, *To Set the Law in Motion*, passim; William Cohen, "Negro Involuntary Servitude in the South, 1865–1940: A Preliminary Analysis," *Journal of Southern History* 42 (1976): 31–60.

33. Lawrence Smith to E. B. Seabrook, December 17, 1869, and Joseph Sanders to Johnson Hagood, May 17, 1877, Legislative Records, Penal System File, South Carolina Archives.

34. Franklin Johnson, *The Development of State Legislation Concerning the Free Negro* (1919; Westport, Conn.: Greenwood Press, 1969), 75, 96, 105, 124, 126, 150; Gilbert T. Stephenson, *Race Distinctions in American Law* (1910; New York: Negro University Press, 1969), 183; Foner, *Reconstruction*, 469–73; James M. McPherson, "Abolitionists and the Civil Rights Act of 1875," *Journal of American History* 52 (1965): 493–510.

35. "Resolutions of the Civil Rights Mass Meeting Held at Lincoln Hall [Washington, D.C.] October 22, 1883," in Aptheker, ed., *Documentary History*, 1:658–59.

36. Valeria W. Weaver, "The Failure of Civil Rights, 1875–1883 and Its Repercussions," *Journal of Negro History* 54 (1969): 368–82.

37. J. Morgan Kousser, *Dead End: The Development of Nineteenth-Century Litigation on Racial Discrimination in Schools* (Oxford: Oxford University Press, 1986), 5–16.

38. Roger A. Fischer, *The Segregation Struggle in Louisiana, 1862–1877* (Urbana: University of Illinois Press, 1974), 139–42; Victor B. Howard, *Black Liberation in Kentucky: Emancipation and Freedom, 1862–1884* (Lexington: University Press of Kentucky, 1983), 169–76; J. Morgan Kousser, "Making Separate Equal: Integration of Black and White School Funds in Kentucky," *Journal of Interdisciplinary History* 10 (1980): 399–428.

39. J. Morgan Kousser, *The Shaping of Southern Politics: Suffrage Restriction and the Establishment of the One-Party South* (New Haven, Conn., and London: Yale University Press, 1974), passim.

40. Charles Lofgren, *The Plessy Case: A Legal-Historical Interpretation* (New York: Oxford University Press, 1987), 28.

41. *Arkansas Gazette* (Little Rock), January 20, 1891 (first quote), February 21, 1891 (second quote), as reprinted in J. Morgan Kousser, "A Black Protest in the 'Era of Accommodation': Documents," *Arkansas Historical Quarterly* 34 (1975): 157–59, 169–78.

42. On the debate over strategy and tactics among blacks, see August Meier, *Negro Thought in America, 1880–1915* (Ann Arbor: University of Michigan Press, 1963); Louis R. Harlan, *Booker T. Washington: The Making of a Black Leader, 1865–1901* (New York: Oxford University Press, 1972); Harlan, *Booker T. Washington: The Wizard of Tuskegee, 1901–1915* (New York: Oxford University Press, 1983); E. David Cronon, *Black Moses: The Story of Marcus Garvey and the Universal Negro Improvement Association*, 2d ed. (Madison: University of Wisconsin Press, 1969); Judith Stein, *The World of Marcus Garvey* (Baton Rouge: Louisiana State University Press, 1986).

43. Quoted in Lawrence Levine, *Black Culture and Black Consciousness: Afro-American Folk Thought from Slavery to Freedom* (New York: Oxford University Press, 1977), 254 (first quote), 251 (second quote).

44. Charles Flint Kellogg, *NAACP: A History of the National Association for the Advancement of Colored People, vol. 1, 1909–1920* (Baltimore, Md.: Johns Hopkins University Press, 1967), 297–98.

45. Mark Tushnet, *The NAACP's Legal Strategy Against Segregated Education, 1925–1950* (Chapel Hill: University of North Carolina Press, 1987), 70–104, 146–55; Richard Kluger, *Simple Justice* (New York: Alfred A. Knopf, 1975), 346 (quotation), 3–26, 346–540.

46. Levine, *Black Culture and Black Consciousness*, 138–40, 441–45.

47. On this transformation see Donald G. Nieman, *Promises to Keep: African-Americans and the Constitutional Order, 1776 to the Present* (New York: Oxford University Press, 1991).

Victorian Moralism and Civil Liberty

in the Nineteenth-Century United States

MICHAEL LES BENEDICT

American legal scholars have long recognized that the law is not independent of social, cultural, and intellectual institutions and ideologies. Consequently, there is a general understanding that the changes that occurred in American constitutional law in the twentieth century, making its contours so different from those of the nineteenth, were related to broader social and intellectual changes. Nonetheless, legal scholars have not done much to explicate the intellectual context in which nineteenth-century law developed. The result has been to leave the nineteenth century still a kind of dark age of constitutional law. Not that we don't know its basic shape, of course, but it is hard to understand how people could accept legal doctrines that seem to us so obviously flawed and unfair.

In important studies Lawrence Friedman and Calvin Woodard have explained this conundrum by suggesting that Americans simply did not expect law to provide what Friedman calls "total justice."[1] Nineteenth-century people had only a limited ability to control their environment. It was a time when the daily vicissitudes of life were beyond humans' capacity to control and great social problems beyond their capacity to combat, when people were equally likely to be blessed by good fortune or struck by disaster. As Friedman put it, "Life was a drama of tremendous uncertainty," in which "there was no general expectation of justice or fairness." Law reflected life. There could be "no general expectation of justice in every circumstance." Other scholars, such as Morton Horwitz, argue that nineteenth-century Americans eschewed the notion that law should embody moral principles: "Law, once conceived of as . . . a paramount expression of the moral sense of the community, had come to be thought of as facilitative of individual desires and as simply reflective of the existing organization of economic and political power."[2]

Yet anyone who reads nineteenth-century cases must see that judges were obsessed with doing justice and suffused with moralism. As a leader of the American bar told his students, the American lawyer should be "the asserter of right, the accuser of wrong, the protector of innocence, and the terror of crime."[3] What Friedman and others surely mean is that the inability to control the physical environment affected how jurisprudents defined what was just and what was moral. But in fact, nineteenth-century Americans thought they had unprecedented ability to control their environment. It was an age of immense confidence, not uncertainty.[4] Rather than a resigned acceptance of injustice, what we perceive as the shortcomings of nineteenth-century American constitutional law were reflections of cultural understandings and values that came under severe attack in the early and middle twentieth century.

These understandings have been resurrected in the form of modern American social conservatism. As a result, legal historians have been able to recover the intellectual foundation of laissez-faire constitutionalism, for example.[5] But they have not yet done the same for other facets of nineteenth-century constitutional law. This essay is an initial attempt to do so. In it I hope to convey the understandings about human nature and the role of government that predominated among the elites who had the most influence in shaping law and public policy. It may be that other groups held radically diverging views, but if so, they did not establish the contours of law and public life.

The predominant cultural understandings of nineteenth-century America may be termed Victorian moralism. Perceived as progressive in their own day, Victorian ideas represented a bold, democratic, egalitarian alternative to traditional, hierarchical philosophies of society and government. Throughout the Western world reformers and revolutionaries were inspired by the democratic implications of these ideas. In Great Britain and the United States they precipitated a wave of humanitarian reform that reshaped social life. Nonetheless, throughout the nineteenth century there had been dissent to various tenets of Victorianism in America, and by the 1880s and 1890s more and more Americans concluded that Victorian ideals were out of touch with the reality of American life. Challenged by new perceptions of society, Victorian ideas came to be viewed as traditional and conservative; they remain the foundation of what we call conservatism today.

At the heart of Victorian moralism lay an understanding of human nature that stressed the constant struggle between people's animal needs and passions and their higher qualities. Orthodox Christianity—Catholic, Anglican, and Calvinist—had presumed human depravity. As Calvin himself put it, "We know that man is so perverse and crooked a nature, that everyone would scratch out his neighbors eyes if there were no bridle to hold them in."[6] Influenced by the evangelical movement that swept America and Britain (and other regions of Europe) in the late eighteenth and early nineteenth centuries, Victorians rejected the view that men were hopelessly depraved and could be saved only by divine grace or through the ritual performance of the sacraments. Certainly human beings shared some characteristics with animals: they required food and shelter; they had an instinct for survival, procreation, and physical pleasure. But in animals these were the driving forces, untempered by other qualities. What separated human beings from animals was their capacity to transcend mere bestiality. Made in God's image, they shared some of the attributes of the divine. As the great Unitarian minister William Ellery Channing said in a sermon revealingly titled "Likeness to God," the Bible itself offered "perpetual testimonies to the divinity of human nature."[7] Human beings had the opportunity, indeed the duty, to cultivate their divine nature, to reach perfection. "We have to choose between . . . those qualities which man possesses in common with the brute, and those which he possesses in common with his creator," reformers urged.[8]

Even as rationalism gradually supplanted religion after 1860, Victorians retained this dualistic notion of human nature. Humans had intellectual and moral qualities that, if nurtured while animal instincts were suppressed, set them apart from the animal world. Thus Victorian moral philosophers insisted on a distinction between mind and body. The mind was the repository of human nature, whose essence was moral. It was the repository of conscience, which enforced moral principles against the natural passions and needs of the body.[9] The irreligious young Abraham Lincoln reflected the common notion when he enthused at a temperance meeting, "Happy day, when, all appetites controled, all passions subdued, . . . *mind* . . . shall live and move monarch of the world! Glorious consummation! Hail fall of Fury! Reign of Reason, all hail!"[10]

This dualistic conception of human nature pervaded society. It explains the tendency of popular literature and drama to present situations and characters in starkly black-and-white terms. Dickens made the conception concrete in his *Tale of Two Cities,* in which Sidney Carton and Charles

Darnay are physically identical but moral opposites competing for the love of the virtuous Lucy Manet. Robert Louis Stevenson provided a paradigm of the common conception in his chronicle of Dr. Jekyll, who separated his bestial qualities from his human nature and thus created the vicious Mr. Hyde.[11]

In his popular manual *Self Culture*, Channing advised readers that "to raise the moral and intellectual nature, we must put down the animal." [12] To nineteenth-century Americans, the essence of humanity was this ability to subdue one's animal passions and transcend selfish desires. While animals demanded immediate gratification of their needs and desires, men were able not only to delay gratification but to weigh mere physical needs and desires against moral values. Thus, as Simon Legree vented his anger and lust in animal brutality, the physically powerful Uncle Tom demonstrated his superior humanity by his patient self-restraint. It is an indication of the distance between nineteenth- and twentieth-century values that, to twentieth-century Americans, Tom's acceptance of abuse seems more a fault than a virtue. But the immense popularity and profound influence of *Uncle Tom's Cabin* attests to the consummate skill with which Harriet Beecher Stowe drew upon contemporary convictions about human nature and morality.[13]

Uncle Tom dies rather than descend to the brute level of Simon Legree— a powerful symbol of humankind's ability to transcend material desires. In fact, man's noblest characteristic was the capacity for sacrifice, through which he most nearly approached the example of Christ himself. In the "Battle Hymn of the Republic" Julia Ward Howe urged northern soldiers, "As He died to make men holy, let us die to make men free." A similar sacrifice made John Brown an icon to northern antislavery people and served to convert the ambivalent to the cause. Everywhere tears were shed over the reformed Sidney Carton's sacrifice for Charles Darnay and Lucy Manet, and over innumerable similar sacrifices in the poor imitations of popular sentimental fiction.

Of course, in real life people were not expected to make the ultimate, Christlike sacrifice. But they were expected to control their desires and overcome the brute's single-minded concentration on self. Honesty and charity were manifestations of humans' ability to place other values ahead of their own desires. Indeed, "selfishness [is] the root of depravity," the influential minister Henry W. Bellows orated. It was "the mother of human evils" and "finds its chief outlets in the . . . passions of men." [14]

As a scholar recently observed of Victorians, "Man, in their view, was an animal whose dangerous instincts were ready to surface at every opportunity. Once man succumbed to those instincts he was forever lost in a morass of passion and impulses. There was but one way man could overcome his animal nature—self-control." [15] With control of the animal passions so important, Victorian Americans often seemed to value moderation above all other virtues. The Victorian home trained boys in self-discipline and girls in modesty, a feminization of the same concept. [16] The paradigmatic case was that of sex. Victorians felt the force of sexual passion as fully as we do, [17] but they were determined to conquer it. To help control that most rampant of instincts they imposed upon themselves a prudery that has become legendary. [18] "Sensuality is the abyss in which many souls are plunged and lost," Channing warned. "Whoever would cultivate the soul must restrain the appetites." [19]

Medical science provided physiological underpinnings to the Victorian philosophy of restraint. Disease and debilitation were the result of "undue excitements and exercises of the mind and of the passions" and "excessive indulgences of the appetites," wrote the popular health reformer Sylvester Graham. Naturally, sexual excess was particularly debilitating. [20]

Men and women who could not control their passions inevitably fell into vice. People referred to the "dangerous class," which was "vicious" in the literal sense—given over to vice, the unrestrained indulgence of passion. Unable to discipline themselves to hard work, they were the first laborers dismissed in hard times. They fell to gambling and then crime. Uncontrolled passions made them violent and sexually promiscuous. Inevitably, their vices left them defenseless against the diseases rampant among them. [21] Thus discipline, order, and morality were the central Victorian values.

Originating in a powerful religious movement, the Victorian moral code remained even after religious belief failed, sustained by a new and almost idolatrous faith in the ability of science and empirical investigation to discern truth. Having reached maturity during a powerful religious revival, Victorians still sought certainty from outside authority. Even in the wake of the famous Victorian crisis of religious faith, while "denial of Christianity was common" and "denial of God was fairly common, . . . doubt was rare." [22] As Walter E. Houghton has written, "The will to believe overrode the desire to question." Moral principles were accepted as the necessary conclusions of empirical analysis, making dogmatism a prime characteristic of Victorian thought.[23] Confident of their ability to arrive at truth, Victorians were "certain that moral judgments applied with equal sureness in literature, art, politics, and all other areas." [24]

Nineteenth-century economic understandings, articulated with typical confidence, reflected and reinforced the tenets of Victorian moralism. Natural laws governed human economic relations as surely as they governed the physical universe. Whether they were instituted by a benevolent deity or were the inevitable consequence of human nature, if left to work without interference economic laws guaranteed success and happiness to those who exercised discipline and led moral lives. The labor, the products, and the services of moral and hardworking men would be in demand. Their virtues would be rewarded through the compensation they received for their service. By the same natural economic laws, the vicious and brutal would end their lives in poverty, disease, shame, and degradation. Moral philosophers taught that "the universe was so constituted that there was a pre-established harmony between virtue and happiness, vice and misery." [25]

Indeed, through natural economic laws, man's base desires—his love of comfort and luxury—became an engine to promote his higher qualities. Only through hard work, good morals, discipline, and sacrifice could he hope to achieve material success. The very effort to secure material well-being served to enhance men's moral faculties. "The ethics of human society are a part of the grand order of the universe," lawyer and philosopher John B. Stallo observed. "There is an eternal law, according to which industry tends to develop the virtues of frugality and honesty . . . [and] social commerce between men fosters charity, mutual forbearance and truthfulness." [26]

Obviously, such beliefs militated against special privileges based on birth or caste. The link between good character and success necessitated a society where everyone had an equal opportunity to succeed. Therefore, hierarchy and special privilege were inconsistent with the most critical requirement of a good society. The great virtue of American society was that it operated on this principle of equal opportunity. No aristocracy received special privileges; "equal rights and no special privileges" was the watchword of American politics, government, and constitutional law. One of the primary responsibilities of government was the prevention of monopoly and restraint of trade.[27] In America, as nowhere else in the world, nineteenth-century Americans believed every man rose as far as his skill and perseverance could take him, with no artificial barriers to stand in his way.[28]

The natural consequence of such ideas was a firm belief that in the United States, wealth was earned and poverty was deserved. Poverty, disease, crime, promiscuity, and other ills were due primarily to flaws in individual character. No improvements in the society at large could cure these evils. Thus William Lloyd Garrison warned against the "absurd and dangerous dogma, that men are 'the creatures of circumstance'—not sinful but unfortunate." "Internal regeneration must precede the external salvation of mankind from sin and misery," he insisted.[29] As James Walvin has written, Victorians were convinced that good morals, hard work, and self-discipline were "the inevitable route to personal and collective salvation." These provided "the antidote to the major ills of individuals and therefore of society."[30] Therefore the only way to reform society was to reform individuals, again in the literal sense—to form their characters anew. YMCAs, the Salvation Army, slum "missions," the missionary impulse that sent thousands south after the Civil War, and even prison reform attest to the force of this perception.[31]

In the twentieth century Americans slowly reached the conclusion that poverty caused vice. But Victorians believed just the opposite. Therefore to combat social evils by interfering with the way the free market distributed resources was worse than useless. It would give wealth to the undeserving and take it away from the worthy, destroying the essential link between natural economic laws and individual morality, between virtue and economic success. This was "class legislation," the use of government to secure unearned privileges to whoever controlled it.

Sharing such beliefs, most Americans watched nervously as new ideas of socialism spread throughout Europe and to the United States. Such a perversion of government inevitably would appeal to the vicious and profligate, they worried, and there were demagogues and corrupt political bosses aplenty to cater to them. Their concern grew as newly enfranchised freedmen supported corrupt carpetbag regimes in the South, as immigrants sustained corrupt political machines in the cities, as workingmen began to demand a state-sanctioned eight-hour workday, and as farmers and small businessmen demanded regulation of railroad shipping rates. By the mid-1870s, any legislation that seemed to redirect resources raised the specter of class legislation seemed to carry the taint of socialism. "Laissez-faire—let economic matters alone," seemed the only safe rule for government to follow.[32]

By the term *social reform* Victorians did not mean restructuring society to eliminate the causes of vice, crime, and disease. They meant removing from the social environment those elements that subverted the effort to lead a moral life, that seduced men and women into lives of self-gratification. In this Victorians demonstrated the moral basis of their attitudes toward the proper role of government, for hard-line laissez-fairists took the position articulated by Henry George: "It is not the business of government to make men virtuous or religious, or to preserve fools from the consequence of their folly."[33]

"It is to the defects of our social organization, to the multiplied and multiplying temptations to crime that we chiefly owe the increase of evil doers," Dorothea Dix argued. The problem, said fellow prison reformer William H. Channing, was that "the sight of evil, as if by contagion, awakens the desire to commit evil."[34] Of course, even Victorians recognized that extreme poverty corroded moral restraints. "Preaching and tracts are of little use to the girl who has nowhere to lay her head except in the brothel, or to the boy, who can only keep himself from starving by stealing," wrote Charles Loring Brace.[35] But Brace and other reformers meant their words to be taken literally. Extreme want negated the effect of moral instruction, and therefore the truly destitute had to be provided with asylums—poorhouses, orphanages, and the like—where such instruction would be effective. They certainly never intended to suggest a program of wealth redistribution.[36]

To eliminate temptations Victorians proposed such social reforms as prohibition of the sale of alcoholic beverages—"the giant whose mighty arm prostrates the greatest numbers, involving them in sin and shame and crime and ruin"[37]—and the suppression of gambling, lotteries, boxing, cockfighting, and other brutal sports, pornography, birth control, and prostitution.[38] As a symbol of social commitment to morality and religion, and to help religion promote morality, they sustained laws barring work and entertainment on Sundays.[39] They called for asylums for those who had already succumbed to the combination of their own weakness and the vice around them, or for those, like orphans, in special jeopardy. Their characters could be formed or reformed in environments free of the seductions of social evil.[40]

In the view of nineteenth-century Americans the purpose of social institutions was to promote the moral life that led to material success and social well-being. Naturally, one of the most potent of these institutions was Christianity. Only the character of Christianity could explain the difference between the United States and pagan nations in the conditions of people and the prevalence of vice.[41] And within Christianity, Protestantism was most conducive to the development of moral character. Since their catalog of virtues and vices was greatly influenced by their northern European Protestant background, most Americans viewed Catholicism with distaste. Catholics seemed too reconciled to human frailty, too willing to indulge weakness of character with absolution, too focused on ritual, and too little concerned with reform. As Protestants saw it, Catholicism "looks only to the . . . religious nature of man, while the Protestant has gone farther, and embraced, not only that, but his mental and moral instruction."[42] The Catholic church's hierarchical organization, which was imposed in the United States only in the mid-nineteenth century, seemed to militate against the equality of opportunity implicit in the Victorian worldview. The reactionary pronouncements of Popes Pius IX and Leo XIII and the Vatican Council of 1870 confirmed most Americans' opinions. Protestant religion, on the other hand, inculcated all the virtues that promoted success in life.[43]

Like the church, the family played a key role in inculcating the moral values essential to personal, and ultimately social, well-being. The home was where the "finest sympathies, tastes and moral and religious feelings are formed and nourished," Victorians believed.[44] "The domestic fireside is the great guardian of society against the excesses of human passions."[45] Indeed, as belief in orthodox religion waned, the family was seen more and more as the most important locus of moral training. And within the family, the wife's role was crucial. By the mid-nineteenth century, women were more and more adopting the roles of ministers. Not only were they responsible for the moral training of their children, women were the catalysts of the moral regeneration of their husbands.[46] Thus, as so many historians have observed over the past twenty years, women moved in a "special sphere," with a special social mission. Since social welfare depended on the character of its individual members, women played the crucial role in maintaining it. If they were to abandon that role, "the beautiful order of society . . . shall break up and become . . . chaos."[47]

Schools were crucial to augment or, if necessary, substitute for the moral training provided at home. Theodore Parker expressed the common belief that "the community owes each child born into it a chance for education, intellectual, moral, and religious."[48] Therefore, as Victorian moralism spread through the United States in the first half of the nineteenth century, so did the idea of state-supported, free public education. Studies of that development have made historians well aware that nineteenth-century Americans considered the obligation of schools to inculcate self-discipline and proper moral values at least as important as their obligation to instill knowledge. "Education judiciously conducted preserves the human mind from depravity," Bronson Alcott said, expressing the common conviction.[49] States enjoined college, secondary, and primary schools, in the words of Massachusetts's school law, to teach "the principles of piety and justice and a sacred regard for truth; . . . sobriety, industry and frugality; chastity, moderation and temperance; . . . and, also, to point out to them the evil tendency of the opposite vices."[50]

The schools were supposed to be free of sectarian influence, but in fact they were permeated by the values of American Protestantism. Reading from the King James Bible was almost universal, but even where school boards began to change the practice in deference to Catholics, Jews, and freethinkers, teachers and texts such as McGuffey's *Readers* continued to drum the Protestant virtues into their pupils.[51]

If nothing else, the arts promoted morals by providing alternatives to "vicious indulgences," poet and journalist William Cullen Bryant pointed out.[52] But most Victorian Americans—Bryant included—assigned them a far loftier mission than that. The purpose of the arts was to instill an appreciation of the beautiful, the spiritual, the moral—to cultivate the finer elements of human character, "to call forth, in the highest degree possible, the sentiment of the moral sublime."[53] "Their great sphere is that *beau ideal* that lifts us above the grovelling, the vile, and the sensual"; the arts were "a salvation from merely material luxury and sensual enjoyment."[54]

The didactic purpose of American painting and sculpture was clearest when artists portrayed biblical or great historical subjects. Artists were to aspire to the ideal, to present the world's great underlying moral truths, not mundane realities.[55] Thus Alexander Everett praised Horatio Greenough's statue of Washington, which was placed in the Capitol rotunda, for placing moral truth ahead of mere realism: "The colossal size—the antique costume—the more youthful air of the face—are circumstances which, without materially impairing the truth to nature, increase very much the moral impression."[56] Rembrandt Peale designed *The Court of Death,* which toured the United States for more than a decade, to be "a Great Moral Painting," in which innocence and purity, symbolized by a beautiful woman, gazed heavenward unterrified by the grim monarch Death, surrounded by his agents War, Intemperance, and Disease.[57] Likewise Hiram Powers's famous Statue, *The Slave,* toured the nation—the beautiful, chained nude's evocation of wronged innocence stirred Victorians' deepest emotions. "There should be a moral in every work of art," Powers wrote.

As long as it served such moral purposes, nudity did not offend Victorian sensibilities.[58]

In the same way, the great American landscapes were "a vehicle for moral imperatives, spiritual inspiration, and didactic formulas."[59] Nature "is fraught with lessons of high and holy meaning," wrote influential landscape artist Asher B. Durand. Again, mere realistic reportage was not the artist's goal. By selecting from nature and composing the parts into an ideal whole, the artist made manifest "the work of God in the visible creation." Representations of the American wilderness offered men and women the opportunity to contemplate God's creation undefiled by human changes and thus lifted them beyond the "senseless idolatry of their own follies," enthused America's premier landscape artist, Thomas Cole. Washington Allston, another leading painter, echoed him. "The master Principle," he wrote, was "to testify to the meanest, most obliquitous mind . . . that there *is* such a thing as *good without self*."[60] Cole's friend William Cullen Bryant eulogized him as "not only a great artist but a great teacher; the contemplation of his works made men better."[61]

Landscape architecture had the same purpose as landscape painting. James Jackson Jarves, an influential art critic and collector, reflected that conviction when he lauded Central Park as "a great free school of the people," which "elevates and refines the popular mind," allowing all a glimpse of "the clear vault of heaven" and teaching the "salutary lessons in order, discipline, and comeliness."[62]

As Jarves's enthusiastic comment indicates, besides spiritual lessons art conveyed the inherent order and harmony of the universe. It was impossible to contemplate the "inexpressible beauty and grandeur" of nature "without arriving at the conviction . . . that the Great Designer of these glorious pictures has placed them before us as types of the Divine attributes." By such contemplation, men

To the beautiful order of his works
Learn to conform the order of our lives.[63]

Genre painting—folk and popular art—likewise conveyed moral lessons by idealizing order, work, and noble sentiment.[64]

Even as they rejected heavy-handed moralizing after the Civil War, American artists continued to believe that "he is the noblest artist who succeeds in reproducing the greatest and truest feelings and conveying to the beholder the noblest emotions." The purpose of art remained to elevate.[65]

Architecture and design served the same purpose. Architects and de-

signers stressed order and harmony in general. Asymmetry had its place—
it suggested rusticity and sometimes power—but a truly beautiful form
must involve "harmonious expression." It required "proportion, symmetry, harmony."[66] The styles of public architecture were derived from
the past and expressed timeless ideals—the simple virtue of the classical
Greeks, the dignified grandeur of the Romans, or the spiritualism of the
Gothic Middle Ages.[67]

In their domestic architecture Victorians sought to provide an environment suitable for Christian nurture. They warned against homes "built
only with a view to animal wants." A home should show through its architecture "that it is intended not only for the physical wants of man, but
for his moral, social, and intellectual existence."[68] Even as Americans lost
their taste for architectural simplicity after the Civil War, they redoubled
their commitment to an architecture that reflected "structure, discipline,
and control."[69]

Literature and drama also both reflected the Victorians' moral universe
and were expected to reinforce it. Poetry harnessed emotions—potentially
so dangerous—to the promotion of virtue and morality.[70] It inspired men
to transcend the selfishness that encouraged vice. The novel likewise served
to promote morality. "The tests are very plain and simple," explained
William Dean Howells. "If a novel flatters the passions, and exalts them
above the principles, it is poisonous. . . . [U]nmoral romances, . . . where
the sins of the senses are unvisited by the penalties following . . . are deadly
poison."[71]

In drama, "the tragic muse should love to sing of successful virtue, of
triumphant heroism, and of defeated iniquity," authors and critics agreed.
"The lessons taught must be those of patriotism, virtue, morality, religion."[72] The masthead of the literary and dramatic magazine *The Fly*
carried a paraphrase of Shakespeare:

Plays are mirrors where mankind may see
How bad they are, how good they ought to be.[73]

With rare exceptions (unsurprisingly considered by modern critics to
be the true classics of the period), virtue was portrayed as beautiful, vice
as ugly. Virtue was rewarded, evil defeated. The distinctions were stark,
reflecting the Victorian conviction that good and evil, the bestial and the
humane, were separate entities warring for dominance in every heart. Characters were good or bad; innocence was unsullied and villainy unqualified.
On stage, heroes and heroines wore white; villains wore black. Always,
good triumphed over evil.[74]

Of course, the colors were symbolic, the characters overdrawn, and the endings predictable. But to Victorians, their literature and drama (what we now scorn as romance and melodrama) conveyed deeper truths than would the more ambiguous shadings of mundane reality.[75] Indeed, to suggest that good did not triumph over evil, to suggest that the good and evil in men's character were so inextricably mixed as to defy separation and suppression of the bad, seemed profoundly *un*realistic. Moreover, such representations, if accepted as true, would erode the underpinnings of morality; they would teach people that there was no link between character and success in American society—a notion as false, in the view of Victorian Americans, as it was dangerous. Thus they worried about "pernicious literature" such as the beautiful but scandalous productions of Lord Byron, which subverted rather than promoted control of animal passions, which were "a fan to the flame of secret desires."[76]

What was true of the other arts was true of music as well. Popular music was characterized by extreme sentimentality, "descending to bathos," as a modern scholar has described it.[77] Classical music was "to be appreciated for its . . . moral, spiritual, or aesthetic values."[78]

In sum, the central Victorian values were restraint, order, and the transcendence of individual desires. That is not a mix likely to put a premium on individual liberties, and inevitably these values affected how judges and other jurisprudents interpreted constitutional rights. Indeed, judges "ought to feel in their full force those deep underlying principles of nationality, of morality, and of religion which constitute the basis of the existing order of things in every country," an eminent judge told law school graduates.[79]

As already noted, the connection between character and success, and the persistent danger that the vicious and profligate coveted the property of the virtuous and successful, made any proposal to redistribute wealth suspect. This was true not only of proposed economic legislation but also of such legal notions as fault and contract. Given Victorian worldviews, it was logical that the only justification for taking one person's property and giving it to another was a promise made by contract or a liability incurred by a wrongful act. Victorians arrived at such doctrines as contributory negligence and the fellow servant rule not because of a utilitarian desire to promote economic development, or because they felt powerless in the face of random catastrophes, but for precisely the opposite reason: they were convinced that people were independent moral agents who controlled their own destinies. Those responsible for losses should bear them, and none other. Refusing to enforce bad bargains, spreading the losses due to injury across society, or imposing them on those best able to pay or on employers, regardless of fault, would have embodied a forced redistribution. If required by legislation, it would deprive the unoffending of their property without due process of law, a perception maintained in courts after much of society had abandoned it.[80]

This did not prevent various groups from advocating policies that amounted to such redistribution. Many farmers and small businessmen favored railroad rate regulation, for example; labor reformers wanted reduced working hours without corresponding reductions in pay. But the general commitment to laissez-faire provided a powerful basis for resistance to these demands. Each group found a justification for its demands within a generally laissez-faire system.[81] Not until critics challenged the basic belief that there was a cause-and-effect relationship between character and economic success could they mount a successful attack on laissez-faire. In the meantime, such redistributive legislation as legislatures did enact faced close scrutiny from judges who fully shared the dominant philosophy.[82]

Victorians were individualists in the sense that they considered each person to be a free moral agent, responsible for his or her own success or failure. But it should be clear that they were not individualists in the modern sense. Truth and morals were not indeterminate to Victorians. They did not concede to each person the right to live freely according to his or her own moral code so long as they injured no one else. And since society as a whole depended on the character of its individual members, it had a legitimate interest in promoting morality, suppressing immoral behavior, and fostering those institutions that inculcated moral virtue.

Although opposed to government favoritism among Christian (or at least Protestant) sects and denominations, the universal belief that religion was essential to morality led Americans to wrestle with the problem of how much support government should give religion. State constitutions enjoined, "Religious morality . . . being essential to good government, it shall be the duty of the legislature to make suitable provisions for the protection of all religious denominations in the peaceable enjoyment of their modes of worship."[83] But it was unclear how far states could go to carry out such injunctions before crossing the line to unacceptable discrimination among sects. Some Whigs and Republicans, with their close links to Protestant evangelicals, favored close relations between the state and religion, while Democrats, with their "equal rights" philosophy, antireli-

gious establishment heritage, and openness to Catholics, urged greater distance.[84] Everywhere, religious institutions were exempt from taxation, for
example, with no complaints.[85] Sunday closing laws were more controversial, but they were almost everywhere sustained by courts, the main issue
being whether antiestablishment clauses of state constitutions required
special arrangements for Jews, Seventh-Day Adventists, and others.[86] As
of 1887, thirty-three states barred business on Sundays, with only thirteen making alternative provisions for Jews and other minorities. Three
more barred recreation. Only two states had no such legislation, except
to bar the sale of liquor.[87] The courts likewise sustained antiblasphemy
laws, although by mid-century actual prosecutions ceased as the offense
was subsumed into "disorderly conduct."[88]

The role of religious training in public institutions was widely accepted.
Public schools, orphanages, poorhouses, asylums, prisons, and reformato-
ries were expected to provide religiously based moral training. Evangelical
Christians, the prime movers in the establishment of these institutions,
remained deeply involved in their operations.[89]

Only in the schools did this reality raise constitutional conflict. State
constitutions clearly associated religious training, morality, and education
in such declarations as that of Mississippi: "Religion, morality, and knowledge being necessary to good government, the preservation of liberty, and
the happiness of mankind, schools . . . shall forever be encouraged in this
state."[90] By the 1870s there were calls for truly nonsectarian education.
To this, traditionalists responded that education must reflect "our proper
humanity, whereby, besides being animals, we have a rational, moral, and
accountable nature. . . . Some men may dehumanize themselves; . . . but is
that a reason for the state's adopting a method of education for its children
which discards or ignores the crown of their humanity?"[91]

Anxious to keep Catholic children in the public schools, educators tried
to create nonsectarian schools that would still inculcate moral values. But
they could not shed the conviction that the King James Bible remained the
best source of moral principles that transcended mere sectarianism. As a
result, by the mid-nineteenth century a large proportion of Catholics had
withdrawn from the public schools and had established their own.[92]

Occasional legal challenges to Protestant Bible reading in the schools
failed. Indeed, one of the most celebrated local trials of the nineteenth
century grew out of the Cincinnati school board's effort to woo Catholics
back into the system by ending Bible reading and hymn singing. Protestant parents denied the board's power to end the practice, pointing to the

state constitution—similar to Mississippi's—which explicitly linked religion and education as "essential to good government."[93] The local court sustained the plaintiffs. If Ohio's schools were to fulfill their function of teaching morality, they must utilize an authoritative source of moral principles, one of the judges explained. "Without the teaching of the Holy Scriptures there is . . . no unvarying standard of moral duty."[94]

Opponents of Bible reading considered it a great victory when Ohio's supreme court reversed the decision, thus permitting a school board to eliminate Bible reading from the curriculum if it wished to do so.[95] The established rule remained that school boards had wide latitude to choose how to fulfill their obligations to provide moral training, including reading of any version of the Bible they felt appropriate.[96] Angry Catholics—driven, they felt, from the public schools—began to demand a share of the public school funds to sustain their own systems. In response, states passed laws and constitutional amendments barring the expenditure of state funds on sectarian educational institutions, in effect ensuring that school funds remained in the hands of Protestant educators.[97]

Blasphemy cases, legal challenges to Sunday closing laws, and protests against religious teaching in the schools raised the question of the relationship between Christianity and the state. Many nineteenth-century Americans urged that the law formally recognize that the United States was a Christian nation. A movement to incorporate such a declaration into the Constitution gained ground in the mid-nineteenth century but ultimately failed to secure its objective.[98]

Nonetheless, throughout the century courts regularly declared that Christianity was to some degree part of the common law, although some—most pointedly the Ohio Supreme Court—rejected the notion.[99] In 1892, in a once-celebrated decision, the U.S. Supreme Court pointed to the continuous and widespread support the American states had given to religion since the Revolution, to such customs as beginning government activities with prayers and adjourning for the Sabbath, and to the pervasiveness of Christian organizations and charities. "These, and many other matters which might be noticed," the Court declared, "*add a volume of unofficial declarations* to the mass of organic utterances *that this is a Christian nation.*"[100] In the same year Congress conditioned its appropriation in support of the Chicago World Columbian Exposition upon its closing on Sundays.[101]

Naturally the law also reflected the crucial role Victorians assigned to the family, and especially to women, in inculcating the moral values essential to a healthy society. Nowhere was divorce consensual. It was available as a remedy only to the innocent party and, with the exception of impotence, only on grounds demonstrating the moral shortcomings of the guilty spouse: infidelity, desertion, fraud, conviction of felony, drunkenness, or extreme cruelty. Evaded through subterfuges by unhappy couples, these rigid laws remained on the books well into the twentieth century—expressing Victorian norms and making divorce humiliating and expensive.[102]

In these circumstances Mormons' arguments that their religious commitment to polygamous marriage took precedence over other Americans' moral beliefs never had a chance of success. In 1878 the Supreme Court sustained the power of the national government to outlaw the practice, and in the 1880s it sustained draconian federal laws that annulled the church's articles of incorporation in Utah territory, confiscated its property, and precipitated the prosecution of over a thousand Saints. Marriage was "a sacred obligation," while polygamy was "contrary to the spirit of Christianity and of the civilization which Christianity has produced in the Western world," the justices said.[103]

Nineteenth-century judges were hardly going to overturn as civil rights violations state laws that reinforced women's primary role as moral preceptor within the family. "The civil law . . . has always recognized a wide difference in the respective spheres and destinies of man and woman," Justice Joseph Bradley wrote in the most quoted courtroom articulation of the Victorian view of woman's role. "The constitution of the family organization, which is founded on the divine ordinance, as well as in the nature of things, indicates the domestic sphere as that which properly belongs to the domain and functions of womanhood. . . . The paramount mission and duty women are to fulfill are the offices of wife and mother." The Court declined to interfere with legislative regulation based on that understanding.[104]

American constitutional law also reflected Victorian understandings of the role of literature and the fine arts. Government had an obligation to make sure that the arts served their purpose of elevating men and women rather than degrading them. Local government enforced laws against pornography in literature; they made certain that painting and sculpture reflected modesty and virtue and that plays were wholesome. In 1842 Congress banned the importation of "indecent and obscene" lithographs and prints. In the 1870s Anthony Comstock and other warriors for decency persuaded the national government to ban not only pornography but also information about birth control and birth control devices from the mail. They then succeeded in securing "little Comstock acts" in the states.[105]

Courts uniformly upheld such regulations, as well as common-law prosecutions for obscenity. "The courts are guardians of the public morals," Pennsylvania judges held in an early and leading case. Francis Wharton's treatise on the criminal law reported that it was indictable at common law to publish an obscene book, to print or utter obscene language, or to do anything "tending to corrupt the morals of the people." [106] American courts accepted the standard of obscenity adopted in the English case of *Regina* v. *Hicklin:* distribution of a work of art or piece of literature could be punished when any part of it had a "tendency . . . to deprave and corrupt those whose minds are open to such immoral influences." [107] Likewise the Supreme Court upheld the Comstock law, sustaining Congress's power to inhibit "the distribution of matter deemed injurious to the public morals." [108]

Confident of their ability to arrive at truth and relying on authority for its exposition, Victorians placed scant value on people's right to challenge orthodoxies. During the Civil War, patriots were quick to challenge the loyalty of those who doubted the wisdom of trying to suppress the rebellion by force.[109] As radicals challenged the late nineteenth-century political and economic order, state after state passed laws making it illegal to espouse "criminal syndicalism." Courts agreed that speech could be suppressed if it had the "bad tendency" of encouraging illegal activity. Likewise they sustained broad discretion in local officials to regulate speech in the exercise of ordinary police powers.[110]

Convinced that crime was a manifestation of the most profound kind of moral failing, Victorians had scant sympathy for the criminal.[111] Police shared the beliefs, prejudices, and values of Victorian society. "They twisted formal law . . . in accordance with everyday values, ideas, and sentiments," the authors of an important local study found. They were, to say the least, "not legalistic." [112] "Police brutality," another wrote, "was a form of 'delegated vigilantism' by which the middle class tolerated and even approved violence against the outcasts of society." [113]

Criminal behavior was a matter of individual responsibility, and that was that. Victorians simply could not conceive it to be a matter of social injustice. The fact that most criminal defendants were poor and ignorant (of their rights among other things) did not suggest a discriminatory law enforcement system; they were poor because poverty was the natural consequence of indiscipline, immorality, and crime. That such defendants were ignorant of their constitutional rights, were served poorly by lawyers, and received short shrift from juries—that the courts, in short, "administered injustice"—hardly troubled the average judge.[114] Judges were strongly committed to the complex rules of criminal procedure, especially in the first half of the nineteenth century. As in civil law pleadings, form was extremely important. Judges regularly threw out indictments for various technical failures of language. They strictly enforced rules against coerced self-incrimination and attended closely to arcane rules of evidence. Many jurisdictions took broad views of what constituted forbidden double-jeopardy; however, these were treated as matters of procedure and not as constitutional rights. Although defense attorneys appealed to every technicality of pleading and the law of evidence in efforts to reverse convictions, it hardly ever occurred to them to appeal on constitutional grounds.[115]

A party dissatisfied with state judges' inattention to civil rights could expect no greater sympathy from the federal courts. Although the Supreme Court became progressively more willing to guard property rights against redistributive legislation, it shared most Victorians' unconcern about other rights. In a series of decisions after the Civil War it carefully declined jurisdiction over such matters.[116]

From the perspective of mid-twentieth-century liberalism, this record seems terribly dismal. The civil libertarianism of our own times has grown out of understandings of human nature, society, and culture utterly different from those accepted by Victorians. Modern liberalism is heir to ideas that challenged the essentials of Victorian moralism with increasing force from the 1870s through the first half of the twentieth century. The philosophy of pragmatism rejected Victorian confidence in the determinacy of truth. Therefore it rejected formalism in legal reasoning. At the same time it mandated toleration of alternative beliefs and the free expression of challenges to orthodoxy. Freudian psychology put a premium on flexibility rather than order and challenged the notion that men and women must repress animal instincts. New nondidactic justifications of art for its own sake encouraged realism rather than idealism in literature and the fine arts. Rebellious intellectuals repudiated order, symmetry, and harmony as ultimate ideals, whether in art or behavior. Deductive reasoning about society gave way to scientific inquiry made possible by the development of new tools, especially modern statistical techniques that permit rigorous testing of hypotheses.[117]

The result was to cut away the philosophical underpinnings of Victorian-era law—the framework that made it intellectually respectable. Those who continued to adhere to its tenets seemed irrational to those with a more modern outlook. Only relatively recently have we been able to rediscover that lost world, to see that nineteenth-century law must be understood as the principled application of nineteenth-century ideas, and not condemned as a failure to apply our own modern values.

NOTES

1. Lawrence M. Friedman, *Total Justice* (New York: Russell Sage, 1985); Calvin Woodard, "Reality and Social Reform: The Transition from Laissez-Faire to the Welfare State," *Yale Law Journal* 72 (1962): 286–328.

2. Woodard, "Reality and Social Reform," 50–51; Morton Horwitz, *The Transformation of American Law, 1780–1860* (Cambridge, Mass.: Harvard University Press, 1977), 253.

3. David Hoffman, *A Lecture Introductory to a Course of Lectures, Now Delivering in the University of Maryland*, reprinted in *The Legal Mind in America: From Independence to the Civil War*, ed. Perry Miller (Ithaca, N.Y.: Cornell University Press, 1962), 84–91 (quote at 87). See, for example, David Gold, "John Appleton of Maine and the Commercial Law: Freedom, Responsibility, and Law in the Nineteenth-Century Marketplace," *Law and History Review* 4 (Spring 1986): 55–69; Gold, *The Shaping of Nineteenth Century Law: John Appleton and Responsible Individualism* (New York: Greenwood Press, 1990). As the title of Gold's book indicates, nineteenth-century lawyers and judges assumed that individuals—with the exception of defined groups such as women, children, and the mentally incompetent—controlled their actions and thus could be held accountable for them. Justice therefore consisted in requiring people to live up to their commitments, which by definition were freely made; making those responsible for accidents and damages bear the loss; and punishing those who willfully hurt others. See also Craig Haney, "Criminal Justice and the Nineteenth-Century Paradigm: The Triumph of Psychological Individualism in the 'Formative Era,'" *Law and Human Behavior* 6 (1982): 191–235.

4. Arthur A. Ekirch, *The Idea of Progress in America, 1815–1860* (New York: Columbia University Press, 1944); Irving H. Bartlett, *The American Mind in the Mid-Nineteenth Century*, 2d ed. (Arlington Heights, Ill.: Harlan Davidson, 1982), 27–34.

5. Robert Goedecke, "Justice Field and Inherent Rights," *Journal of Politics* 27 (April 1965): 198–207; Robert E. Garner, "Justice Brewer and Substantive Due Process: A Conservative Court Revisited," *Vanderbilt Law Review* 18 (March 1965): 615–41; Alan Jones, "Thomas M. Cooley and the Michigan Supreme Court, 1865–1885," *American Journal of Legal History* 10 (1966): 97–121; and Jones, "Thomas M. Cooley and 'Laissez-Faire Constitutionalism': A Reconsideration,"

Journal of American History 53 (March 1967): 751–71; Charles M. McCurdy, "Justice Field and the Jurisprudence of Government-Business Relations: Some Parameters of Laissez-Faire Constitutionalism, 1863–1897," *Journal of American History* 61 (March 1975): 970–1005; John E. Semonche, *Charting the Future: The Supreme Court Responds to a Changing Society, 1890–1920* (Westport, Conn.: Greenwood Press, 1978); Michael Les Benedict, "Laissez-Faire and Liberty: A Re-Evaluation of the Meaning and Origins of Laissez-Faire Constitutionalism," *Law and History Review* 3 (Fall 1985): 293–331; William Forbath, "The Ambiguities of Free Labor: Labor and the Law in the Gilded Age," *Wisconsin Law Review* (July–August 1985): 767–817; and Gold, *Shaping of Nineteenth Century Law*.

6. Quoted in Michael Walzer, *The Revolution of the Saints: A Study in the Origins of Radical Politics* (Cambridge, Mass.: Harvard University Press, 1982), 33.

7. William Ellery Channing, "Likeness to God," in *Works of William Ellery Channing,* 6 vols. (Boston: James Munroe, 1846), 3:227–55 (quote at 231).

8. I. B. Sears, "Our Candidates as Reformers, Genuine and Spurious," *National Quarterly Review* 25 (September 1872): 372; Theodore Parker, "The Three Chief Safeguards of Society," in *Speeches, Addresses, and Occasional Sermons,* 2 vols. (Boston: Crosby and Nichols, 1855), 2:360–61; Horace Mann, *Lectures on Education* (Boston: Ides and Dutton, 1855), 87–89. See Claude Welch, *Protestant Thought in the Nineteenth Century,* 2 vols. (New Haven, Conn.: Yale University Press, 1972), 1:127–37; Timothy L. Smith, *Revivalism and Social Reform: American Protestantism on the Eve of the Civil War* (New York: Abingdon Press, 1957); for Britain, Gertrude Himmelfarb, *Victorian Minds* (New York: Alfred A. Knopf, 1968), 275–92.

9. D. H. Meyer, *The Instructed Conscience: The Shaping of the American National Ethic* (Philadelphia: University of Pennsylvania Press, 1972), 43–50.

10. Abraham Lincoln, "Temperance Address," February 22, 1842, in *Collected Works of Abraham Lincoln,* 9 vols., ed. Roy P. Basler (New Brunswick, N.J.: Rutgers University Press, 1953), 1:279.

11. Charles Dickens, *A Tale of Two Cities* (London: Chapman and Hall, 1859); Robert Louis Stevenson, *The Strange Tale of Dr. Jekyll and Mr. Hyde* (London: Longmans, Green, 1886).

12. William Ellery Channing, "Self Culture," *Works,* 2:374.

13. Harriet Beecher Stowe, *Uncle Tom's Cabin; or, Life among the Lowly* (Boston: John P. Jewett, 1852). See Jane Tomkins, "Sentimental Power: *Uncle Tom's Cabin* and the Politics of Literary History," in *Ideology and Classic American Literature,* ed. Sacvan Bercovitch (Cambridge, U.K.: Cambridge University Press, 1986), 267–92.

14. Henry Whitney Bellows, *The Relation of Public Amusement to Public Morality, Especially of the Theatre to the Highest Interests of Humanity* . . . (New York: C. S. Francis, 1857), 10.

15. Phillip A. Gibbs, "Self Control and Male Sexuality in the Advice Literature of Nineteenth-Century America 1830–1860," *Journal of American Culture* 9 (Summer 1986): 39.

16. Ibid.; Barbara Welter, "The Cult of True Womanhood: 1820–1860," *American Quarterly* 18 (Summer 1966): 154–58; John S. Haller and Robin M. Haller, *The Physician and Sexuality in Victorian America* (Urbana: University of Illinois Press, 1974), 102–13.

17. Carl N. Degler, "What Ought to Be and What Was: Women's Sexuality in the Nineteenth Century," *American Historical Review* 79 (December 1974): 1467–90; Nancy S. Landale and Avery M. Guest, "Ideology and Sexuality among Victorian Women," *Social Science History* 10 (Summer 1986): 147–70.

18. Walter E. Houghton, *The Victorian Frame of Mind* (New Haven, Conn.: Yale University Press, 1957), 356–57; Himmelfarb, *Victorian Minds*, 305–6; Gibbs, "Self Control and Male Sexuality," 37–41; Haller and Haller, *Physician and Sexuality in Victorian America*, 91–113, 134–41.

19. Channing, "Self Culture," *Works*, 2:374; Channing, "Self Denial," *Works*, 4:105–21.

20. Sylvester Graham, *Lecture on Epidemic Diseases Generally, and Particularly the Spasmodic Cholera* (New York: M. Day, 1833), 10–11; Jayne A. Sokolow, *Eros and Modernization: Sylvester Graham, Health Reform, and the Origins of Victorian Sexuality in America* (Rutherford, N.J.: Fairleigh Dickinson University Press, 1983), 77–99; Haller and Haller, *Physician and Sexuality in Victorian America*, 195–211.

21. Parker, "Sermon on the Dangerous Classes of Society," *Speeches*, 1:201–7; E. C. Wines, "Crime: Its Causes and Cure," *Princeton Review*, 4th ser., 1 (May 1878): 784–814; Francis A. Walker, "The Causes of Poverty," *The Century* 55 (December 1897): 210–11; Benjamin J. Klebaner, "Poverty and Its Relief in American Thought, 1815–1861," *Social Service Review* 38 (December 1964): 382–99; Clifford Clark, "Religious Beliefs and Social Reforms in the Gilded Age: The Case of Henry Whitney Bellows," *New England Quarterly* 43 (March 1970): 59–78; Robert H. Bremner, *From the Depths: The Discovery of Poverty in the United States* (New York: New York University Press, 1952), 5–6; David J. Rothman, *The Discovery of the Asylum: Social Order and Disorder in the New Republic* (Boston: Little, Brown, 1971), 161–65; Graham, *Lecture on Epidemic Diseases*, 10–11; John Duffy, *The Healers: The Rise of the Medical Establishment* (New York: McGraw-Hill, 1976), 190–92.

22. A. O. J. Cockshut, *The Unbelievers: English Agnostic Thought, 1840–1890* (New York: New York University Press, 1966), 32; Gertrude Himmelfarb, *Victorian Values* (New York: Alfred A. Knopf, 1968), 276–77, 303; Meyer, *The Instructed Conscience*, 89–90; Henry F. May, *The End of American Innocence: A Study of the First Years of Our Own Time 1912–1917* (New York: Oxford University Press, 1959), 10–14.

23. Houghton, *The Victorian Frame of Mind*, 96–99 (quote at 94), 137–60.

24. May, *End of American Innocence*, 9.

25. Meyer, *The Instructed Conscience*, 99–107 (quote at 99); May, *End of American Innocence*, 14.

26. Argument of J. B. Stallo, *Minor v. Board of Education of Cincinnati*, in *The Bible in the Schools: Arguments before the Supreme Court of Cincinnati in the Case of Minor v. Board of Education of Cincinnati (1870)* . . . , ed. Robert G. McCloskey (New York: DaCapo Press, 1967), 101.

27. Benedict, "Laissez-Faire and Liberty," 300–301, 317–22.

28. Eric Foner, *Free Soil, Free Labor, Free Men: The Ideology of the Republican Party before the Civil War* (New York: Oxford University Press, 1970); Gabor S. Boritt, *Lincoln and Economics of the American Dream* (Memphis, Tenn.: Memphis State University Press, 1978).

29. Garrison, in *The Liberator*, January 5, 1854, quoted in Ronald G. Walters, *The Antislavery Appeal: American Abolitionism after 1830* (Baltimore, Md.: Johns Hopkins University Press, 1976), 66. See generally ibid., 21–37, 62–67.

30. James Walvin, *Victorian Values* (Athens: University of Georgia Press, 1987), 140.

31. Smith, *Revivalism and Social Reform*, 151–52 and passim; Walters, *The Antislavery Appeal*, 21–37; David J. Rothman, *The Discovery of the Asylum*, 162–65; Haney, "Criminal Justice and the Nineteenth-Century Paradigm," 209–26.

32. Benedict, "Laissez-Faire and Liberty," 298–314; Eric Foner, *Reconstruction: America's Unfinished Revolution* (New York: Harper and Row, 1988), 460–524.

33. Henry George, *Social Problems* (Chicago and New York: Belford, Clarke and Company, 1883), 237.

34. Dorothea Dix, *Remarks on Prisons and Prison Discipline in the United States*, 2d ed. (Philadelphia: J. Kite and Company, 1845), 25; Channing, in New York Prison Association, *First Annual Report* (1845), 34–35.

35. Charles Loring Brace, "The Outcast Children," *New York Tribune*, June 21, 1852.

36. Thus M. J. Heale is wide of the mark when he suggests such reformers were "Harbingers of Progressivism: Responses to the Urban Crisis in New York, c. 1845–1860," *Journal of American Studies* 10 (April 1976): 17–36. See Rothman, *Discovery of the Asylum*, 169–79 and passim; Ronald G. Walters, *American Reformers, 1815–1860* (New York: Hill and Wang, 1978), 193–211.

37. Channing, in New York Prison Association, *First Annual Report*, 34–35.

38. Walters, *American Reformers;* Clifford S. Griffin, *Their Brothers' Keepers: Moral Stewardship in the United States, 1800–1860* (New Brunswick, N.J.: Rutgers University Press, 1960); Martin E. Marty, *Righteous Empire: The Protestant Experience in America* (New York: Dial Press, 1970), 89–99; Paul S. Boyer, *Purity in Print: The Vice-Society Movement and Book Censorship in America* (New York: Scribner's, 1968), 1–22; Michael Grossberg, *Governing the Hearth: Law and the*

Family in Nineteenth-Century America (Chapel Hill: University of North Carolina Press, 1985), 187–93; Heywood Broun and Margaret Leech, *Anthony Comstock, Roundsman of the Lord* (New York: Literary Guild of America, 1927); David Jay Pivar, *The Purity Crusade: Sexual Morality and Sexual Control, 1868–1900* (Westport, Conn.: Greenwood Press, 1973); Carol F. Brooks, "The Early History of the Anti-Contraception Laws in Massachusetts and Connecticut," *American Quarterly* 18 (Spring 1966): 3–23; Carl N. Degler, *At Odds: Women and the Family from the Revolution to the Present* (New York: Oxford University Press, 1980), 279–97.

39. Manfred Jonas, "The American Sabbath in the Gilded Age," *Jahrbuch für Amerikastudien* 6 (1961): 89–114.

40. Rothman, *The Discovery of the Asylum.*

41. See, for example, Edward Everett, "Address before the Massachusetts Bible Society, May 27, 1850," in Everett, *Orations and Speeches,* 3 vols. (Boston: Little, Brown, 1850), 2:664; Argument of George R. Sage, *Minor v. Board of Education,* in McCloskey, ed., *The Bible in the Public Schools,* 157; Lois Banner, "Religious Benevolence as Social Control: A Critique of an Interpretation," *Journal of American History* 60 (June 1973): 38–39.

42. Frederic W. Sawyer, *A Plea for Amusement* (New York: D. Appleton, 1847), 251.

43. Channing, "On Catholicism," *Works,* 2:261–87; Josiah Strong, *Our Country,* ed. Jurgen Herbst (Cambridge, Mass.: Harvard University Press, 1963; from rev. ed., 1891), 59–88; Marty, *Righteous Empire,* 14–17, 127–30; Lloyd P. Jorgenson, *The State and the Non-Public School, 1825–1925* (Columbia: University of Missouri Press, 1987), 129–32; Morton J. Keller, *Affairs of State: Public Life in Late Nineteenth-Century America* (Cambridge, Mass.: Harvard University Press, 1977), 137–42.

44. L. E., "Home," *Ladies Magazine* 3 (May 1830): 217–18, quoted in Nancy Cott, *The Bonds of Womanhood: Woman's Sphere in New England, 1780–1835* (New Haven, Conn.: Yale University Press, 1977), 64.

45. *The Young Ladies Class Book,* quoted in Welter, "The Cult of True Womanhood," 162.

46. Maxine Van de Wetering, "The Popular Concept of 'Home' in Nineteenth-Century America," *Journal of American Studies* 18 (April 1984): 5–28; Jan Lewis, "Mother's Love: The Construction of an Emotion in Nineteenth Century America," in *Social History and Issues of Human Consciousness: Some Interdisciplinary Connections,* ed. Andrew E. Barnes and Peter N. Stearns (New York: New York University Press, 1989), 211–15.

47. Jonathan F. Stearns, *Female Influence, and the True Mode of Its Exercise . . .* (Newburyport, Mass.: John G. Tilton, 1837), 18; Cott, *The Bonds of Womanhood,* 63–100; Houghton, *The Victorian Frame of Mind,* 349–53; Degler, *At Odds,* 26–51, 81–85; Pivar, *Purity Crusade,* 78–83.

48. Theodore Parker, "The Public Education of the People," *Speeches*, 1:396.

49. Quoted in Frederic C. Dahlstand, *Amos Bronson Alcott: An Intellectual Biography* (Rutherford, N.J.: Fairleigh Dickinson University Press, 1982), 43; Channing, "Remarks on Education," *Works*, 1:373; Horace Mann, *Lectures on Education*, 87–93, 103–10; Banner, "Religious Benevolence as Social Control," 38; Ruth Miller Elson, "American Schoolbooks and 'Culture' in the Nineteenth Century," *Mississippi Valley Historical Review* 46 (December 1959): 411–34; Carl F. Kaestle, *Pillars of the Republic: Common Schools and American Society, 1780–1860* (New York: Hill and Wang, 1983), 75–103, 96–98.

50. *Massachusetts Revised Statutes* (1860), p. 216, sec. 10.

51. Timothy L. Smith, "Protestant Schooling and Nationality, 1800–1850," *Journal of American History* 53 (March 1967): 679–707; David Tyack, "The Kingdom of God and the Common Schools: Protestant Ministers and the Educational Awakening in the West," *Harvard Education Review* 36 (Fall 1966): 477–79; Jorgenson, *The State and the Non-Public School, 1825–1925*, 20–68.

52. Bryant, "Music in the Schools," in *Prose Writings of William Cullen Bryant*, 2 vols., ed. Parke Godwin (New York: D. Appleton and Company, 1889), 2:204.

53. Alexander H. Everett, "Greenough's Statue of Washington," *United States Magazine and Democratic Review* 14 (June 1844), quoted in *American Art, 1790–1960: Sources and Documents*, ed. John W. McCoubrey (Englewood Cliffs, N.J.: Prentice-Hall, 1965), 82. This compilation provides an excellent entrée to contemporary understandings of American art, and I have gratefully utilized its selections.

54. William Dunlap, *History of the American Theater and Anecdotes of the Principle Actors*, 2 vols. (London: R. Bentley, 1833), 1:1; Horatio Greenough, *Travels, Observations and Experiences of a Yankee Stonecutter* (New York: G. P. Putnam, 1852), 17. See also James Jackson Jarves, *The Art-Idea* (1864; Cambridge, Mass.: Harvard University Press, 1960), 35–36, 281; John F. Weir, "American Art: Its Progress and Prospects," *Princeton Review*, 4th ser., 1 (May 1878): 827, 829.

55. Allston, *Lectures on Art*, 3–8; Jarves, *The Art-Idea*, esp. 210–11, 215–16, 225.

56. Everett, "Greenough's Statue of Washington," quoted in McCoubrey, ed., *American Art*, 82.

57. Rembrandt Peale, *Letter on the Court of Death*, reprinted in McCoubrey, ed., *American Art*, 53–56.

58. Powers, quoted in Oliver Larkin, *Art and Life in America* (New York: Rinehart and Company, 1960), 180. See Margaret Farrand Thorp, "Rediscovering a Lost Chapter in the History of Nineteenth Century Taste: The Nudo and the Greek Slave," *Art in America* 49, 2 (1961): 46–47.

59. John Wilmerding, *American Art* (New York: Penguin Books, 1976), 76; Larkin, *Art and Life in America*, 141–43; Earl A. Powell, "Luminism and the American Sublime," in *American Light: The Luminist Movement, 1850–1875*, ed. John Wilmerding (New York: Harper and Row, 1980), 69–94; Barbara Novak,

Nature and Culture: American Landscape and Painting, 1825–1875 (New York: Oxford University Press, 1980), 3–17 and passim.

60. Asher B. Durand, "Letters on Landscape Painting," *The Crayon*, January 17, 1855, 34–35, and June 6, 1855, 354; Thomas Cole, "Essays on American Scenery," *American Monthly Magazine*, n.s., 1 (January 1836): 3; Washington Allston, *Lectures on Art and Poetry*, ed. Richard Henry Dana, Jr. (New York: Baker and Scribner, 1850), 69.

61. William Cullen Bryant, *Funeral Oration on the Death of Thomas Cole before the National Academy of Design, May 4, 1848*, quoted in McCoubrey, ed., *American Art*, 96–97.

62. Jarves, *The Art-Idea*, 248.

63. Durand, "Letters on Landscape Painting," 35. Allston referred to "the sovereign principle [of] Harmony" as the basis for appreciation of the beautiful (Allston, *Lectures on Art and Poetry*, 16).

64. Theodore C. Stebbins, *A New World: Masterpieces of American Painting 1760–1910* (Boston: Museum of Fine Arts, 1983), 106–7.

65. Kenyon Cox to Jacob D. Cox, January 1878, in *An American Art Student in Paris: The Letters of Kenyon Cox, 1877–1882*, ed. H. Wayne Morgan (Kent, Ohio: Kent State University Press, 1986), 57–58.

66. Andrew Jackson Downing, *The Architecture of Country Houses* (New York: D. Appleton, 1850), 31.

67. Larkin, *Art and Life in America*, 154–77.

68. Ibid., 9, 23; Jarves, *The Art-Idea*, 92–93. See, generally, Clifford Clark, "Domestic Architecture as an Index to Social History: The Romantic Revival and the Cult of Domesticity in America, 1840–1870," *Journal of Interdisciplinary History* 7 (Summer 1976): 33–56; Clark, "American Architecture," in *The Bible in American Arts and Letters*, ed. Giles Gunn (Philadelphia: Fortress Press, 1983), 110–13.

69. Geoffrey Blodgett, "The Architectural Psychology of the Gilded Age," *Hayes Historical Journal* 7 (Spring 1988): 9–13.

70. Bryant, "Lectures on Poetry," *Prose Works*, 1:14–24.

71. Howells, in *Harper's Magazine* 74 (April 1887): 825.

72. *The Aeronaut*, September 1, 1816, 321; Dunlap, *History of the American Theater*, 1:129.

73. Quoted in David Grimsted, *Melodrama Unveiled: American Theater and Culture, 1800–1850* (Berkeley: University of California Press, 1987), 39.

74. Ibid., 111–36, 171–248; Herbert Ross Brown, *The Sentimental Novel in America, 1789–1860* (Durham, N.C.: Duke University Press, 1940); Peter Brooks, *The Melodramatic Imagination: Balzac, Henry James, and the Mode of Excess* (New York: Columbia University Press, 1985), 28–33. Again, it is a sign of the great gap separating our times from the Victorians that we consider that era's greatest classics to be those works in which the distinctions between good and

evil were most ambiguous, or better yet, where conventional order and morality were challenged outright, such as Nathaniel Hawthorne's *The Scarlet Letter* and Herman Melville's *Moby Dick* and *Billy Budd.*

75. Brooks, *The Melodramatic Imagination,* 12–13.

76. Anthony Comstock, *Traps for the Young,* ed. Robert H. Bremner (Cambridge, Mass.: Harvard University Press, 1967), xxv; Elizabeth Blackwell, *Counsel to Parents on the Moral Education of Their Children* (New York: Brentano's Literary Symposium, 1879), 116–17; Gibbs, "Self Control and Male Sexuality," 39; Welter, "Cult of True Womanhood," 166.

77. C. Wiley Hitchcock, *Music in the United States: A Historical Introduction* (Englewood Cliffs, N.J.: Prentice-Hall, 1969), 151.

78. Ibid., 43.

79. Charles A. Kent, *Closing Address Delivered to the Senior Class, Law Department of the University of Michigan* . . . (Ann Arbor: Fishe and Douglas, 1874), 20–21.

80. Gold, "John Appleton of Maine and the Commercial Law"; Lawrence M. Friedman, *Contract Law in America: A Social and Economic Case Study* (Madison: University of Wisconsin Press, 1965), 98–101; Morton J. Horwitz, "The Historical Foundations of Modern Contract Law," *Harvard Law Review* 87 (March 1974): 917–56; Gary T. Schwartz, "Tort Law and the Economy in Nineteenth-Century America: A Reconsideration," *Yale Law Journal* 90 (July 1981): 1717–75; G. Edward White, *Tort Law in America: An Intellectual History* (New York: Oxford University Press, 1980), 15–19. Schwartz finds courts much more willing to find corporations liable in tort actions than Horwitz and White do, but all three stress the centrality of negligence or a freely assumed obligation as the element that justifies recovery.

81. Morton Keller, *Affairs of State: Public Life in Late Nineteenth Century America* (Cambridge, Mass.: Harvard University Press), 162–96. The major justification was that the group seeking legislation faced monopolistic power, a violation of a key tenet of laissez-faire. Therefore the dominant post–Civil War economic reform movement was "antimonopoly." "Greenbackism" also proceeded on the conviction that powerful interests were using the government to monopolize the supply of money. In general, critics of Gilded Age economic life still believed that in a properly ordered economic system there should be "harmony of interests" between employers and employees. They adhered to a philosophy of producerism, which demanded a society of independent small producers in which the market could operate free of concentrated economic power and thus truly reward the moral and industrious. See Solon J. Buck, *The Granger Movement: A Study of Agricultural Organization and Its Political, Economic, and Social Manifestations, 1870–1880* (Cambridge, Mass.: Harvard University Press, 1913); Bruce Palmer, *"Man over Money": The Southern Populist Critique of American Capitalism* (Chapel Hill: University of North Carolina Press, 1980), 111–25; Irwin Unger,

The Greenback Era: A Social and Political History of American Finance, 1865–1879 (Princeton, N.J.: Princeton University Press, 1964), 94–119; Walter Nugent, *Money and American Society, 1865–1880* (New York: Free Press, 1968), 28–31, 209–15.

82. *In re Jacobs*, 98 N.Y. 98 (1885); *Godcharles & Co. v. Wigeman*, 113 Pa.St. 431 (1886); *Ritchie v. People*, 155 Ill. 106 (1895). For a fuller discussion of the link between laissez-faire constitutionalism and morally based Victorian opposition to redistribution of wealth, see Benedict, "Laissez-Faire and Liberty."

83. Constitution of Ohio (1851), Art. 1, sec. 7; Constitution of Massachusetts (1780), pt. 1, Arts. 2, 3; Constitution of Maryland (1867), Art. 36; Constitution of Arkansas (1868), Art. 1, sec. 23. Similar provisions were proposed for the abortive 1858 constitution of Kansas and the proposed constitution of Massachusetts defeated in 1853. See William F. Swindler, ed., *Sources and Documents of United States Constitutions*, 11 vols. (Dobbs Ferry, N.Y.: Oceana, 1975), 4:67, 5:113.

84. Rush Welter, *The Mind of America, 1820–1860* (New York: Columbia University Press, 1975), 253–76. Welter goes too far, I believe, in suggesting that Democrats rejected the religious foundation of morality. The different positions of the Democratic and Republican parties on religion-linked moral issues played a large role in determining their constituencies. See Ronald Formisano, *The Birth of Mass Political Parties: Michigan, 1827–1861* (Princeton, N.J.: Princeton University Press, 1971); Paul Kleppner, *The Third Electoral System, 1853–1892: Parties, Voters, and Political Cultures* (Chapel Hill: University of North Carolina Press, 1979); Kleppner, *The Cross of Culture: A Social Analysis of Midwestern Politics, 1850–1900* (New York: Free Press, 1970); Richard Jensen, *The Winning of the Midwest: Social and Political Conflict, 1888–1896* (Chicago: University of Chicago Press, 1971).

85. Nowadays, repeal of such exemptions would raise a problem of discrimination *against* religion, assuming that exemptions were retained for nonreligious charitable and educational institutions. But before the Civil War, charitable and educational institutions were so universally sponsored by religious organizations that no such distinction was made. Indeed, the question arose whether any charitable or educational institution independent of religion could be created at law. See *Vidal et al. v. Girard's Executors*, 43 U.S. (2 Howard) 127 (1844), and the controversy surrounding the charter of Cornell University, in Walter P. Rogers, *Andrew D. White and the Modern University* (Ithaca, N.Y.: Cornell University Press, 1942), 72–84.

86. H. Frank Way, "The Death of the Christian Nation: The Judiciary and State-Church Relations," *Journal of Church and State* 29 (Autumn 1987): 515–18. The leading cases were *Shover v. The State*, 5 English 259 (Supreme Court Ark., 1850); *State v. Ambs*, 20 Mo. 214 (1854); *Lindenmuller v. The People*, 33 Barbour 548 (Supreme Court N.Y., 1861). In *ex parte Newman*, 9 Cal. 502 (1858), the Califor-

nia Supreme Court ruled that state's Sunday closing law unconstitutional entirely because it discriminated against those who adhered to a different Sabbath.

87. Abram Herbert Lewis, *Sunday Legislation: Its History to the Present Time and Its Results* (New York: D. Appleton, 1902), 209–56.

88. *People* v. *Ruggles*, 8 Johnson's Reports 290 (Supreme Court N.Y., 1811); *State* v. *Chandler*, 2 Harrington (2 Del.) 553 (1837); *Commonwealth* v. *Kneeland*, 20 Pickerington (37 Mass.) 206 (1838); Way, "Death of the Christian Nation," 513–15.

89. Tyack, "The Kingdom of God and the Common Schools"; Smith, "Protestant Schooling and American Nationality"; Jorgenson, *The State and the Non-Public School*, 31–68; Rothman, *The Discovery of the Asylum*, passim; Samuel Walker, *Popular Justice: A History of American Criminal Justice* (New York: Oxford University Press, 1980), 74.

90. Constitution of Mississippi (1832), Art. 7, sec. 14; Constitution of Ohio (1851), Art. 1, sec. 7.

91. Lyman Atwater, "Morality, Religion and Education in the State," *Princeton Review*, 4th ser., 1 (May 1878): 416.

92. Jorgenson, *The State and the Non-Public School*, 20–30, 69–145; Kaestle, *Pillars of the Republic*, 166–71.

93. Constitution of Ohio (1851), Art. 1, sec. 7.

94. *Minor* v. *Board of Education* (1870), in McCloskey, ed., *The Bible in the Schools*, 380.

95. *Board of Education of Cincinnati* v. *Minor*, 23 Ohio 211 (1872); Bernard Mandel, "Religion and the Public Schools of Ohio," *Ohio Archeological and Historical Quarterly* 58 (April 1949): 191–95; Harold M. Helfman, "The Cincinnati Bible War, 1869–1870," *Ohio Archeological and Historical Quarterly* 60 (October 1951): 369–86; Jonathan Lurie, "The Fourteenth Amendment: Use and Application in Selected State Court Civil Liberties Cases, 1870–1890—A Preliminary Assessment," *American Journal of Legal History* 28 (October 1984): 299–302. For another celebrated case see the excellent discussion of *Donohoe* v. *Richards*, 38 Me. 379 (1854), in Gold, *Shaping of Nineteenth Century Law*, 131–35.

96. *Donahoe* v. *Richards; Spiller* v. *Inhabitants of Woburn*, 94 Mass. 127 (1866); *Ferriter* v. *Tyler*, 48 Vt. 444 (1876); Way, "Death of the Christian Nation," 518–21.

97. Jorgenson, *The State and the Non-Public School*, 72–85, 111–45. Jorgenson points out that it was not uncommon, however, for public school systems to take over education within church-owned buildings during school hours, with the church providing religious instruction before or after (ibid., 112–17).

98. Anson P. Stokes and Leo Pfeffer, *Church and State in the United States* (New York: Harper and Row, 1964), 566–67.

99. *Vidal et al.* v. *Girard's Executors; People* v. *Ruggles; Lindenmuller* v. *The People; Updegraph* v. *The Commonwealth*, 11 Sergeant & Rawles 394 (Pa., 1822);

State v. *Chandler; Shover* v. *The State*, 10 Ark. 259 (1850); *State* v. *Ambs; Judefind* v. *State*, 78 Md. 510 (1894). The minority Ohio view was trenchantly expressed in *Bloom* v. *Richards*, 2 Ohio 387 (1833), and again in *Board of Education of Cincinnati* v. *Minor.*

100. *Church of the Holy Trinity* v. *U.S.*, 143 U.S. 457 (1892).

101. *Statutes at Large of the United States* (Washington, D.C.: Government Printing Office, 1892), 27:363.

102. Lawrence M. Friedman, "Rights of Passage: Divorce Law in Historical Perspective," *Oregon Law Review* 63 (1984): 649–69; Lynne Carol Halem, *Divorce Reform: Changing Legal and Social Perspectives* (New York: Free Press, 1980), 18–40.

103. *Reynolds* v. *U.S.*, 98 U.S. 145, 165 (1878); *Late Corp. of the Church of Jesus Christ of Latter-Day Saints* v. *U.S.*, 136 U.S. 1, 49 (1890); Grossberg, *Governing the Hearth*, 120–27; Kenneth David Driggs, "The Mormon Church–State Confrontation in Nineteenth-Century America," *Journal of Church and State* 30 (Spring 1988): 273–89; Gustave O. Larson, *The "Americanization" of Utah for Statehood* (San Marino, Calif.: Huntington Library, 1971); Edwin Brown Firmage and Richard Collin Mangrum, *Zion in the Courts: A Legal History of the Church of Jesus Christ of Latter-Day Saints, 1830–1900* (Urbana: University of Illinois Press, 1988), 129–209.

104. *Bradwell* v. *Illinois*, 83 U.S. 130, 141 (1873) (Bradley, concurring). The Supreme Court of Illinois had articulated the same views. *Bradwell* v. *State*, 55 Ill. 535 (1870). It should be noted that the courts did *not* suggest that legislatures would be overstepping their power to ordain equality, but only that judges would not overturn legislation based on the Victorian conception of women's role as a violation of women's civil rights. See Martha Minow, " 'Forming Underneath Everything That Grows': Toward a History of Family Law," *Wisconsin Law Review* 1985 (June–July): 843–45.

105. Boyer, *Purity in Print*, 1–22; Donald H. Gilmore, *Sex, Censorship, and Pornography, vol. 1, The Past* (San Diego, Calif.: Greenleaf Press, 1969), 134–50; Grossberg, *Governing the Hearth*, 170–78; Brooks, "Early History of Contraception Laws in Massachusetts and Connecticut"; Mary Dennett, *Birth Control Laws: Shall We Keep Them, Change Them, or Abolish Them?* (New York: DaCapo Press, 1970), 11–14.

106. *Commonwealth* v. *Sharpless*, 2 Sergeant & Rawles 91 (Pa. 1815); Francis Wharton, *A Treatise on the Criminal Law of the United States*, 3 vols. (Philadelphia: Kay and Brother, 1870), sec. 2547.

107. *Regina* v. *Hicklin*, 3 Queen's Bench 360, at 371 (1868); *U.S.* v. *Bennett*, 24 Federal Cases 1093 (no. 14,571) (Circuit Court So. District N.Y., 1879); *Commonwealth of Pennsylvania* v. *Landis*, 8 Phila. 453 (1870); *People* v. *Muller*, 96 N.Y. 408 (1884); *Commonwealth* v. *Havens*, 6 Pa. County Court Reports 545 (1888);

David M. Rabban, "The First Amendment in Its Forgotten Years," *Yale Law Journal* 90 (January 1981): 548–50; Grossberg, *Governing the Hearth*, 187–93.

108. *Ex parte Jackson*, 96 U.S. 727, at 736 (1877).

109. George Fort Milton, *Lincoln and the Fifth Column* (New York: Vanguard Press, 1942), 47–55, 73–76, and passim; Harold M. Hyman, *The Era of the Oath: Northern Loyalty Tests during the Civil War and Reconstruction* (Philadelphia: University of Pennsylvania Press, 1954).

110. Alexis J. Anderson, "The Formative Period of First Amendment Theory, 1870–1915," *American Journal of Legal History* 24 (January 1980): 56–75; Rabban, "The First Amendment in Its Forgotten Years," 543–48, 555–59.

111. Haney, "Criminal Justice and the Nineteenth-Century Paradigm."

112. Lawrence M. Friedman and Robert V. Percival, *The Roots of Justice: Crime and Punishment in Alameda County, California, 1870–1910* (Chapel Hill: University of North Carolina Press, 1981), 75; Wilbur F. Miller, *Cops and Bobbies: Police Authority in New York and London* (Chicago: University of Chicago Press, 1977), 58–73.

113. Walker, *Popular Justice*, 63. See also David R. Johnson, *Policing the Urban Underworld: The Impact of Crime on the Development of the American Police, 1800–1887* (Philadelphia: Temple University Press, 1979), 122–33 and passim; Miller, *Cops and Bobbies*, 140–48.

114. Walker, *Popular Justice*, 117–23, passim (quoted at 117); Friedman and Percival, *Roots of Justice*, 75, 113–34; Miller, *Cops and Bobbies*, 58–59, 77–78.

115. For procedural strictness, see David J. Bodenhamer, *The Pursuit of Justice: Crime and Law in Antebellum Indiana* (New York: Garland Publishing, 1986), 31–35. A general study of nineteenth-century criminal procedure badly wants doing. For the absence of appeals on constitutional grounds, see Friedman and Percival, *Roots of Justice*, 265–69. In the twenty years that Thomas McIntyre Cooley spent on the Michigan Supreme Court, only two cases came before him challenging the sufficiency of arrest warrants. There were no cases involving the right to counsel or the adequacy of representation. None complained about excessive bail. See John B. Ashby, "Reflections: Thomas M. Cooley—The Defendants' Rights Cases," *Cooley Law Review* 3 (September 1985): 523–45.

116. *The Slaughterhouse Cases*, 83 U.S. 36 (1873); *Bradwell v. Illinois; Minor v. Happersett*, 88 U.S. 162 (1875); *Hurtado v. California*, 110 U.S. 516 (1884).

117. The best general descriptions of the sea change in American culture in the early twentieth century remain May, *The End of American Innocence*, and T. J. Jackson Lears, *No Place of Grace: Antimodernism and the Transformation of American Culture, 1880–1920* (New York: Pantheon, 1981). See also Morton White, *Social Thought in America: The Revolt Against Formalism* (Boston: Beacon Press, 1947); Thomas L. Haskell, *The Emergence of Professional Social Science: The American Social Science Association and the Nineteenth-Century*

Crisis of Authority (Urbana: University of Illinois Press, 1977); Gerhard O. W. Mueller, *Crime, Law and the Scholars: A History of Scholarship in American Criminal Law* (Seattle: University of Washington Press, 1969), 82–108, passim; F. H. Matthews, "The Americanization of Sigmund Freud: Adoption of Psychoanalysis before 1917," *Journal of American Studies* 1 (April 1967): 39–62; John C. Burnham, "The New Psychology: From Narcissism to Social Control," in *Paths into American Culture: Psychology, Medicine, and Morals* (Philadelphia: Temple University Press, 1988), 69–93.

Drug Laws and Drug Use

in Nineteenth-Century America

DAVID T. COURTWRIGHT

Consider a mystery. During the nineteenth century, Americans' consumption of alcohol declined by more than two-thirds, from 6.6 gallons per person of drinking age per year to only a little more than 2 gallons. Most of the decline came before the Civil War; from 1870 onward consumption was stable and, by historical comparison, low. At the same time, beer, a more beneficent form of beverage alcohol, was gaining rapidly in popularity over hard spirits, the per capita consumption of which declined by one-half between 1870 and 1900. Yet a powerful and well-organized prohibition movement emerged during these same decades, a movement that by 1903 had thirty-five million Americans living under some form of prohibition regime.[1] The law was being applied in coercive fashion to a social and medical problem that seems to have been getting better rather than worse.

Consider a second mystery. The pattern of American drug consumption and abuse was in many respects the reverse of alcohol use during the nineteenth century. Opiate addiction was a rarity in the early 1800s, and cocaine use of any sort was nonexistent. But after 1860 there was a major, sustained epidemic of opiate addiction, and after 1885, a national cocaine binge that peaked in the early 1900s. Yet the legal response to all of this was delayed, fragmentary, and generally ineffectual. Municipalities with substantial Chinese populations enacted ordinances against opium dens, but enforcement efforts were infrequent and of short duration. A correspondent who walked through San Francisco's Chinatown in 1887 saw hundreds of Chinese "smoking in full view of the street, and nothing is thought of it. The police disturb them not."[2] Festive opium smoking among New York City's Chinese residents was likewise quite open. If whites, particularly white women, were seen to be smoking with the Chinese, then there might be a temporary police crackdown, as happened in Denver in 1880. The real motives behind such actions were revulsion against miscegenation—the racial stereotype was of a fiendish, long-fingernailed Chinese man preying upon a wayward, narcotized young beauty—and the desire to protect whites from acquiring an alien vice. All that was achieved, however, was a measure of segregation; the dens themselves were soon back in business.[3] An opium-smoking subculture flourished well into the twentieth century.

The control of medicinal narcotics was even more lax. European doctors who came to the United States blamed much of the addiction epidemic on the ready availability of drugs like morphine. It was one of the disadvantages, a Danish physician tartly remarked, of being "the freest country in the world, [where] everybody can do as he pleases."[4] A 1903 report of the American Pharmaceutical Association conceded that in many drug stores customers could obtain cocaine and morphine as easily as Epsom salts.[5] The same was true of needles and hypodermic syringes. Until the New York legislature finally enacted a law in 1911, addiction specialist Charles Towns recalled, "a boy of fifteen could buy a syringe as easily as he could buy a jack-knife."[6] Those who preferred discretion could make such purchases through mail-order catalogs.

Most states did not enact comprehensive drug control laws until well after 1900. These laws typically restricted the sale of opium and cocaine products (and, in some places, of cannabis and chloral hydrate) to those having a prescription written by a licensed practitioner. The pharmacists who sold the drugs had to make a permanent record of the transaction. Only patent or proprietary medicines having very small amounts of the regulated drugs were exempt from the prescription and record-keeping requirements. On paper, this represented a reasonably thorough system of control. In reality, state laws were passively and sporadically enforced. Drugs were mailed directly to users or sold by pharmacists who knew that their chances of being detected and prosecuted were nil. As late as 1915 the U.S. Public Health Service's resident expert on drug laws, Martin I. Wilbert, complained that direct state appropriations for the enforcement of antinarcotic legislation were practically nonexistent.[7]

The federal government failed to address the problem until 1906, the year of the passage of the Pure Food and Drug Act and the District of Columbia Pharmacy Act.[8] It was not until 1919 that the most important coercive aspect of federal policy—the denial of legal drugs to addicts—

was firmly in place and upheld by a (narrow) majority of the Supreme Court. When the axe fell, it fell hard, but the puzzle is why there was such a long delay, in view of the vigor of the alcohol prohibition movement. Why was it that late nineteenth-century Americans did practically nothing in the midst of a drug epidemic, even as they used the law to attack an alcohol problem that was at a historically low level?

To begin to answer this question it is necessary to understand something of the origins and development of the widespread usage of opium and coca products and preparations in nineteenth-century America. Opium was above all a medicine, the one indispensable item in the armamentarium. It was unsurpassed as an analgesic and very effective in the treatment of diarrhea, a serious and potentially fatal disease of which our ancestors much complained. Opium and its alkaloids were thus often used in medical preparations prescribed by physicians, purchased as nostrums, or concocted by the patients themselves. "Recipe for Cure of Cholera, Diarrhea, Dysentery, Cramp Cholic and Cholera Morbus," Confederate artilleryman Miles Bennet wrote confidently in his diary, "*Certain* cure— One pint of good Brandy, one ounce of Laudanum [tincture of opium], one ounce of gum Camphor, half ounce of Cayenne pepper. Mix well together and for dose take teaspoonful." [9]

The risks of medication with opiates were overdose and, if the treatment continued too long, addiction. What happened to "Mrs. B.," a thirty-four-year-old mother and widow who lived near Rochester, New York, was typical. She suffered from a uterine disorder that she palliated with laudanum, to which she became addicted. In the course of six years she consumed upward of an ounce of laudanum a day. She tried repeatedly to quit but always relapsed because she craved the drug and because of the stress of having to raise her young children alone.

Mrs. B.'s case appeared in the medical literature in 1871.[10] Over the next three decades she was joined in her misfortune by tens of thousands of other addicts—with one important difference. They generally became addicted through the injection of morphine rather than the ingestion of opium solutions. The 1870s and 1880s were the flush times of hypodermic medication. American doctors of this era were notorious for their willingness to inject patients with morphine, the principal active alkaloid of opium. Injection was a more immediate, powerful, and pleasure-producing experience, hence more likely to lead to addiction. Since patients could easily acquire drugs and syringes on their own, they could continue the injections even after the physician had ceased giving them. Those who suf-

fered from a chronic, painful affliction or injury were particularly likely
to do so. Numerous Civil War veterans became addicted, although they
never made up the majority of addicts. We know this because several sur-
veys published after 1878 showed that 60 to 80 percent of those addicted
to medicinal opiates were female.[11]

The hows and whys of narcotic addiction were much discussed. The
condition was blamed on everything from defective heredity to nervous
exhaustion to professional carelessness. What is striking is that this discussion was carried on mainly within the context of medicine rather than
law or criminology. Chinese opium smokers may have been regarded with
contempt, as were white criminals and prostitutes who became addicted
to drugs, but the medical addicts, who were in the majority, were regarded
more sympathetically. They were sick, or victims of unlabeled patent medicines, or they had been introduced to drugs under therapeutic auspices.
Those whose addiction was of medical origin were not at all likely to behave violently or spread the habit to others. On the contrary, they were
highly secretive. Mrs. B. went ten miles out of her way to purchase her
laudanum so that her neighbors would not suspect her dependence on the
drug. Post–Civil War Americans were unlikely to demand the rigorous
exercise of the state or local police power, let alone the inchoate powers of
the federal government, against persons who engendered no compelling
threat to others. When, by contrast, the owners of rendering plants asserted their "private rights" to go on operating their fetid establishments,
New York City's Metropolitan Board of Health did not hesitate to prosecute, for the noxious odors they released were feared as a potent source of
deadly disease.[12]

The relatively sympathetic attitude toward medical opiate addicts also
reflected the values of the larger culture. Then, as now, Americans were
much concerned with blameworthiness. The poor, the incapacitated, and
the homeless were afforded only the meanest of charity if they were held to
be responsible for their own plight. Yet disabled servicemen and their families were given generous pensions, and victims of disasters like the 1871
Chicago fire received prompt financial help from all over the country.[13]
The difference lay in the perception that they were not at fault.

This same preoccupation with blame and unworthy behavior helps to
explain why prohibitionists were able to rapidly advance their cause.
Drunkards were drunkards not because they took alcohol as a medicine but
because they frequented saloons and imbibed for pleasure. Their language
was foul and their behavior obstreperous, just the opposite of the secretive,

heavily tranquilized opiate addicts. Drunkards were also men, often of immigrant, Catholic, or lower-class backgrounds. Narcotic addicts were largely women, native-born, Protestant, and outwardly respectable. The prohibition movement had a pronounced nativist and middle-class bias. This is not to say that prohibition was simply a matter of prejudice; alcoholism was by any rational criterion a more serious problem than opiate addiction. The social costs it generated seemed to justify strong measures. Even reformers who balked at prohibition espoused the disfranchisement and incarceration of alcoholics in specially designed institutions where they might be forced to learn "useful habits" while recovering from the ravages of drink.[14] A drunkard was a menace and a burden. An addict was someone's mother.

This situation changed, and as it did, the moral and emotional basis for stricter narcotic laws was laid. During the 1890s and early 1900s, medical journals, textbooks, and educators broadcast the dangers of the excessive administration of opium and morphine. At the same time new and safer therapies were popularized, such as the use of acetanilid for rheumatic and neuralgic disorders or naphthalene for diarrhea.[15] Fewer narcotic prescriptions were written and fewer new medical addicts were created. Self-medication with patent medicines abated, thanks to the labeling provisions of the Pure Food and Drug Act and the efforts of muckraking journalists to alert the public to the dangers of their habit-forming ingredients. Opiate addicts began to decline in number—except in the underworld, where opium smoking persisted along with the use of morphine and, after 1910, heroin.

As the less blameworthy medical addicts diminished in number relative to the nonmedical addicts, perceptions of who drug users were and how they behaved inevitably began to alter. They were more often described as criminally inclined, psychopathic, and otherwise deranged men of the lower orders.[16] They were like drunkards, though they had enslaved themselves to a different drug. The suggestion made in all seriousness by a Newark, Ohio, physician in 1889—that everyone would be far better off if alcoholics were converted into morphine addicts—would have struck middle-class Americans of thirty years later as risible.[17] By 1919, drink and narcotic drugs were both firmly identified with dangerous and deviant behavior.

Attitudes toward cocaine use and addiction underwent a similar transformation, although within a more compressed span of time. Cocaine was the miracle drug of the 1880s. During that decade glowing articles testifying to cocaine's manifold usefulness appeared in European and American medical journals. Sigmund Freud's 1884 paper "Über Coca" recommended the drug for stomach upsets, tuberculosis, typhoid fever, asthma, the treatment of opiate addiction and alcoholism, and as a local anesthetic.[18] On this last point his advice was sound: cocaine's anesthetizing properties were of great utility in eye, nose, and mouth surgery. The problem was that Freud and other enthusiasts touted cocaine in virtually panacean terms. They recommended it for too many conditions—everything from depression to hay fever—and without adequate attention to its potential for abuse and dependence. No less an authority than William Hammond, the former surgeon general, discounted the possibility of full-blown addiction to cocaine. It was, he said, more like the tea or coffee habit than addiction to opium or its derivatives.[19]

The results of this may be readily guessed. There was a wave of iatrogenic (literally, "doctor-produced") cocaine addiction. By the early 1890s medical journals were publishing numerous case histories of men, women, and even children who had become "cocainists." Many of the men were doctors who had unwisely treated their own ailments with liberal applications of the miracle drug. There were also reports of cocaine overdose deaths, as in the case of an Arizona man who died from convulsions an hour after his dentist injected his gums with four grains of cocaine.[20]

The early, cautionary articles about cocaine are of as much interest for what they do not say as for what they do say about the dangers of misapplying the drug. No one proposed a crusade against cocaine, or anything like a prohibitionist stance. As with the opiates, the debate was initially conducted within a medical and scientific framework: doctors gave advice (sometimes sharply) to other doctors about whether, how, and with what precautions a new alkaloidal remedy should be used.

The tone soon changed. Articles appearing in the popular and medical press from the mid-1890s onward emphasized that while iatrogenic cocaine addiction was still a reality it was rapidly being supplanted by a more sinister pattern of abuse. E. R. Waterhouse, a St. Louis physician, remarked that few people knew the true extent of the cocaine habit in the lower walks of city life. He described a local drug store that was in reality a "cocaine joint" where pulverized cocaine crystals were wrapped in paper and sold to prostitutes for ten cents apiece. Admitted through a portiere to a dimly lit back room, the prostitutes sniffed their purchases on the premises, ringing a bell when they wanted a clerk to bring them more. A woman reporter who managed to peek into the room spied a dozen lower-class prostitutes, black as well as white, seated on benches or sprawled across the floor. They were, Waterhouse commented, lost in a sort of dreamy intoxication, "not unlike the Chinaman 'hitting the pipe' in Dope Alley." Although the proprietor of the cocaine den was arrested under a statute regulating the sale of poisons, Waterhouse noted that the establishment was still going full blast, and hundreds of other people were buying the drug and sniffing it in the privacy of their own homes. "Some law," he concluded, "should be made to reach this new state of affairs." [21]

In using the expressions "joint" and "den" and "hitting the pipe," Waterhouse was drawing an explicit analogy between cocaine sniffing and opium smoking. That he did so is revealing, since opium smoking was virtually the only form of opiate use that was universally condemned and subject to prosecution. Morally, the cocaine sniffers he described were indistinguishable from the opium smokers: both groups used the drug as an intoxicant, were prone to vice and crime, and—no small matter in the St. Louis of 1896—were known to keep mixed racial company.

Waterhouse's allegation that cocaine use was fast becoming an indulgence of the vicious and criminally minded of both races and his belief that legislative action was needed to control its use were often repeated by doctors and public officials over the next several years. New details were added to the story. The declining price of cocaine, by 1897 a mere two dollars an ounce, had greatly increased its nonmedical use, especially among "the tramp and low criminal classes" of the cities. Many of cocaine's underworld devotees had used and become addicted to other drugs before discovering cocaine. When their funds were exhausted by their cocaine appetite, they resorted to petty theft and other crimes to obtain funds to purchase more of the drug.[22]

The growing popularity of cocaine among blacks, who would purchase a nickel's worth of the drug and go on a "coke drunk," caused the greatest concern. Editorials in two leading professional journals, the *Journal of the American Medical Association* and the *American Druggist and Pharmaceutical Record,* pointed to increased cocaine use by blacks as a justification for restrictive legislation.[23] "I am convinced," declared Colonel J. W. Watson of Georgia in 1903, "that if some stringent law is not enacted and enforced against [cocaine sniffing] the habit will grow and extend to such proportions that great injury will result; in fact, great injury has already resulted, for I am satisfied that many of the horrible crimes committed in the Southern States by the colored people can be traced directly to the cocaine habit." [24]

Whether and to what extent there was a cocaine-inspired crime wave at the turn of the century has been much debated by historians. It is possible that the allegations of Watson and others were exaggerated as a disingenuous way of attacking prohibition, the idea being that voters might balk at banning liquor if they thought that drinkers would turn to cocaine instead. "I am not an advocate of whiskey," the colonel slyly observed, "but I am fully convinced that if a man feels he must have a stimulant, the best thing he can do is to get a bottle of liquor."[25] Whatever the merits of this bold assertion (and they are dubious), it is striking that cocaine should be compared so unfavorably with alcohol. Only two decades earlier doctors had been urging the opposite course, that coca preparations could be successfully used in treating alcoholics.[26]

In the end we are left with an excellent illustration of the principle, which Harold Hyman was wont to drill into his students, that legal history cannot be properly studied apart from social history. The presence or absence, the enforcement or nonenforcement, and the content and timing of antidrug laws are not fully comprehensible without an understanding of who was using drugs and why they had begun using them. One of the primary reasons that the bulk of legislation came after 1900 was the growing perception that opiate and cocaine use and addiction were moving from private misfortune to public threat, from the respectable province of medicine and middle-class ladies to the fallen masculine world of alleys and dives. This was not, to be sure, the only reason. Twentieth-century drug laws were something more than the inevitable, legally codified expression of prejudice against disliked or deviant groups. They were also configured by diplomatic, constitutional, and political pressures, particularly at the federal level.[27] The worsening social characteristics of the drug-using population are best understood as a necessary, rather than a sufficient, cause for the emergence of a police-oriented system of narcotic control—a system that by the 1920s and for many decades thereafter was among the most punitive in the world.

NOTES

1. Mark Edward Lender and James Kirby Martin, *Drinking in America: A History* (New York: Free Press, 1982), 87–132, 196.

2. Letter from "J. F. M.," reprinted in Samuel B. Collins, *Theriaki: A Treatise on the Habitual Use of Narcotic Poison: How the Habit Is Formed, Its Consequences and Cure* (Laporte, Ind.: n.p., 1887), 64.

3. "The Chinese New Year: Idolatry in Baxter Street—Feasting and Smoking Opium," *New York Times*, February 16, 1874, 5; Henry O. Whiteside, "The Drug Habit in Nineteenth-century Colorado," *Colorado Magazine* 55 (1978): 52–54. In Los Angeles the police left Chinese smokers alone; only white smokers were occasionally prosecuted. See C. W. Bonyge to Hamilton Wright, August 8, 1908, Records of the U.S. Delegation to the International Opium Commission and Conference, 1909–1913, Record Group 43, National Archives, Washington, D.C. A partial exception to this generalization is Chicago, where police raids in the 1880s were reportedly more successful in breaking up public opium dens. Rather than ceasing, however, opium smoking apparently shifted to private quarters. See Charles Warrington Earle, "Opium-Smoking in Chicago," *Chicago Medical Journal and Examiner* 52 (1886): 105–6.

4. C. Steensen, "Misbrug af Opium og Morfin i Amerika," *Ugeskrift for Laeger* 7 (1883): 165–67.

5. E. G. Eberle et al., "Report of Committee on the Acquirement of Drug Habits," *Proceedings of the American Pharmaceutical Association* 51 (1903): 476.

6. Charles B. Towns, "The Peril of the Drug Habit and the Need of Restrictive Legislation," *Century* 84 (1912): 582.

7. Martin I. Wilbert, "Efforts to Curb the Misuse of Narcotic Drugs: A Comparative Analysis of the Federal and State Laws Designed to Restrict or to Regulate the Distribution and Use of Opium, Coca, and Other Narcotic or Habit-Forming Drugs," *Public Health Reports* 30 (1915): 893–923 (comment on enforcement appropriations at 898).

8. A year earlier, in 1905, Congress passed a law gradually prohibiting the nonmedical use of opium in the Philippines, but this did not affect the continental United States.

9. Miles S. Bennet diary, 71, Eugene C. Barker Research Center, University of Texas, Austin. Women often kept similar formulas in their recipe books; e.g., *Mrs. McKenney's Cook Book* (MS, n.d., probably 1830s–1860s), 77, 83, 88, 91, 92, Daughters of the Republic of Texas History Research Library, San Antonio, Texas.

10. In Alonzo Calkins, *Opium and the Opium Appetite* (Philadelphia: J. B. Lippincott and Company, 1871), 152.

11. For more details on the nature and extent of medically related opiate addiction see chapters 1 and 2 of David Courtwright, *Dark Paradise: Opiate Addiction in America before 1940* (Cambridge, Mass.: Harvard University Press, 1982).

12. Details in the board's *Annual Report* (New York: Westcott, Union Printing House, 1866), 36–37. Harold M. Hyman, *A More Perfect Union: The Impact of the Civil War and Reconstruction on the Constitution* (Boston: Houghton Mifflin, 1975), 306, summarizes prevailing postwar attitudes toward state and federal power.

13. Robert H. Bremner, *The Public Good: Philanthropy and Welfare in the Civil War Era* (New York: Alfred A. Knopf, 1980), 150, 191.

14. David T. Courtwright and Shelby Miller, "Progressivism and Drink: The Social and Photographic Investigations of John James McCook," *Journal of Drug Issues* 15 (Winter 1985): 105.

15. J[ames] F. A. Adams, "Substitutes for Opium in Chronic Disease," *Boston Medical and Surgical Journal* 121 (1889): 351–56.

16. For example, V. V. Anderson, "Drug Users in Court," *Boston Medical and Surgical Journal* 176 (1917): 755–57.

17. J. R. Black, "Advantages of Substituting the Morphia Habit for the Incurably Alcoholic," *Cincinnati Lancet-Clinic*, n.s., 22 (1889): 537–41.

18. Translated and reprinted in Robert Byck, ed., *Cocaine Papers*, with notes by Anna Freud (New York: Stonehill, 1974), 48–73.

19. "Remarks on Cocaine and the So-called Cocaine Habit," *Journal of Nervous and Mental Disease* 13 (1886): 757.

20. Robert W. Haynes, "The Dangers of Cocain [sic]," *Medical News* 65 (1894): 14. See also H. G. Brainerd, "Report of Committee on Diseases of the Mind and Nervous System: Cocaine Addiction," *Transactions of the Medical Society of the State of California*, n.s., 20 (1891): 193–201; and J. B. Mattison, "Cocainism," *Medical Record* 42 (1892): 474–77, and 43 (1893): 34–36.

21. "Cocaine Debauchery," *Eclectic Medical Journal of Cincinnati* 56 (1896): 464–65.

22. T. D. Crothers, "Cocaine-Inebriety," *Quarterly Journal of Inebriety* 20 (1898): 369–70. Many of the urban narcotic addicts who adopted cocaine did not abandon morphine but continued to use the two drugs together. The use of opiates and cocaine in combination quickly became a sign to public health officials that they were almost certainly dealing with a case of nonmedical origin.

23. "The Cocain [sic] Habit," *Journal of the American Medical Association* 34 (1900): 1637; and " 'Cocaine Alley,' " *American Druggist and Pharmaceutical Record* 37 (1900): 337–38.

24. "Cocaine Sniffers," *New York Times*, June 21, 1903, 11.

25. Ibid., 11. See also Edward Huntington Williams, "The Drug-Habit Menace in the South," *Medical Record* 85 (1914): 247–49.

26. H. F. Stimmel, "Coca in the Opium and Alcohol Habits," *Therapeutic Gazette* 5 (1881): 132; Freud, "Über Coca," in Byck, ed., *Cocaine Papers*, 72.

27. For more details see Arnold Taylor, *American Diplomacy and the Narcotics Traffic, 1900–1939: A Study in International Humanitarian Reform* (Durham, N.C.: Duke University Press, 1969); and David F. Musto, *The American Disease: Origins of Narcotic Control*, exp. ed. (New Haven, Conn.: Yale University Press, 1987), chaps. 2–7.

Commitment Law, Family Stress,

and Legal Culture: The Case

of Victorian Alabama

JOHN S. HUGHES

As the Confederacy's founding fathers were meeting in Montgomery, Alabama, to launch their revolutionary regime, a far less dramatic
and almost unheralded reform was commencing in the university town of
Tuscaloosa in 1861. In April the Alabama Insane Hospital, the first and
only such institution in the state's history, opened its doors and encouraged families to commit their disturbed members. Fittingly enough, the
first inmate was a forty-eight-year-old Confederate recruit who suffered,
perhaps understandably, from a madness brought on by the "political
excitement."[1]

Unlike this inaugural inmate, most of the seven thousand Alabamians
committed over the next forty years suffered from derangements that were
more private and less connected with public affairs. Private grief and family
distress more often eclipsed political turmoil in the lives of average folks.
Even while the war was under way, the commitment dramas of Alabama's
families only rarely reflected the political or economic circumstances. Private, even deliberately hidden, realities, it seems, contributed at least as
much to shaping the emerging Victorian legal culture of southerners as did
the public and powerful forces of disunion, war, and Reconstruction.

Commitment provided a powerful and unprecedented process that expanded the legal options of average people.[2] In less than a generation
Alabamians came to accept commitment as a solution to many problems in
their families' lives. In doing so, they subtly changed their legal culture—
that is, the ideas and behaviors that gave vitality to their legal system.

Moreover, this reliance on commitment came to alter their perceptions of where private and social problems diverged.

Victorian southerners had at their disposal few charitable institutions designed to alleviate either personal or social distress. Above the local level, which provided often haphazard church support and public poor relief, there was an absence of alternatives for families experiencing distress. Age-old problems caused by senile elders, deranged members, spouse abuse, drug use, excessive drinking, embarrassing eccentricity, petty criminality, or the unwelcome dependence of unmarried adult daughters all created stress within Alabama's families. As genuine and deeply troubling to relatives and neighbors as these concerns often were, few would have considered them social problems. Legitimate and respected public institutions to meet these concerns were still lacking.

The opening of the Alabama Insane Hospital provided the institutional framework for translating family distress into recognizable social problems. Thereafter, when families proved unable to care for the disturbed, when they simply became exasperated, or when the person's condition became a public nuisance, they could look to outsiders, in this case doctors and the courts, to help them vent their frustration. Physicians and the courts rather than the family thus came officially to be recognized as the ultimate experts in what was best for the afflicted.

Alabama's history of commitment shows, however, that this translation of family distress into a social problem by no means left families powerless. In a wholly unexpected way the process actually empowered families. As we shall see, insanity was an amazingly vague category. Lay persons certainly had no precise meaning for the concept. Neither, it turns out, did the medical authorities. And, unlike in criminal proceedings, the courts offered no definition at all. But the lack of clarity in the diagnosis of insanity meant that a great many conditions—indeed, all those noted above—could be and on occasion were subsumed under the label. In an ironic way, then, the deference to authority required by this medical-legal process actually empowered Alabama's inexpert families to formulate their own conclusions about behavioral deviance. In doing so they exploited the new commitment process and thereby placed many kinds of domestic distress in a realm reachable by law.

RAPID ACCEPTANCE OF THE HOSPITAL

Dr. Peter Bryce, the asylum's only superintendent until his death in 1892, promised the state's families that if they committed patients soon after the disease appeared, a cure was possible, even likely.[3] Within a short time Alabamians embraced his optimism. No matter how many new inmates Bryce received, there were always more families pleading for the admission of wayward members. According to an economy of insanity, as it were, the public's demand grew even more rapidly than the hospital's ability to supply space. In July 1862, only about a year after its opening, the asylum held but 31 inmates. By 1869, at the height of Reconstruction and amidst fiscal peril, the inmate population climbed to 191, in 1875 to 356, and by 1886 there were 733 inmates. In 1896 the then seriously overcrowded Insane Hospital housed 1,215 patients and was turning away as many applicants as it accepted. In 1900 Bryce's successors had managed to make room for 1,486 deranged Alabamians. No amount of expansion ever solved the problem of crowding.[4]

Architecturally, the asylum itself impressed its beholders as few buildings anywhere in the South.[5] By the 1890s it constituted the largest single structure anywhere in Alabama, and probably anywhere for hundreds of miles in all directions. No traveler on the busy Black Warrior River bordering the hospital on the north, or on the railroad that stopped at its front gate to the south, could easily forget the Insane Hospital or the images of authority and permanence it projected.

Even the many who never saw the asylum in person had heard of it. In his annual report for 1897 the superintendent boasted that the asylum was "by far the largest public charity in the State; there is hardly a hamlet or family that is not interested in us."[6] Even those who had not committed members acknowledged the hospital's place in their society when they offered distressed neighbors words of support and condolence, or when they whispered gossip about the hidden history of an acquaintance's lunacy. By the 1880s hundreds of former inmates had drifted back into the larger society, carrying tales of the asylum and providing constant reminders of the institution's presence.

In a single generation Alabama's residents passed from an age when the state lacked any respectable public, or even private, institution to care for the insane. Commitment to the hospital had become one of the most important and most familiar legal mechanisms for dealing with domestic distress. A century after Peter Bryce admitted his first patient, Alabama novelist Harper Lee observed casually in *To Kill a Mockingbird* that her silent and peculiar character Boo Radley might have profited from a "season in Tuscaloosa."[7] Few Alabamians would have failed to catch her meaning.

THE HOSPITAL AS A LEGAL INSTITUTION

Though promoted exclusively as a medical establishment and viewed as such by the state's families, the Alabama Insane Hospital was fundamentally a legal institution. Few families probably gave much thought to the legal framework that supported the institution. They understandably cared little about the considerable extent to which medicine had become an adjunct to law. But statutory provisions for commitment— the people's link to the hospital—were essential because the institution held virtually all of its patients against their wishes. Almost every patient who passed through the asylum before 1900 came at the behest of others who acted in what they believed to be the best interests of the patient, the patient's family, and neighbors. As a house of incarceration, then, the hospital relied absolutely on the support of the free society's laws and courts. It was, in this narrow sense at least, not unlike a prison.

Historians, sociologists, and others have long made much of the similarities between asylums and penitentiaries; and in a great many respects the comparison is apt. In both, inmates ordinarily live highly regimented lives in carefully constructed, artificial environments designed by their keepers to amend deviant behavior. In antebellum America the founders of both kinds of institutions projected an optimism that through benevolent authoritarianism, the lives of the wayward could be salvaged, disciplined, and rendered productive. By the century's end most of this optimism had eroded, leaving behind only a residue of authoritarianism and discipline. Few of the keepers still preached a philosophy of cure; most focused instead on the onerous chore of maintaining the growing numbers of the state's wards.[8]

The literature comparing asylums and prisons has focused principally on the common aspects of daily life and the inmates' "careers." Less attention has been directed to the crucial process by which outsiders became transformed into inmates. In this regard, criminals and lunatics alike followed paths that passed through legal institutions and procedures that legitimated the loss of freedom and incarceration.

For the most part the similarity ended there. Legal procedure for accused criminals' cases was far more rigorous than for the allegedly insane. Prospective hospital inmates received none of the traditional guarantees accorded to accused criminals. Unlike criminals, supposed lunatics traveled their paths to confinement under no presumption of "innocence." In most states during the late nineteenth century families and friends could commit a person on the certificate of one or two respectable physicians (only one was required in Alabama). The majority of the insane were indigent, and in their cases the law also required papers from the county probate judge that were to be drawn after an investigation of the person's supposed insanity. In Alabama private patients (the minority whose families rather than the state paid for their maintenance) needed no order from the probate court. State law required only a certificate of insanity, advance payment, and a proper bond.[9]

Civil proceedings for the indigent insane bore no resemblance to a criminal trial. With some important exceptions, few states during the nineteenth century required the presence of the supposed lunatic before the judge who officially sanctioned the confinement. Often the prospective patient received no notice at all of the legal proceeding. Some patients, in fact, learned of it only when they arrived at the asylum. Probate judges generally accommodated families in such matters of secrecy and took care to reduce any unnecessary exposure of private grief.

Commitment proceedings and criminal trials differed in another quite significant respect. In addition to formal notice and the opportunity to defend themselves, criminal defendants were accused of a violation of a law that was clearly spelled out. Whether it be larceny, assault, or murder, for example, all parties generally accepted the court's definition. And because crimes were offenses subject to definition, they likewise could be challenged through the presentation of evidence according to prescribed rules. Only clear and compelling evidence sufficed in criminal trials to warrant the taking of a person's freedom. The burden of proof lay with those seeking to take away liberty.

For prospective mental patients the legal journey to incarceration was more muddled. Insanity, unlike criminality, lacked anything approaching definitional precision. Legal, medical, and lay notions of insanity varied widely. Moreover, few procedural obstacles existed to prevent families from making expansive use of the term. The general practitioners who supplied the certificates of insanity possessed no real expertise in mental disease. Even as late as the 1890s a great many of Alabama's doctors were only marginally trained. A few had graduated from respectable institutions, but most had attended haphazard proprietary medical schools known for their easy admission policies, ill-organized lectures, and high graduation rates. A good many older physicians at the turn of the century were only apprentice trained. But in a larger sense, the supposed quality of the doctors' training was beside the point. Even the best medical schools offered lectures on insanity only on an elective basis.

The incarceration of insane persons was acceptable to a society that otherwise jealously guarded the ideal of liberty because the insane person, unlike the criminal, engendered pity rather than contempt. Those responsible for the forced confinement of family members or friends—whether that person be a parent, child, neighbor, family doctor, probate judge, or hospital superintendent—could rest assured that their act, trying and painful as it often was, could be defined as humane and altruistic. In support of the concept of insanity as a disease were the legitimating forces of the state's public policy, its medical elite, and the law.

ROUTINE COMMITMENT IN ALABAMA: LAW WITHOUT LAWYERS

As is true of many procedures that operate outside public scrutiny, the actual process of commitment in Victorian Alabama often lapsed into a ritual so informal as hardly to merit being called a proceeding. Under state law the probate judge could, if he chose, call a jury to determine whether the person under investigation was actually insane. Careful reading of the thousands of judge's orders in the hospital's records office reveals, however, that this practically never occurred. More often the judge, usually from a rural county, knew personally or by reputation some or all of the parties involved. In such cases the calling of a jury would have risked the suggestion that the judge, an elected official, suspected something dishonorable. Most judges acknowledged their own ignorance of insanity and showed considerable deference to families, who were often neighbors and were always constituents, and to the doctors who lent their prestige to the process.[10]

Many probate judges had no legal training; none was required. In addition, families only rarely sought out counsel.[11] As a result, this increasingly important process of law developed largely without the routine participation of lawyers. Institutional incentives to require procedural rigor were consequently limited. Just as there were no real experts in insanity to oversee this new and emerging process, neither were there experts in law.

Superintendent Bryce, however, stopped short of admitting everyone whom the nonexpert families and courts considered proper inmates. From its inception the hospital's statutes gave preference to persons suffering from acute mental disease (that is, from insanity of recent standing and thus presumably more curable). Bryce personally urged this policy, and with good reason. He realized that if he admitted large numbers of the chronically insane he would soon have no other kinds of patients populating his wards. The chronically insane seldom improved, and once admitted often occupied valuable bed space until they died.[12]

Despite his unflagging efforts, Bryce could not keep out chronic cases entirely. Statutes forced him to accept them whenever he had space available and no acute case had presented itself. As a result, more and more incurables found their way into the asylum. Though Bryce and his successors tried hard to release many of the harmless incurables, they seldom succeeded. In most cases families either disappeared, abdicated all responsibility, or steadfastly refused to care again for these chronic unfortunates. Dr. James T. Searcy, who took over as superintendent after Bryce's death, complained to the trustees in 1897 that "many efforts are made to get into the Hospital persons who are simply dependent characters, sick, or feeble objects of charity. We have necessarily to guard with great care this point in accepting patients. We have had to decline some even after they were brought to our door, because their applications grossly misrepresented them in this particular." [13]

State law provided Bryce and Searcy with only one imperfect way to alleviate the problem of admitting these incurables. Before any commitment could proceed, someone at the place of commitment (usually a family member but sometimes the doctor or the judge) was required to respond to a printed questionnaire that solicited specific information about the length of the current attack, how the insanity was manifested, and whether the person was dangerous, clean or filthy, and so on.[14] Given this information, the hospital's staff could screen unfit patients and give preference to acute over chronic patients. But those who responded to the questions generally had no previous experience with insanity. In addition, some general practitioners and judges acquired experience with these questionnaires and counseled families on what kinds of responses had succeeded in the past. As a result, the hospital always faced the growing problem that Searcy bemoaned in 1897: unfit applicants showing up at the door. And more often than not, the feeble and incurable were not turned away. Charity dictated that a place be made for them.

The hospital's questionnaire had another, more powerful, effect on the commitment process. According to the statutes governing commitment, judges submitted the answers to the superintendent before they took any other action. Only after the superintendent agreed to admit the patient was the judge authorized to investigate the person's sanity. "When informed that the patient can be received," the Alabama code of 1876 stated, "the judge must call one respectable physician and other credible witnesses and fully investigate the facts in the case."[15] This assured that the probate judge's investigation would be only a formality, because everyone knew that the hospital's experts considered the facts sufficient to warrant confinement. In most cases the superintendent's willingness to accept the application created a clear presumption that the person involved was truly insane. It was indeed a rare probate judge who ruled at this point that the party was sane.

Contributing further to making the judicial process only a technical formality, the statutes did not require that the judge give the supposedly insane person any notice of the proceedings. Neither was the judge required to order the person to be presented in court. Many judges committed persons they had never seen. Ordinary commitments, then, shared these features: the hospital approved the patient before any legal proceeding; and when that proceeding occurred, the person about to be committed received no notice, appeared before no magistrate, and marshaled no "defense."

A quarter of a century ago sociologist Erving Goffman offered a sort of sociology of commitment in his famous study of asylums as total institutions: "The society's official view is that inmates of mental hospitals are there primarily because they are suffering from mental illness. However, in the degree that the 'mentally ill' outside hospitals numerically approach or surpass those inside hospitals, we could say that mental patients distinctively suffer not from mental illnesses, but from contingencies." By "contingencies" Goffman meant largely the changing circumstances of the prospective patient's domestic situation.[16] In discussing this same issue, Goffman's fellow sociologist Edwin M. Lemert said in 1946 that families committed certain of their members not so much for mental illness per se as for "deviations . . . from customary role expectations which increase [their] social visibility."[17]

When it opened in 1861, the Alabama Insane Hospital offered a new remedy to families distressed by the deranged, eccentric, violent, or embarrassing behavior of their members. Moreover, by defining behavioral deviance (like alienation of affection, subtle threats, actual violence, delusions, and so on) as a disease curable at the hospital, Alabama's families acquired a new and potent perspective on age-old problems. A lax legal process made the new medical intervention possible. Indeed, the legal system's uncritical acceptance of insanity as disease facilitated doctors' appropriation of the problem. But unlike other medical concerns such as tuberculosis or yellow fever, the object of the intervention lacked any clear definition. Consequently, when legal process opened this remedy to Alabama's lay families, it empowered them to reach a wide range of "contingencies."

RATIONALES FOR COMMITMENT

While it is true that commitment served many ends, there exists little evidence to support the familiar melodramas of false imprisonment. Alabama seems to have been largely lacking in sinister and grasping relatives who lurked in its shadows and schemed to lock up innocent family members in order to exploit some hard-earned life savings. To be sure, not all who sought to confine family members operated from unalloyed altruism. Many acted from ulterior motives that mingled with and supported reasons more justifiable in humanitarian terms. But within the complexity of motivations one point seems fairly consistent: most who sought out the probate judge to commit a family member saw it as a burden and took up the heavy task out of distress, exasperation, and often love.[18]

Most did not, however, act from medical necessity. Sociologists Goffman, Lemert, and others were correct; the clinical classification of a person's behavior as a "mental disease" was largely irrelevant. Most of the persons responsible for committing others to the hospital understood nothing of insanity as a disease, except perhaps that medical and legal elites assured them that it was such. Ordinary people knew only of changed behavior in a loved one and of the domestic distress that the change had caused.

In most cases families tried to solve their problems at home and sought the help of the hospital only after more private remedies failed. In 1865, while the asylum was still quite small, Bryce admitted twenty-one patients. The average length of their present attack was over four years.[19] These data, while inexact, offer some valuable insights. Bryce got his information on the duration of his patients' insanity through answers to the questionnaire filled out by family members or their doctors. Reports of insanity lasting for years, then, came not from physicians specializing in insanity as a clinical entity but from relatives measuring the duration of distress.

For patients admitted in 1870 the length of attacks remained high, at slightly over five years. A decade later, however, the average plummeted to only four months, reflecting Bryce's success in keeping away chronic cases. The figure also reveals that the hospital, which was quite crowded in 1880, had begun to turn away many cases of long standing. Bryce's success in restricting admissions to recent cases was short-lived. By 1890 the average length of attack had reached two and a half years.[20]

In summary, Alabama's families generally sought out the probate judge after having coped for a protracted period with a member's insanity. Despite doctors' commonplace analogies to physical diseases such as tuberculosis or typhoid,[21] management of insanity followed a rather different course. Families only occasionally were reacting to something analogous to a medical emergency. More often, they were responding to problems that had eroded patience.

MARRIAGES IN TROUBLE

Commitment histories of this period frequently told stories of unhappy marriages. To modern eyes these nineteenth-century cases appear better suited to divorce court than to probate court. But divorce remained rare in Alabama throughout the period, even though it was becoming more common in the United States during the late nineteenth century.[22] Residents could file for divorce in chancery courts, but only on narrow grounds: physical incapacity to consummate the marriage, adultery, desertion (for at least two years), imprisonment (for at least two years with a term lasting at least seven), crimes "against nature," and, beginning in 1870, habitual drunkenness. Needless to say, a great many sources of matrimonial friction failed to make this rather scant list.[23]

In any event, few Alabamians viewed legal divorce as a workable solution to an unhappy marriage. Some who faced exceptional problems relieved their distress by committing their spouses to the hospital in Tuscaloosa. Several factors made this a viable alternative. First, commitment statutes set out no grounds for insanity. Courts, in fact, left definition of the condition almost entirely up to others, mostly family members and their doctors. As we have seen, even lawyers were largely absent from the process. Statutes governing divorce, on the other hand, defined quite clearly the requisite grounds, regulated what evidence was admissible, and made the presence of an attorney practically essential. Commitment to the asylum could also be carried out quietly, even without the knowledge of the other spouse.

Second, divorce in Alabama's male-dominated society generally left former wives financially vulnerable. Cast by convention into a financially dependent status and generally debarred from a livelihood, women sought divorce only as a last resort in this era when alimony awards were small and rarely enforced. Civil commitment, however, could benefit a distressed wife by effecting a desired separation while keeping open her access to her husband's estate.[24]

Finally, divorce and confinement carried different social stigmas. In divorce, the grounds generally amounted to some species of depravity in one of the marriage partners. Even aggrieved spouses often shrank from publicly labeling their partners as depraved. Commitment, although stigmatizing to the patient and perhaps the family, obviated this unpleasant need to discover evil. Since both legal and medical institutions encouraged Alabamians to view insanity as a disease, troubled spouses could formulate their plight in terms of the visitation of inescapable misfortune rather than in acts of willful wickedness. Friends and neighbors who viewed divorced persons with suspicion might well pity and support someone who found it necessary to commit a spouse to Tuscaloosa. In short, divorce required that one spouse or the other accept responsibility for being bad, whereas commitment enabled all concerned to locate the source of trouble outside the partners per se and in the mysterious workings of nature. In Alabama's emerging legal culture, commitment thus provided a bypass around the socially unacceptable divorce process.

During the 1890s the hospital's questionnaire included inquiries about relations between husbands and wives. As a result, many case histories from these years include mention of whether the inmate's marriage had been "happy," "unhappy," "jealous," and so on. For the year 1895, records for all 144 admissions of married persons were examined. Sixty-four case histories included clear references to the marriage (more often than not this space on the form was left blank). Thirty-eight marriages were regarded as happy, while twenty-six were characterized as unhappy. About 40 percent of the admissions for which there is information therefore suggest some marital unhappiness. Few histories clearly indicate whether the unhappiness predated the insanity or resulted from it. Still, a significant number of the hospital's inmates left behind troubled marriages.[25]

True to their Victorian professionalism, physicians at the hospital seldom pried too deeply into the private reaches of their patients' lives. But their records do allow occasional glimpses of marital discord and the insanity associated with it. On November 15, 1889, for example, staff physician W. G. Somerville admitted a thirty-seven-year-old private patient who had been married for only a year. Somerville reported that the man's "wife, without any assigned reason, would permit no approaches and refused to sleep in the room with her husband from the time they were married." At first, the patient had decided that his bride was excessively modest and "submitted to this treatment for several months." When the condition continued, he decided to get a divorce. As it came time to file, however, he changed his mind, "saying it would bring dishonor on his family." In time he became "gloomy & neglected his business, taking little interest in anything." Somerville added that although he was quiet, the patient insisted that he was sane and demanded his freedom. Only with "much difficulty" did the staff get him to remain.[26]

Twenty years earlier, Bryce had admitted a similar case involving almost stereotypical Victorian repression. On March 24, 1869, he examined a man, twenty-nine years old, who five months earlier had married "a good woman" who was "said to be . . . fine looking." She allowed the patient "to remain two nights with her, and it is thought they had no intercourse." At that point she claimed illness and agreed to see only her mother and physician. Her groom, according to Bryce "is said to have been very affectionate, and greatly distressed about his wife's condition. Finally[, he] became insane about three weeks ago." On admission, the young man displayed considerable anger and was hard to manage. Subsequently, the hospital released and then readmitted him twice. He died (still married) in the institution nineteen years later of what his doctors surmised to be "organic disease of the brain."[27]

In another case a husband committed his wife privately in order to prevent her from securing a divorce. Superintendent Searcy admitted the woman in December 1895 after a telegraphed plea from Dr. B. L. Wyman, a former staff physician at the hospital who had entered private practice in Birmingham. According to the case history taken on her admission, the woman "had a stormy time with her husband, who is intemperate." As a result, she filed for divorce, perhaps on the grounds of habitual drunkenness. Incensed at her husband for confining her, she claimed that he was seeking to prevent her divorce and gain control of her estate, which was considerable.[28]

Clearly marked at the top of her case history appeared the following unorthodox instruction: "Note: ———— [the patient] is not to write or receive letters from any persons except her husband and Col. [Sam Will] John [a prominent resident of Birmingham and later a hospital trustee] and her Aunt." Given these restrictions, there was no way that she could contact her lawyers. With the help of Searcy's staff the husband thus succeeded in preventing her from seeking a divorce.[29]

Some inmates came to the hospital not because of a contemplated separation but because their spouses became abusive.[30] In such a case Bryce learned in 1892 of the real history of a woman he had admitted in 1885. He had written to her family, informing them that she was well enough to return home and was anxious to do so. Instead of agreeing to receive the woman, the family unexpectedly attempted to block her discharge. Her grown children quietly approached J. C. Kumpe, the probate judge, and asked him to intercede on their behalf. The judge wrote to Bryce unofficially in September 1892 to try and prevent her discharge, explaining that "it was his [the husband's] unkind treatment and neglect that contributed to place his wife where she is & . . . I join the family in the hopes that he will not be able to get control of her. It would be the most tr[y]ing [thing] that could hapen [sic] for both of them & trust you can prevent him from taking her."[31]

Kumpe, who had presided at the woman's commitment seven years earlier but had been silent on the matter of abuse at that time, pleaded with Bryce in 1892 not to divulge to the husband, who was then escorting another patient to the asylum, that he or the family had blocked his wife's discharge. Everyone had labored hard during the commitment proceedings to divert attention from the husband's "unkind treatment and neglect." Again, years later, the family preferred to work behind the scenes by manipulating the superintendent and misleading the husband in order to keep the woman incarcerated. Confronting the husband would have required coping directly with the tragic reality of abuse. As matters stood, the husband's mistreatment came thereby to be "solved" by the wife's insanity. The strategy worked; the woman remained an inmate for another fourteen years until Searcy released her to her son's custody following her husband's death.[32]

Kumpe's intercession and the hospital's reversal of its decision to discharge this patient point eloquently to the difficult position of the asylum as an outside agent for helping families in distress. On one hand, Bryce's staff made a professional decision to release the patient based on her mental condition and life within the hospital. On the other hand, for reasons beyond the control of the institution or the woman herself, the family refused to take her. As a result, the doctors retained her against her wishes in order to please her relatives and protect her from domestic abuse. It seemed to them the humane alternative; but it was a choice founded primarily on what Goffman called "contingencies," not on medical considerations. Moreover, it was a choice with a cost—the woman's freedom. There is no doubt that she wanted to leave the hospital. In 1892 she wrote to Kumpe, pleading for his help to arrange her return home.[33]

Nor was it always the victim of spouse abuse who ended up in the hospital. Sometimes aggrieved spouses committed the abusive party. On August 6, 1886, a woman and her relatives confined her husband at the hospital because she claimed that he had assaulted her several times, once with a hatchet. In a letter to Bryce she expressed concern that despite these episodes of private criminality, her husband seemed outwardly rational. The admitting physician agreed. When he examined the fifty-five-year-old man, the doctor noted that except for excitement at being brought against his will, the new patient was otherwise rational. His wife reported that his "condition just at this time is not nearly so bad as it very often is." But she cautioned Bryce not to be disarmed: "he is so cunning and plausible that a good many people think there is nothing wrong with him."[34]

Bryce accepted the wife's construction of the case and admitted the man despite his overt signs of rationality. After observing him for a day or two, however, the superintendent had still discerned no insanity and wrote the wife asking for more details. She responded that she "knew pretty well that . . . [her husband] would be so plausible at first that you might be misled a little—Still," she added, perhaps with a touch of pique, "I thought that a Physician of your experience and skill would soon find out where his failure of reason was." But because Bryce had proved unable to divine the nature of the problem, she consented to supply some of the gruesome particulars. Her husband, once "a good man[,] husband & Father," had gradually become "indescribably bad wicked profane." He made obscene threats to their impressionable daughters, and on one occasion had threatened her by holding a pocket knife to her throat. Besides the obscenity and violence, he stole small items from family members and inexplicably refused to eat the food prepared for him or to take his meals with others.[35]

The distressed wife concluded her letter with the following insight: "there is only two constructions to be put on his conduct—he is an insane man or he is a thief a rascal is a brute in Human shape with the most complete powers of dissembling that God has ever give to the Devil power to put into a human beings heart." She pleaded with Bryce that if he had any regard at all for her or their "innocent daughters," he would not release her husband before she could "enforce the civil law by a divorce." "I am affird of him," she repeated.[36]

Despite this urgent plea for help, Bryce proved unable to solve her problem. Weeks later, he wrote to the woman, explaining again that her husband was sane and would have to be discharged. With sad resignation she wrote back and agreed that if her husband was truly sane, then release was only proper. Still, she had hoped that he was really insane:

I must confess that his very proper conduct and pleasant manners to you and others since he has been in the Asylum only goes to prove conclusively that he can behave himself genteely when he sees he is compelled to do so, and therefore filthy and obscene insults to his helpless wife and daughters, was only the cowardly indulgence of a wicked and depraved mind toward those he knew were powerless to resent it.

She closed by refusing to send money for his transport home to Birmingham. He was, she said, debarred "from being received into our home again."[37]

Between writing this note and her husband's release she lost her resolve. She neither sought a divorce nor refused to take him in again. Within a month her son-in-law wrote to Bryce, appealing for help anew. On his release, the man had gone directly home and resumed his abusive habits. According to the son-in-law, there were rages in which he knocked down doors, delivered "kicks and blows" aimed at his wife and daughters, and uttered "terrible and indecent language." Worse, he "expos[ed] his person . . . shamefully before the female members of the family."[38]

Perhaps recognizing the limits of his powers, Bryce refused to become involved again in this sad affair. But ten years later, in 1896, after Bryce had died and memories of this episode had faded, the man's wife committed him again, this time with the authority of a jury verdict declaring him insane. At the time of his trial the man had sent two urgent notes to Superintendent Searcy (who had not worked at the hospital during the earlier confinement), pleading for someone to testify to his sanity. B. L.

Wyman, the former staff physician who now practiced in Birmingham, had testified that the man was sane and wrote to Searcy expressing this view. Searcy consented to admit the man anyway. Along with her husband, the wife sent a letter telling the superintendent of the man's abusiveness. As she had done years earlier with Bryce, she pleaded with Searcy not to release him. For "Auld lang synd [sic]," she urged him to take a personal interest in the case.[39]

Searcy retained the distressed woman's husband, who, as during the earlier confinement, proved to be a model inmate. After four months the man tired again of hospital life and escaped to live with relatives in Lowndes County in the south-central part of the state. Searcy made no effort to retrieve the man; in fact, he packaged and mailed his belongings to him. Surprisingly, though, he neglected to inform the patient's wife in Birmingham. She wrote him two months after the escape when she learned from others that her husband was at large. She expressed her outrage that the hospital had allowed the escape of an abusive man without contacting family members who claimed to be his victims. Like Bryce, Searcy simply let the matter drop. And on that unhappy note the institution ended its involvement in the family's problems.[40]

Returning to Goffmann's analytic framework, it seems that in these cases commitment operated as a device that vented distress in families and, by extension, the society they formed. It provided a legal remedy of last resort for troubled, often abusive, marriages that avoided the pitfalls of a divorce proceeding. Commitment also imparted a particular configuration to the region's legal system and the culture that gave it meaning. Perhaps Alabamians resorted to divorce less often than they otherwise might have. Certainly commitment reduced pressures to reform the rigidity of divorce litigation by accommodating at least some difficult cases.

The commitment process also reinforced a legal culture in which average people dealt with problems obliquely rather than directly. For example, Victorian Alabamians did not come to define abusive marriages as a social problem in need of legal remedy. The state's legal culture embraced the more encompassing, though less specific, problem of insanity. So even though citizens acquired an expanded legal system capable of translating private grief into social problems, their emerging legal culture addressed those new problems only circuitously.

NONMARITAL SOURCES OF DOMESTIC DISTRESS

Commitment ameliorated other sources of distress, also rather obliquely, that could have found no resolution in divorce. Many Alabamians committed during this period experienced domestic trouble that was unrelated to marital turmoil. Some were defiant or abused children. Others were unmarried aunts or daughters. A large number were simply peculiar and eccentric people who embarrassed other family members. Others skirted the edge of criminality and were confined as sick to avoid the stigma of criminal proceedings. More than a few suffered with narcotic or alcohol addictions that alarmed their families.

In a particularly disturbing case of incest, the parents of a seventeen-year-old woman committed her to the hospital in March 1895. During the admitting physician's initial examination, in which he diagnosed her as suffering from acute melancholia, he also reported that "she states, & insists that her father has been criminally intimate with her, & she became pregnant four months ago." The patient added that "her mother produced an abortion upon her about a month ago, by introducing into her uterus 'a long rubber thing' (a catheter probably)." Ordinarily the hospital's doctors, like most people at this time, discounted such tales of sexual abuse, at most referring cryptically to "erotic delusions." But struck by the fact that this marginally literate young woman could so accurately describe an abortion, this doctor added an uncharacteristic comment to his notes, classifying the story as "a coherent & circumstantial account" that "may be true."[41]

Confinement failed to improve the young woman's mental condition. Over the next year she slipped periodically from her melancholia into what the staff described as a catatonic condition; she withdrew entirely and became unresponsive to outside stimuli. Sadly, her physical condition worsened as well. She contracted tuberculosis in the hospital. As a result, thirteen months after her admission, the doctors released her to be escorted home by the same parents whose abuse had placed her under their care. Commitment had thus temporarily transformed the parents' problem of abuse into the problem of their daughter's insanity, which in turn failed to succumb to the hospital's ministrations.[42]

The hardest group of commitments to classify involved no such clear abuse or obvious mental illness. These were single women who had passed the age of a likely marriage. Blocked as they were from pursuing their own livelihood, they often became financially dependent on their families. More than others, these women fit Lemert's categorization of mental patients as those who deviated from "customary role expectations" and thereby increased their "social visibility."[43] One case fitting this category was that of a forty-year-old woman who was committed by a married sister with whom she lived. A college-educated woman, the patient had grown temperamental and, according to Bryce, who interviewed her when she was admitted, had become obsessed with "erotic ideas." Bryce, however, saw no evidence of insanity. Her sister agreed, saying that she "cant [sic] control her affections, yet is too sensitive, & refined in her nature ever to act wrong." Like Bryce, the sister did not consider her insane. In fact, she tricked her sister into going to Tuscaloosa by telling her that she was to be employed in the hospital as a music teacher. To elicit support for the ruse, the sister said to Bryce, "I write to beg you not to put her with insane people but treat her as a boarder." She hoped that with Bryce's "skillfull treatment she may be restored & be useful & happy in her old age."[44]

This middle-aged single woman, peculiar and perhaps sexually curious, ended up a patient in the hospital and remained one most of the rest of her life. Neither the person who committed her nor the doctor who admitted her were convinced that she was insane. Yet both understood, albeit mutely, the domestic stress caused by a dependent, eccentric, and aging female member.

In other cases similar embarrassment to the family played a significant role in the commitment of peculiar or unorthodox women. In an example from October 1893, the hospital received a twenty-eight-year-old woman who, according to the admitting physician, seemed "perfectly rational, displaying no incoherence, dulness, delusions, nor emotional disturbance, beyond a natural depression of spirits." The patient claimed to have "been very unkindly used by her mother and sisters, who drove her from home on account of 'some trouble she got into with a young man.' "[45]

After a month of observation, evidence of insanity remained absent. When the hospital contacted the woman's widowed mother to inform her of this, she responded that her daughter was deceiving them. She must be insane, the mother insisted, because she "wanders into places I do not want her at." The mother told the doctors to keep her daughter at the hospital, "for I am satisfied now, and know she is protected." Without such "protection" she might continue to wander about unsupervised. Before being committed, "she was on her way to Florida when we caught her." In closing, the saddened widow added a note of exasperation: "God knows what I have gone through with her."[46]

The doctors continued to find no evidence of insanity, repeatedly noting in the casebook that she was "quiet, rational, cheerful." After three months they decided that they had no choice but to release her, even though the mother refused to "permit her in the house."[47] Here again is an example of contingencies. A widowed mother exasperated with an unmanageable daughter went through the process of committing her for the "protection" of the daughter's and her own reputation. She found in civil commitment a remedy, albeit a temporary one, for long-standing distress.

In June 1895 the hospital received another rebellious woman with a colorful, although more distressing, past. Ten years earlier, when she was twenty-seven, she had become engaged to marry the son of one of Alabama's senators. When the young suitor tried to "terminate his relations with her, she fired two or three shots at him in the streets of Selma . . . , wounding him slightly." The young man then retreated to Washington to assume a government position. She followed, securing employment as a stenographer and typist in government agencies. For unexplained reasons the romance reignited, only to end in another showdown in the streets when he attempted "to end the matter again." Luckily, her marksmanship had deteriorated and the man escaped injury.[48]

While in Washington she became, according to her own account, "nothing but a prostitute," as were "all the government women." She also commenced a morphine habit, which continued until her confinement in Tuscaloosa. This alarming behavior caused her family to commit her to St. Elizabeths, the federal government's asylum near Washington. Following her discharge in the late 1880s she returned to Alabama, where she resumed her adventurous social life. According to her case history, she soon filed suit against a leading citizen of Selma for breach of a promise of marriage. Another man reportedly "went West" to get away from her. To break this alarming cycle of what the admitting physician called a "checkered" career, her family committed her to the asylum, where she remained for more than two years, only to be readmitted several times thereafter. Evidently, she never managed to meet her family's expectations.[49]

Another inmate, perhaps the most notorious to the hospital's doctors and nurses, embodied many sources of family distress, including the taint of criminality. A single woman, forty-one years old, had been committed in 1890 before her trial for arson on the intercession of her father, a prominent resident of Montgomery, and her brother, the probate judge of Marshall County. The patient, however, denied that she was guilty of the arson and insisted that her lover, with whom she had lived in Marshall County, was responsible. Her father deprived her of any opportunity to prove this, however. In defense of her and the family's honor, he shot and killed "her paramour . . . on account of the intimate relations existing between this man and his daughter."[50]

This woman's career as an asylum inmate lasted for thirty years—until her death. From the outset she assertively defended her sanity, claiming that her family had committed her to avoid further shame and the prospect of a female member wasting away in the penitentiary. Because of her aggressive and intelligent self-defense and her unflagging hatred for the hospital and everyone associated with it, she became infamous to generations of doctors and nurses. During her years in Tuscaloosa she wrote hundreds of letters: to doctors and nurses inside the asylum as well as to numerous dignitaries on the outside. Every governor received at least one letter, and each was struck by her rationality and intelligence. As a sane and presumably criminal woman, she reasoned to these officials that she should be locked up at the penitentiary, not the asylum.[51]

Her doctors at the hospital and her family placed another construction on her case. As one physician remarked in a case note from May 12, 1891, they considered her "to be a woman of considerable intellectual capacity, but devoid of moral stamina."[52] Superintendent Searcy characterized her to one governor who had been troubled by her lucidity as "morally insane."[53]

Regardless of her mental condition, family members accomplished their objective. They saved her (and themselves) from the stigma of a prison term. Moreover, her eccentric and supposedly immoral personality never again became a matter of public scrutiny to cause the family anguish. Indeed, it seems that she died nearly forgotten by all but her keepers. Her brother, for example, occasionally corresponded with the hospital in his capacity as a probate judge, but he never inquired about his sister's welfare. For the family, though not for the patient, the problem of this troublesome daughter and sister thus found solution in a quiet legal process.

Problems of alcohol and drug addiction, like the distress of criminality and the failure to fill role expectations, supplied some families with the rationale for commitment. Bryce and the hospital's trustees, however, never looked favorably on admitting alcoholics and addicts. In October 1869 the board of trustees unanimously resolved that it was "impractible [sic] to admit inebriates and opium eaters into the Insane Hospital." Such patients usually resented their incarceration bitterly and retained the mental acuity to scheme and connive, thereby disrupting the rather rigid routine of asylum life.[54]

Despite this policy, though, addicts often found their way into the hospital's wards. A typical case of alcoholism, from 1869, involved an irregular, largely unlearned physician who practiced medicine in Butler County when he was sufficiently sober to do so. After being confined for a few months at Tuscaloosa, he recovered enough to return to his family. Bryce wrote to L. M. Lane, the probate judge, inquiring about the advisability of sending the man home. Lane responded that the man's family would have no more to do with him: "They say, and I know it to be true, that they kept him here as long as the citizens would stand him." When drunk, it seems, the doctor had "a perfect mania for letting down his pants in the front yards of the best people." If he returned, even sane and sober, Lane feared that his neighbors would harm him. Besides, he concluded, a drunkard practicing medicine posed a danger to the unsuspecting. It was better for all that the man should stay where he was.[55]

Records for drug addicts are more extensive than those for alcoholics. The hospital's doctors often classified "morphinism" or "narcomania" as a clinical entity like mania or melancholia, and thereby left a discernible trail through the records. In the twenty-five years between 1863 (when Bryce admitted the first addict) and 1898 (when, for some reason, record keeping became lax), at least sixty-six users of opium, morphine, or cocaine were admitted (thirty-five men and thirty-one women). Almost all of these (85 percent) were admitted after 1885, many several times each. Typical of their era, all were white, most were from either the middle or upper class, and most were well educated. Many, especially the women, had become addicted as a result of medical treatment. The men were less likely to have started using drugs under a doctor's care and were more likely to have combined the use of narcotics with alcoholism.[56]

A typical patient whose family committed her for opium use was a woman from Mount Meigs, first admitted in early 1887 and then again in 1888. This daughter of a physician had become addicted to morphine in 1880 as a result of medical treatment, and since then her father had tried unsuccessfully to break her of the habit. For many years she had been a source of friction in her rather large extended family. She, her husband, and their children lived in her father's home. When deprived of the drug, she reportedly berated every member of the large household.[57]

Before the woman's second admission, her sister wrote to Bryce, outlining the domestic anguish that necessitated the commitment. In addition to her insatiable appetite for morphine, she had developed an intense dislike of her stepmother. Often, the sister told Bryce, she begged from neighbors, saying that her father's wife refused to feed her. Worse, she "talks principally to negroes, whose company she seems to prefer." To the grieving, exasperated sister it was "mortifying to state all these things," but she forced herself to do so in order to impress upon the doctor the need for confinement.[58]

Another morphine addict was admitted and released six times between 1887 and 1898. Like many others she started using the drug to ease the pain of menstruation. Unlike others, though, she returned voluntarily to the hospital after her first release. In October 1890, for example, she wrote to Bryce, begging to be readmitted: "I want to come back before I have to be sent back publicly." She wanted to protect her young daughters, who would suffer if she continued her habit and had to be committed forcibly. In short, she acted to relieve her family's distress before it grew too great.[59]

In June 1893, a month after returning to the hospital for the third time, she wrote a sad note to the supervisor of her ward, explaining that, as before, she had failed to please her family. "I am in the way here [in the hospital]," she told the nurse, "and my friends and relatives are afraid to trust me out of here." In her depression she begged the supervisor to "get me 25 cents worth of morphine," enough, she believed, to effect an overdose. The supervisor refused to cooperate, and in time the patient improved enough to return to her family yet again. But after several failed trials at home, she returned unescorted by any family member in July 1896. She had resumed taking morphine and told her doctor that she never wanted to leave again, that she was unwanted and useless.[60]

Few drug addicts shared this woman's self-pity or resignation to asylum life. Most bitterly resented their incarceration. Typical of such rebellious patients was a forty-one-year-old, widowed lawyer who was related by marriage to a prominent official of the hospital and was himself a former officer of the asylum. Admitted on three occasions between 1890 and 1892, the man began taking opium in 1879 "as a cure for [the] whiskey habit." By 1890 he was drinking a pint of whiskey and ingesting ten grains of morphine daily, sometimes more. His family committed him each time he began to suffer convulsions and hallucinations. Within days or weeks of admission, however, he typically became lucid and intractable.[61] On July 5, 1892, for example, he had been in the asylum for about a month. His doctor reported that his "headaches have disappeared & he is stronger and less tremulous." As a result, he was "determined to leave the Hospital as soon as possible, even if by habeas corpus if necessary." Two days later, the institution released the troubled lawyer as "improved."[62]

Another recalcitrant patient, a single, forty-year-old schoolteacher, was admitted twice in the 1890s for a laudanum and morphine habit that she had maintained for a dozen years. Her family became alarmed as her physical health deteriorated and she began to be delusional, always smelling chloroform and hearing the voices of what she called "low negroes." She came willingly at first, stayed less than two months, and returned to her family. At home she immediately resumed her habit, causing her family to commit her again three weeks later. This time she resisted and was carried to Tuscaloosa forcibly.[63]

Seven months later, in October 1892, her doctor reported that she had "written to a Huntsville lawyer regarding a writ of habeas corpus." Evidently, she kept up a stream of complaining letters to lawyers and others. Her brother, who was her legal guardian, wrote to Searcy in August 1894 to put a stop to his sister's epistles. The letters, he said, "only advertise her unfortunate condition, and [do] no good to either herself or family." He asked that she be allowed to post letters only to her immediate family. The hospital granted these wishes, and in doing so helped to resolve the family's long-standing distress.

SUMMARY AND CONCLUSIONS

A consensus of sorts has emerged among historians that the profound social changes of the late nineteenth century placed significant pressure on the family. Robert Griswold, Elizabeth Pleck, and Michael Grossberg, among others, have shown that legal doctrine relating to the family (and, by extension, the family itself) experienced new challenges and underwent significant change. And Christopher Lasch has argued that there was, in fact, a "crisis of the family at the end of the nineteenth century." In support of such assertions historians have cited a fifteenfold increase in divorce nationally in the half century after 1870 and a rising perception of emotional and physical cruelty in marriage.[64]

This essay attempts to refine our understanding of the legal response to family distress during this period. Focusing on the consequences rather than the sources of distress, it shows that the legal system was considerably more pliant than an overview of doctrine alone suggests. Consider the area best understood by historians, marriage and divorce. Recent studies have shown that as Victorian America gave way to the Progressive Era, the allowable grounds for divorce expanded and the divorce rate increased significantly.[65] Despite this liberalization, however, the grounds for divorce continued to be narrow, and divorce remained embedded in an adversarial process that made it public, confrontational, and morally charged. Commitment offered some spouses a more private and less adversarial means for solving problems that was clothed with the respectability of objective science. Moreover, the grounds for commitment were hardly precise and almost never articulated.

Thus, while other studies have enhanced our understanding of how the legal system changed and expanded the remedies for marital conflict, this essay suggests that the real expansion of legal remedies was even greater than the statutes and case law would indicate. Commitment offered an alternative course, albeit one that may have been seen as a last resort, for addressing a wide variety of domestic distress, including failed marriages.

The real (as opposed to the ideal) functioning of Alabama's commitment system also has important implications for understanding the relationship between elite reformers and social control.[66] The founders and physicians of the Alabama Insane Hospital fit the definition of humanitarian social controllers so familiar in the historical literature: they hoped to provide a mechanism of reform, both individual and social, over which a small group of doctors, judges, and trustees maintained formal control. But in the half century following the institution's opening something quite unanticipated occurred. Plain folks took the medical-scientific elite's doctrines of madness and the procedures of commitment and fashioned them to meet their own needs. By the century's end it was by no means clear who was controlling whom. The hospital's founders clearly had not anticipated the creative ways in which average families would seize upon insanity's definitional flexibility and the commitment procedure's informal qualities to solve problems of long standing—problems that might otherwise have ended up in divorce court, criminal court, or even beyond the reach of legal remedy of any kind.

Ironically, this expanding framework for defining new social concerns actually limited the potential sources of stress that could attain social visibility. While families did gain a valuable remedy for deranged members, that label's imprecise meaning allowed it to subsume other sources of concern that may not have been best served by its application. Troubled marriages, abusive spouses, addiction to drugs and alcohol, and the social anomaly of often strong-willed and aging single women who failed to meet their communities' role expectations were some of the causes of distress that occasionally came to be labeled insane. The recognized problem, however, never expanded beyond madness. Consequently, concerns about addiction as well as a host of what today are called women's issues never acquired the legal remedies or institutional arrangements that accommodated insanity. Alabama's legal system and the Victorian culture that supported it made no provision for conceptualizing these matters as ones requiring social action, and many years passed before more constructive solutions were sought.

NOTES

1. Entry 1, Admissions Book, Staff Library, Bryce Hospital; file of patient 1, Medical Records Office, Bryce Hospital. The Alabama Insane Hospital became the Alabama Bryce Insane Hospital following the death of Peter Bryce, its first superintendent, in 1892. Today it is simply called Bryce Hospital.

2. In a strict sense commitment was not unprecedented; common law had long provided for the confinement of those who posed a danger to themselves or to others. But in the absence of a place to send lunatics, such commitment was of little value to distressed families. The opening of an avowedly curative institution changed all that. In this basic sense it was indeed a milestone.

3. Bryce's fullest early discussion of insanity's curability is found in his *Annual Report* (Tuscaloosa: John F. Warren, 1867), 9–10. Bryce claimed that 80 percent of all cases treated within the first six months were curable.

4. "Superintendent's Report," July 1, 1862, in "Proceedings of the Board of Trustees," Trustees' Record Book 1, 9, Staff Library; "Superintendent's Report," July 1, 1864, Book 1, 17; "Superintendent's Report," October 1, 1869, Book 1, 43; *Annual Report, 1875* (Montgomery: W. W. Screws, 1875), 21; *Biennial Report, 1886* (Montgomery: Barrett and Company, 1886), 8; *Biennial Report, 1896* ([Tuscaloosa]: Hospital Print, 1896), 12; *Biennial Report, 1900* (Montgomery: Roemer Printing Co., 1900), 8.

5. The *Montgomery Advertiser* reported on August 23, 1907, for example, that "the State Hospital for the Insane [is] the largest single building in Alabama" (see p. 1, col. 1).

6. "Annual Report," 1897, unpublished typescript, p. 2, Documents of State Hospitals, Alabama Department of Archives and History, Montgomery.

7. *To Kill a Mockingbird* (1960; New York: Warner Books Edition, 1982), 15. Interestingly, Boo's father refused to allow his son to be carried to Tuscaloosa, believing that it would mark the family too visibly with a stigma.

8. See, for example, David J. Rothman, *The Discovery of the Asylum: Social Order and Disorder in the New Republic* (Boston: Little, Brown, 1971); and Erving Goffman, *Asylums: Essays on the Social Situation of Mental Patients and Other Inmates* (New York: Doubleday and Co., 1961).

9. For an example of Alabama's law of commitment see *Revised Code of Alabama* (Montgomery: Reid and Screws, 1867), secs. 1041–74.

10. *Revised Code,* 1867, sec. 1053, states that the probate judge is required to "fully investigate the facts in the case, . . . with or without the verdict of a jury." Wording remained nearly identical throughout the rest of the century. See *Code of Alabama, 1876* (Montgomery: Barrett and Brown, 1876), sec. 1482; *Code of Alabama, 1887* (Montgomery: Marshall and Bruce, 1887), sec. 1281; and *Code of Alabama, 1897* (Atlanta: The Foote and Davies Company, 1897), sec. 2553.

11. Families did employ counsel frequently in cases where the maintenance of property required guardianship, but it was usually clear that the advice pertained only to estate matters, and not to commitment per se.

12. *Code,* 1867, sec. 1053; see also *Code,* 1876, sec. 1478.

13. "Superintendent's Report," November 17, 1897, Trustees' Record Book 2.

14. *Code,* 1876, sec. 1482.

15. Ibid.

16. Goffman, *Asylums,* 135.

17. "Legal Commitment and Social Control," *Sociology and Social Research* 30 (1946): 371.

18. A fine study that touches on commitment rationales and the broader context of commitment during the period is Constance M. McGovern, "The Myths of Social Control and Custodial Oppression: Patterns of Psychiatric Medicine in Late Nineteenth-Century Institutions," *Journal of Social History* 20 (Fall 1986): 3–24.

19. This sample is based on entries in the Admission Book, which includes information on, among many other things, the length of current attacks of patients' insanity.

20. Ibid.

21. In 1872 Bryce wrote in his annual report that "insanity is the result, in every case, of a diseased condition of the brain, just as dyspnea or shortness of breath results from a deposition of tuberculous matter in the lungs"; see *Annual Report, 1872* (Tuscaloosa: Meteor Print [Alabama Insane Hospital], 1872), 33. Another printing of this report was made in Montgomery by W. W. Screws, state printer, also in 1872, but it has a different pagination.

22. For a general discussion of divorce during the late nineteenth and early twentieth centuries see William L. O'Neill, *Divorce in the Progressive Era* (New Haven, Conn.: Yale University Press, 1967), in which the author offers explanations for the rise in divorce during the Victorian period. He suggests that the rise of patriarchal families that placed high values on chastity, monogamy, fidelity, privacy, and so on, required something like divorce as a safety valve. A fine study of divorce is Elaine Tyler May, *Great Expectations: Marriage and Divorce in Post-Victorian America* (Chicago: University of Chicago Press, 1980).

23. *Code,* 1876, sec. 2685.

24. O'Neill, *Divorce in the Progressive Era,* 24, says that alimony was rarely awarded in Victorian America.

25. This sample from 1895 is based on cases in Case History Book 8, Medical Records Office.

26. "Examination" form, November 15, 1889, in file of patient 3691, Medical Records Office.

27. Case History Book 1, 292. Subsequent history for this patient is from Case History Book 4, 448. There was no autopsy recorded for this case. Consequently, the diagnosis of brain disease was at best conjectural. It does, however, point to the fact that doctors in the hospital believed as an article of faith that all insanity was essentially physical.

28. Case History Book 8, 525 (patient 5439).

29. Ibid. After seven months this patient was released, her "condition much improved," to the care of her husband (see Continued History Book, 480, Medical Records Office).

30. The best study on the wider context of domestic violence is Elizabeth Pleck, *Domestic Tyranny: The Making of Social Policy Against Family Violence from Colonial Times to the Present* (New York: Oxford University Press, 1987). See especially her chapter 8, "Psychiatry Takes Control."

31. Kumpe to Superintendent, September 21, 1892, in file of patient 2399 (admitted April 25, 1885).

32. See letter from son of patient 2399 to Searcy, February 11, 1906, in file.

33. This patient (2399) so disliked her husband that she wrote to the governor, telling him that the man was "Treacherous[,] untrue and unkind to me." This letter, which was intercepted before it left the hospital, also included the claim that she had married a male patient in the asylum. Despite her alleged entanglement in the institution she nonetheless wished to be released. (See patient 2399 to Governor Jones, July 7, 1893, in file.)

34. Wife of patient 2707 to Bryce, August 6, 1886, in file. See also the "Examination" form in the file.

35. Wife of patient 2707 to Bryce, August 10, 1886, in file.

36. Ibid. Emphasis in the original.

37. Wife of patient 2707 to Bryce, September 26, 1886, in file.

38. Son-in-law of patient 2707 to Bryce, October 25, 1886, in file.

39. Wife of patient 5563 (formerly 2707) to Searcy, April 10, 1896, in file.

40. Wife of patient 5563 to Searcy, October 18, 1896, in file.

41. Patient 4627, Case History Book 7, 289.

42. Ibid.

43. See Lemert, "Legal Commitment and Social Control."

44. Sister of patient 2669 to Bryce, June 3, 1886, in file. This patient was not treated as a boarder, as her sister had hoped. She received the same care as did other women of her social station.

45. Patient 4757, Case History Book 7, 419.

46. Mother of patient 4757 to Searcy, quoted in entry for November 9, 1893, in Case History Book 7, 419.

47. Letter from mother of patient 4757, quoted in entry for January 9, 1894, Continued History Book, 296.

48. Patient 5291, Case History Book 8, 377.

49. Ibid.

50. Patient 3910, Case History Book 6, 185.

51. The letters she wrote to the governors are missing, but see the governors' responses: Governor William C. Oates to Searcy, December 26, 1895; and Governor J. T. Johnston to patient 3910, July 19, 1897, in file of patient 3910.

52. Case History Book 6, 224.

53. Searcy to Governor William C. Oates, January 1, 1896, in file of patient 3910.

54. Minutes, October 29, 1869, "Proceedings of the Board of Trustees," Trustees' Record Book 1, 38.

55. Lane to Bryce, May 23, 1889, in file of patient 3440.

56. This sample of drug addicts was compiled from several sources: first, the Admission Book, which lists "exciting causes" of insanity such as "opium eating" or "morphinism"; second, analysis of existing files, which include letters and, in some cases, physicians' diagnoses; and, third, the case history books. It gives a very conservative number of addicts. Family and doctors alike appear not to have discussed the problem readily.

57. See letter of sister of patient 3354 to Bryce, October 31, 1888, in file. The patient had formerly been patient 2799 (see Case History Book 4, 281).

58. Letter of sister of patient 3354 to Bryce, October 31, 1888, in file.

59. See patient files 2837, 4011, and 6370, all of which are for this woman. Quotation from letter from patient 4011 to Bryce and E. D. Bondurant, an assistant physician, October 28, 1890, in file of patient 4011.

60. Case History Book 6, 290.

61. See patient files 3832, 3987, and 4440. Quotation from "Examination" form, April 12, 1890, in file of patient 3832.

62. Patient 4440, Case History Book 7, 102.

63. See patient files 4212 and 4382. See also Case History Book 6, 477.

64. Robert Griswold, *Family and Divorce in California, 1850–1890: Victorian Illusions and Everyday Realities* (Albany: State University of New York Press, 1982), provides an excellent account of divorce and its impact on the family. See also Griswold, "The Evolution of the Doctrine of Mental Cruelty in Victorian American Divorce, 1790–1900," *Journal of Social History* 20 (Fall 1986): 127–48; Elizabeth Pleck, *Domestic Cruelty: The Making of Policy Toward Domestic Cruelty from Colonial Times to the Present* (New York: Oxford University Press, 1987); Michael Grossberg, *Governing the Hearth: Law and the Family in Nineteenth Century America* (Chapel Hill: University of North Carolina Press, 1985).

The quotation is from Lasch, *Haven in a Heartless World: The Family Besieged* (New York: Basic Books, 1977), 8.

65. In addition to studies by Griswold and Grossberg, William O'Neill's *Divorce in the Progressive Era* (New Haven, Conn.: Yale University Press, 1967) is important, arguing that the increase in divorce offered a "safety-valve" to the legal rigidity of the Victorian marriage.

66. For a good discussion of social control in late nineteenth-century hospitals see Constance McGovern, "The Myths of Social Control and Custodial Oppression: Patterns of Psychiatric Medicine in Late Nineteenth-Century Institutions," *Journal of Social History* 20 (Fall 1986): 3–24. McGovern's essay does not focus directly on the commitment process but rather on the system of care for custodial patients, and therefore does not explore the way family members used the commitment process. The most prominent discussions of social control include Rothman, *The Discovery of the Asylum;* Goffman, *Asylums;* and Michel Foucault, *Madness and Civilization: A History of Insanity in an Age of Reason* (New York: Random House, 1965).

Creative Necessity: Municipal

Reform in Gilded Age Chicago

HAROLD L. PLATT

In his annual report for 1892, Mayor Hempstead Washburne, scion of Republican stalwart Elihu Washburne, cried out against Chicago's "hydra-headed system of county, city and town government." [1] The mayor was lamenting the bewildering existence of 392 distinct public agencies in the metropolitan area, including 38 separate units of government within the city boundaries. This extremely fragmented structure had grown like Topsy since 1870, when a new state constitution had imposed severe limitations on legislation designed for Illinois's urban centers. Forced to work around these constitutional barriers, Chicago's elite businessmen responded creatively to pressing demands of the fast-growing metropolis for public works improvements and essential services by adding layer upon layer of special tax districts such as park, library, school, and sanitary boards.[2]

The Chicago experience highlights the need for historians to give greater emphasis to these mugwump reformers of the Gilded Age because they forged important links of continuity between the reform initiatives of the Civil War era and the rise of urban progressivism. In the case of Chicago, they established the first permanent organization in the United States devoted to municipal reform, the Citizens' Association, and outlined an innovative program of governmental improvements in the late 1870s that continued to dominate public debate into the 1890s. Unfortunately, however, most accounts of the period still blindly follow Lord Bryce's famous dictum of a century ago that municipal government represented "the one conspicuous failure of the United States." [3] This approach has obscured the important contributions of the mugwumps to the improvement of city services, the modernization of public administration, and the effort to ameliorate the environmental damage caused by industrialization. In part, the historians' myopia stems from their low opinions of the genteel reformers, who are invariably cast in an unfavorable light compared with the more modern "progressives." Summing up the reputation of the two generations, one scholar notes that "against the bright sunlight of the Progressive Era, mugwumpery seems like something out of the dark ages of social reform."[4]

But a very different picture emerges when causal links are restored to show the uninterrupted flow of structural reform ideas and political tactics from one period to the next. In 1984 Jon C. Teaford opened up this frontier of scholarship in his book *The Unheralded Triumph*. He argues that "late nineteenth-century urban government was a failure not of structure but of image."[5] Teaford highlights the successes of the mugwumps in coping with an unprecedented set of environmental and fiscal problems that accompanied the rise of the industrial city. Although his study provides a badly needed counterweight to conventional interpretations, a single-minded effort to catalog the accomplishments of the mugwumps ultimately creates an equally false impression of municipal reform during the Gilded Age. The pathetic images of "how the other half lives" photographed by Jacob Riis and recorded by Jane Addams in her Hull House diary belie any description of city government as a triumph of reform. Building on Teaford's pioneering work, historians now need to construct a balanced model of urban innovation in the post–Civil War decades.

In broad strokes, this essay examines the process of municipal reform in Chicago from the state constitutional convention of 1870 to the decisive defeat in 1907 of a "home rule" movement for a consolidated charter of metropolitan government. This periodization helps us assess the successes and failures of mugwump reformers more fairly than previous accounts. It enables us to see that while elite reformers devised important practical measures to cope with the problems generated by rapid growth, their reforms had the unintended consequence of strengthening the grip of localistic politicians and their party organizations on the reins of power. The result was a fragmented structure of government that fed the insatiable appetites of the parties for more elected positions and patronage jobs.

During the Gilded Age, Chicago's German and Irish immigrants and a semifrontier, boomtown spirit combined to give the city a vibrant political culture, best described as anarchistic democracy. Mobilizing these voters along ethnocultural and class lines at the polls, ward-centered politicians effectively locked the civic elite out of city hall. Unable to rule at home,

Chicago's reformers were forced to create new tactics that reached beyond the council chambers and mayor's office to the state legislature and the courts. With the Washburne administration, a new generation of elite reformers began taking over the effort to reverse the Gilded Age legacy of structural fragmentation. They tried with remarkable persistence to bring about "efficient" municipal government, and with equally remarkable consistency they were thwarted by the well-entrenched ward bosses and their immigrant constituencies.[6] Despite this failure, mugwump reformers left their imprint on the city's politics. In the late 1880s and the 1890s, as other groups adopted the tactics pioneered by the Citizens' Association, a new type of issue-oriented, coalition politics that would characterize urban progressivism emerged.

MOVING THROUGH THE CROSSROADS: FROM THE CIVIL WAR TO THE GILDED AGE

In *A More Perfect Union,* Harold Hyman calls attention to the dramatic effects of the Civil War on American governmental and legal institutions.[7] Abraham Lincoln's determination to create a more perfect union, Hyman argues, gave rise to new theories of the adequacy of the Constitution to cope with the emergency. As Hyman shows, Lincoln's "new birth of freedom" not only spawned broader definitions of individual liberty as embodied in the postwar amendments but also generated faith in the positive use of government to effect social reform. In a masterful chapter appropriately entitled "The New Era," he shows how the lessons of the war were applied after Appomattox at the state and local levels, including such urban reform innovations as New York City's Health Board, Metropolitan Fire Commission, and Society for the Prevention of Cruelty to Animals.[8]

Despite the undercurrent of constitutional adequacy and social reform that emerged from the war, by the 1870s the prevailing tidal forces of localism, laissez-faire, and racism inexorably gained the ascendancy in the formation of public policy. In *The Affairs of State,* Morton Keller explains how laissez-faire constitutionalism and the mechanical application of supposedly immutable principles of law served well to protect vested rights and to impose a sense of order on a tumultuous period of economic and social upheaval.[9] Yet this sweeping synthesis largely ignores the cities, where rapid demographic, geographic, and industrial growth created a

Table 1. Population of Chicago,
1850–1900

Year	Population
1850	29,963
1860	122,172
1870	298,977
1880	503,185
1890	1,099,850
1900	1,698,575

Source: U.S. Census, 1850–1900.

pragmatic necessity for innovation in government institutions and the delivery of essential public services. Keller seems deflected by his disdain for the mugwumps from pursuing the logic of his analysis to the local level.[10]

Nonetheless, the urban mugwumps' contributions in an otherwise conservative age represent an important source of continuity in the history of American federalism and the tradition of social reform. The spirit of reform remained alive, not latent, in the budding metropolitan centers of the United States. In Chicago, for example, a virtual doubling of the population every ten years sparked crisis after crisis in public administration (see table 1). With a population explosion from 300,000 residents in 1870 to 1,700,000 in 1900, Chicagoans were repeatedly forced to reshape the scope and scale of governmental operations in order to safeguard public health and safety, the ballot box, and their own fortunes.[11]

During the postwar decade, municipal reform and politics in Chicago were characterized by a dynamic tension between incessant practical demands for the expansion of the public sector and countervailing cultural pressures for the restrictions of a laissez-faire constitutionalism. The city's incredible growth prolonged the community's status as a boomtown and sustained its political culture of anarchistic democracy. After Appomattox, temporary allegiances to the two major parties quickly dissolved and were replaced by shifting loyalties to ethnic and class interests. Unlike older cities in the East, Chicago had no long-established or well-entrenched elite when large numbers of politically articulate Irish and German immigrants began arriving in the United States. The result was a raw struggle among the city's various classes and groups to establish a legitimate right to rule. This continuing contest for the reins of power made Chicago a "city on the make," to quote Nelson Algren.[12]

The Civil War's impact on constitutional thought about the positive use of government to advance both personal fortunes and civic goals helped to reorient political attention from national issues back to state and local forums. The origin of the Union Stock Yard in 1864–65 illustrates how ideas of constitutional adequacy gave rise to Chicago's most distinctive private enterprise as well as to innovative public policies. Learning how to supply the Union army with meat taught Chicagoans how to prepare dressed beef and distribute it over a national market area. But the stench, filth, and pollution of the air and water from the existing slaughterhouses in the built-up areas of the city soon became intolerable. The incorporation of the Union Stock Yard and Transit Company helped solve the environmental drawbacks of economic growth without limiting its rich opportunities for private profit. The new corporation allowed a wide variety of vested interests to be included in the new enterprise as shareholders.

Initiatives to make positive use of government for private gain were matched by innovations in the public sector. In February 1865, before ground was broken on the 320-acre Union Stock Yard site just outside the city limits, municipal reformers obtained a second state act to "provide sanitary measures and health regulation for the City of Chicago" and a four-mile ring around it. The act directed the city council to appoint a health officer, who was to be given extensive powers. In November the aldermen followed up by enacting a license ordinance with strict pollution controls for a variety of businesses.[13] In this case, Chicagoans used the powers of the state government to achieve both public and private goals.

Keeping up with urban growth kept the attention of Chicago reformers focused on improving the urban environment. Finding the means to finance an insatiable demand for public works projects and utility extensions was one of the greatest challenges facing the mugwumps. The creation of a park system for Chicago is a good example of how reformers translated the lessons of the war into progressive public policies. And like the stockyards scheme, the parks plan incorporated a mix of private benefits and civic goals. In 1869 lawmakers dutifully passed a series of bills establishing three special-purpose tax districts, corresponding to the three traditional geographical divisions of the city and its surrounding suburbs. The independent governing boards of the South, West, and North [Lincoln] park districts were entitled to exercise extensive powers to build and maintain recreational facilities, besides levying taxes in order to pay their debts and expenses.[14]

The reformers responsible for the parks plan drew upon their experi-

ences as war managers in groping for innovative ways to promote the public welfare and fatten their own pocketbooks at the same time. This type
of "city boosterism" represents a typical case of the blurred line between
the public and private sectors in the mid-nineteenth century. Real estate
developer Paul Cornell initially sponsored the park proposals as a way to
boost land values in his suburban subdivision, Hyde Park. Cornell's plan
soon attracted other postwar reformers who were excited about the idea
of using the government as a positive instrument of social reform. Most
prominent among the park system's supporters were war-bred sanitarians,
including the bill's author, Ezra B. McCagg. An attorney and civic activist,
McCagg had headed the North Western Sanitary Commission. Moreover,
fellow sanitarian Dr. John Rauch became a leading spokesman during the
referendum campaign to gain voter approval of the legislation.[15] By the
end of the decade, however, the mad rush by individuals and localities for
similar special privileges and aid from government was producing a sense
of political vertigo, a dizzy feeling that public policy was spinning out of
control.

   In 1870 a backlash against the accelerating momentum of government
activism led to the triumph of conservative constitutionalism in Illinois.
The use of the public sector to release creative energies and advance the
public welfare had culminated during the 1869 session of the legislature.
Lawmakers passed 1,188 private acts, primarily for the benefit of business and municipal corporations, but only 385 general acts. In addition
to the special parks laws, the creative session enacted many other provisions for Chicago's benefit, ranging from incorporation of the German
Savings Bank, the Chicago Library, Art, and Social Association, and the
Chicago Dock and Canal Company to approval of a $3 million bond issue
for water and sewage improvements. The sheer volume of these private
laws—which filled 3,350 pages of text—provoked cries of outrage and
demands for constitutional reform to curb the perceived abuses of the
legislative power.[16]

   The postwar era's dominant motif of constitutional conservatism with
an underlying theme of administrative innovation was clearly evident by
December 1869, when the Illinois convention met to draft a new constitution. With the heresy of state secession still fresh in their minds, the
delegates reacted in knee-jerk fashion to the freewheeling legislative activism of the previous session. One alarmed member of the convention, for
example, called for a blanket prohibition of special legislation because "it
has been, and while it remains it must ever be, the ground work of corrupt,

ring legislation. . . . It fills the lobbies of our state capitol with corruptionists."[17] The convention agreed heartily but adopted a more cautious,
shopping-list approach that eventually enumerated twenty-three varieties
of proscribed legislation. The list tied lawmakers' hands in several areas
affecting Illinois's subdivisions, including bans on special city charters,
county seat relocations, street railway franchises, and public utility mo-
nopolies. State legislators were also prohibited from writing special laws
for local elections and pay scales as well as from interfering in the administrative affairs of individual counties, townships, and justices of the
peace. Finally, to safeguard their work against the corruptionists, the delegates placed nearly insurmountable roadblocks in the path of the amendment process, which was narrowed in any case to a single proposal every
two years.[18]

The convention did not neglect to shackle local officials, who were
rapidly earning a reputation for corruption second only to the state solons.
The most conspicuous abuse of power in the communities involved an infectious mania to finance railroad construction and improvement projects
with public credit. "The experience of the last ten years has taught us . . .
that the counties, towns, and municipalities have donated, appropriated,
and lent credit to an extent that has proven, in many instances, almost
ruinous," warned a rural representative. He argued that constitutional
checkreins had to be placed on the communities, or "the people will be
swallowed up by the presistent [sic] demands of unscrupulous and merce-
nary [railroad] monopolists."[19] After considerable debate over the proper
remedy, the delegates decided to impose a maximum debt limit. No local
subdivision could extend its credit beyond 5 percent of its assessed property values. This restriction, more than any other, forced the mugwumps
to resort to the creation of overlapping special tax districts, each with
independent authority to issue bonds up to the 5 percent ceiling. At the
convention, however, the measure to throttle local financial obligations
provided an acceptable answer to the conservatives' charge that "we had
better limit these municipal corporations somewhere."[20]

This drive to circumscribe the powers of local government requires a
more subtle explanation than a simple revolt of the hayseed Grangers
against the city slickers. Few delegates tried to stop the conservative bull-
dozer from erecting higher constitutional barriers around local government. But in spite of Chicago's alarming growth to metropolitan proportions during the wartime boom, there is little evidence of an antiurban
movement at the convention. Only the most controversial issue—pub-

lic aid to the railroads—divided the convention along traditional party lines between southern-bred Democrats from downstate and transplanted Yankee Republicans from the Chicago region. Even in this exceptional case the debate actually pitted the "have" against the "have-not" areas of transportation services rather than the metropolitans versus the provincials. A spirit of cooperation prevailed for the most part because the Chicago delegation had shrewdly agreed beforehand to form themselves into a nonpartisan block. With Democrats and Republicans chronically segregated into two sectional camps of equal strength, the Cook County delegates held the balance of power. Compromise and logrolling tactics ensured that both the farmers and the urbanites achieved their most important reform objectives. In several instances these goals coincided, including the convention's most original creation, the independent regulatory commission. Growers, shippers, and dealers found common cause in attacking warehouse operators like the Munn brothers and other middlemen whose unscrupulous business practices undermined Chicago's emerging role as the national center of the grain trade.[21]

The most striking example of innovation in the structure of government, the Railroad and Warehouse Commission, exposed an undercurrent of reform that would soon surface full-blown in the wake of the Chicago fire of 1871. Originally drafted by the Chicago Board of Trade, an elite group of businessmen, the proposal to establish the commission departed from the past by empowering a regulatory agency for the first time to set rates and enforce its rulings independently of the legislature. Both agricultural producers and traders felt a dire need to restore honesty in the commodity markets. "One of our most extensive grain buyers told me," a rural representative of the Grangers reported, "that with all his stealing, the Chicago warehousemen always beat him, for he never could make a load hold out weight."[22] In other words, the warehousemen shortchanged the farmers in spite of their brokers' inflated claims.

Not only did urban and rural delegates unite behind the reform, but they also found an ingenious way to target a general law to apply exclusively to a single locality, Chicago. Drawing on the constitutional model of Iowa, Joseph Medill—editor of the *Chicago Tribune* and Republican warhorse—suggested a classification scheme designed to circumvent the ban on special legislation. Permitting legislation applicable to cities of 100,000 inhabitants allowed legislators to enact ostensibly general laws that applied only to Chicago. A fellow delegate and legal expert, John C. Haines, objected to this perversion of mechanical jurisprudence, but his protest was buried under practical needs to solve the unique problems of the state's only big city. Similar logrolling politics ensured the inclusion of several other special provisions for Chicago, including extra courts and greater representation on the county board of commissioners.[23]

Drawing upon the experience of the much maligned, albeit imaginative, legislative session of 1869, municipal reformers actually had little difficulty circumscribing the new constitutional limitations. After the park acts were upheld by the Illinois Supreme Court the year following the convention, the pieces of a complete fiscal system fell quickly into place. Chicago reformers used this constitutional precedent to build an effective money machine to pay for progress. In addition to affirming the right of the legislature to establish the new type of tax district, the court went on to declare that it was "a public municipal corporation." This flexible interpretation allowed reformers to fashion a series of agencies with tightly defined functional arenas but enjoying the same broad fiscal authority of the municipal government itself. By 1873 they had spread the heavy expense of city building among several semiautonomous agencies, including the Library Board, the Board of Education, and the three park districts. Gaining control of ten of the fifteen seats on the Cook County Board of Commissioners at the constitutional convention, Chicagoans were also able to transform this subdivision into a specialized agency, one that carried most of the burdens of the city's welfare costs. The resulting system of overlapping tax districts was cumbersome, inefficient, and a rich breeding ground for patronage politics. But it also offered a creative approach to public finance in a conservative age.[24]

The Chicago fire underscored the practical necessity of counterbalancing legal formalism with structural flexibility. Typical of American disasters, the emergency of October 1871 served as a catalyst for reform by emphasizing long-standing deficiencies in the organization, cost, and delivery of government services. The unprecedented crisis galvanized Chicagoans to set aside (at least temporarily) their ethnic and class differences and unite behind the city's business leadership. With municipal elections scheduled for the following month, the city's elite presented voters with a nonpartisan, "fire-proof" slate of candidates, headed by Joseph Medill. He agreed to serve, but only after securing promises of support for a proposed state act to significantly strengthen the mayor's powers. In November, Medill and his ticket were swept into office on a wave of civic boosterism.[25]

With Medill's sponsorship, state lawmakers loosened the rigid structure of constitutional limitations imposed on the cities in order to help Chicago rebuild. The origins and enactment of Medill's "Mayor's bill" suggested the emergence of a new pattern of municipal reform in an age of legal formalism. Medill sidestepped the legislative process at the local level by drawing on the expertise of the city's elite lawyers. Even before his inauguration Medill persuaded Murray F. Tuley, a politically influential jurist, to write a structural reform bill for the consolidation of administrative power in the mayor's office. Tuley also took charge of lobbying his bill through the legislature.

In March 1872 Tuley's success in Springfield encouraged reformers to promote a series of special laws for Chicago's unique benefit. Over the next two years the legislature dutifully passed measures to deal with the need for special procedures to restore the city's burned real estate records, to fund the construction of a new courthouse, to relieve Chicago from paying its share of the Illinois and Michigan Canal debts, and to install better machinery to assess and collect property taxes. In some cases these acts were framed as general legislation that any subdivision could use under similar emergency conditions. In other cases the use of a classification scheme based on the size of the locality's population provided the most convenient method to get around the new constitution's formal restrictions against special legislation.[26]

But closer to home, Medill soon found to his dismay that a political consensus was virtually impossible to maintain. Less than six months after Chicagoans elected Medill, two policy issues shattered the consensus and reignited the passions of ethnocultural and class conflict. The establishment of a fireproof-building code was the first priority of Medill's new administration. In December the mayor sponsored a bill to prohibit wooden structures within the city limits. North Side residents, however, protested vehemently that more costly building materials would effectively deny them the opportunity of home ownership. North Siders—80 percent of whom were foreign-born skilled workers and small proprietors—also pointed out that brick structures required expensive basement foundations, while wooden homes were light enough to get by without them. On January 15, 1872, the protestors marched to city hall, stormed the council chambers, and frightened the aldermen into amending the building regulations to allow wooden structures outside the central business district.[27]

During the same year, the liquor question, that lightning rod of ethnocultural politics, further reinforced the role of the ward-centered politicians as the legitimate voice of the people. In this case, a postwar faith in the positive use of government to effect social reform backfired politically for Chicago's native-born Republicans. They prodded a reluctant Mayor Medill to enforce an 1872 state law requiring saloons to close at midnight and all day on Sunday. This set off a divisive struggle between the council and the mayor over the control of the police force, and the battle resulted in the wholesale defection of Chicago's Germans from the Republican party to the Democrats. In the 1873 general elections this political shift spelled the defeat of the businessmen's Union ticket by a People's party. Although the contest for control of city hall continued without relief for six years, the business elite suffered defeat after defeat. The first president of the Citizens' Association, Franklin MacVeagh, summed up the frustration of Chicago's best men: "So long as the present city-political system prevails in America—a system that practically disfranchises the better portion of the community—we conceive it to be needful to have what we can of a supplemental political organization like this, that will to some extent, represent these disfranchised people."[28]

NEW PATHS OF REFORM:
THE CITIZENS' ASSOCIATION AND
THE SPECIAL INTEREST LOBBY

Frozen out of policy formation at city hall, Chicago's mugwumps responded by pioneering new tactics of municipal reform. After the fire, Philip Armour, Marshall Field, Potter Palmer, and other large property owners had formed an ad hoc group to promote the rebuilding of a fireproof city, the securing of an adequate water supply, and the establishment of a professional fire department. With these initiatives thwarted at city hall by the ward politicians and their immigrant constituencies, the business elite was forced to blaze new paths of reform in order to achieve its objectives.

The formation of the Citizens' Association in 1874 was the first step in creating a permanent special interest group lobby. Its founding is significant because the organization supplanted the previous episodic efforts of reformers in Chicago and other American cities with a more effective, continuous campaign for municipal improvement. Composed of one hundred top businessmen and leading attorneys, the association set up standing committees to study various urban problems such as cleaning up the environment, financing public works projects, and safeguarding the ballot box. Equally important, the group formed a committee to draft model laws and another to lobby these bills through the legislature. By establishing a permanent organization, the mugwumps were now able to sponsor investigations by doctors, engineers, lawyers, and other technical experts. The value of the new approach to municipal reform was reflected in the evolution of the group's increasingly sophisticated reports, legislative proposals, and legal briefs.[29]

Over the next five years the Citizens' Association developed a lengthy agenda of structural improvements for the city and a new set of tactics to achieve its reform goals. At first, the mugwumps continued to focus on the local arena, where political battles raged over the control of city hall, the balance of power between the council and the mayor, and the enforcement of the blue laws. During these years of economic depression and labor strife, culminating in the shocking violence of the national railroad strike of 1877, mounting social tensions produced a potentially explosive situation.

Chicago's political culture entered an era of extreme fragmentation and polarization. A decade later, the proliferation of radical groups for armed revolution and an infectious paranoia about conspiracies to defraud the ballot box would lead to the fatal confrontation at Haymarket Square and its equally tragic repercussions. In this highly charged atmosphere of anarchistic democracy, the members of the Citizens' Association began shifting their attention from rearguard actions at city hall to more receptive forums such as the state legislature and the courts, where they hoped to regain the initiative in the formation of public policy. The election of a Democrat, Carter Harrison, to the mayor's office in 1879 hastened their retreat from electoral politics. Frustrated by Harrison's broad appeal (he was elected to four consecutive terms between 1879 and 1887) and encouraged by their success in lobbying and litigation, the business elite came to rely almost entirely on the tactics of the special interest lobby to promote its agenda.[30]

After three years of experimentation, a new configuration of reform began to crystallize within the Citizens' Association. In 1877, as table 2 indicates, Chicago's businessmen formulated a comprehensive list of reform objectives for the first time. And their reform tactics worked surprisingly well; nine of the fifteen bills sponsored by the Citizens' Association were enacted during the 1877 session. Anticipating another "very favorable" outcome at the following session, the organization's vice president, Edson Keith, crowed that "Cook county can obtain any desired measure of [legislative] relief, under the constitution, which does not conflict with the manifest rights and interests of smaller communities." With two members

Table 2. Chicago Citizens' Association Legislative
Reform Program

Year	Proposed legislation	Passage
1877	Amend Municipal Incorporation Act of 1872 (Art. 4:1—election date)	yes
	Amend Municipal Incorporation Act of 1872 (Art. 4:2—increase number of elected officers)	yes
	Collection of back taxes (special assessments for streets and water)	yes
	City treasury warrants as tax payments	yes
	Reorganization of city courts	yes
	Create state board of health	yes
	Create police and firemen's relief fund	yes
	Criminal vagrancy law	yes
	Criminal conspiracy to defraud the city law	yes
	Amend Township Reorganization Act (Art. 7:7—township elections)	no
	Township tax collection books to county government	no
	Create probate courts in Cook County	no
	Jury reform	no
	General Revenue Act reform	no
	Create state militia	no
1879	County commissioner elections	yes
	City voter registration	yes
	Park Commission and Driveways Authority	yes
	Two percent city tax limit	yes
	Tax collection enforcement power	yes
	Create state militia	yes
	Consolidate townships in Chicago	no
1881	Tenement house inspection and sewage law	yes
1883	[Saloon tax issue produces stalemate]	
	Amendment of Constitution (consolidation of government units in Chicago)	no
	Jury reform	no
	Criminal code reform	no
	Primary election law	no
	General Revenue Act reform	no
1885	Primary election law	yes
	Creation of revenue study commission	yes
	Amendment of Constitution (consolidation of government units in Chicago)	no

Table 2. Continued

Year	Proposed legislation	Passage
	Create sanitary district	no
	Create civil service system	no
	Food adulteration regulation	no
1887	Criminal mob, riot, and conspiracy laws	yes
	Pension fund for police and firemen	yes
	Real estate title abstracts books law	yes
	Amend burned records law	yes
	Property owners' consent to street railroads	yes
	Chicago annexation law	yes
	Reorganization of county government	yes
	Create jury commission [defeated in local referendum]	yes
	Redistrict wards	no
	Create sanitary district	no
	Create civil service system	no
	Create state board of supervisors for the insane	yes
1889	Create sanitary district	yes
	Reform General Revenue Act	no
	Create jury commission	no
	Pawners' bank regulation	no
	Building and loan association regulation	no
	Consolidation of townships in metropolitan Chicago	no
1891	Election law reform	yes
	Chicago park system reform	yes
	Columbian Exposition law	yes
	Chicago School Board reform	yes
	Building and loan association regulation	yes
	Create real estate titles commission	yes
	Call for a constitutional convention	no
1893	Special assessment tax reform	yes
	Chicago park system reform	yes
	Gas Trust investigation	yes
	Real estate titles commission reform	no
	Justice of the peace court reform	no
	Call for a constitutional convention	no

Source: Chicago Citizens' Association, *Annual Report* (1876–94).

of the group acting as a permanent lobby during the 1879 session, Edson's prediction of easy victory was verified by the passage of six of seven bills for Chicago's benefit.[31]

A closer examination of a single reform measure sheds light on the inner workings of the special interest group lobby. In the Gilded Age, efforts to purify the ballot box represented a running battle of parry and thrust between the mugwumps and the ward heelers. After imposing a voter registration law on Chicago in 1879, the Citizens' Association discovered that the politicians were adapting to the new law ingeniously by inventing new ways to stuff the ballot box. Over the next five years the registration rolls swelled with the names of hundreds of ghost voters. In 1884 a grand jury found vote irregularities in 164 of the city's 171 precincts. The Citizens' Association decided it had to plunge back into this "hideous vortex" of election fraud. It sponsored a conference attended by two hundred representatives of Chicago's elite organizations, set up a committee headed by lawyer A. M. Pence to draft remedial legislation, and formed the Non-Partisan League to help enforce the new laws.[32]

In June 1885 the state legislature passed three measures to close the loopholes in the city's registration and voting rules. The key act shifted control of the registration rolls from the politicians serving on the board of county supervisors to the new bipartisan Election Commission appointed by the county judiciary. Pence used an 1872 New York law as a model to build an elaborate structure of procedural safeguards against vote fraud. A second law further advanced this goal by setting the maximum size of a precinct at 450 voters. Equally important, perhaps, a final reform act brought the parties' primary contests under the regulation of law for the first time. Taken together, the legislative package went a long way toward addressing the most glaring faults in Chicago elections.[33]

The tactics of reform wrought by the Citizens' Association extended beyond the special interest group lobby in the legislature to the courts and the administration of the law. In July 1885 Judge Richard Prentergast began mobilizing the city's "well known lawyers" to plot strategy for a test case. By the time of the municipal elections the following April, the mugwumps had raised a proper legal challenge, which afforded the state supreme court an opportunity to affirm the act's constitutionality. The Non-Partisan League sprang into action after the act's passage and purged the registration rolls. Eventually the reformers obtained convictions for vote fraud under the new law.[34]

Of course, the election reforms of 1885 did not eliminate vote fraud altogether, but the presence of a permanent special interest group lobby made a difference on the side of fair and honest elections. Citizen's Association president Edwin Lee Brown proclaimed that it was safe again to vote because "the active measures taken to redeem the city from the vile influences which have heretofore controlled the elections have produced good and abundant results: the local political events of the last twelve months have assumed the importance and proportions of a revolution." [35] Building on the structural reforms of 1885, watchdog groups such as the Non-Partisan and Ballot Reform leagues began to gain the ascendancy over the ward heelers in the battle to purify the ballot box. Chicago continued to make steady strides in this direction, including the institution in 1891 of the "Australian," or secret, ballot. [36]

The value of the special interest group lobby in the legislature and the courts was especially evident in the area of environmental planning and sanitary reform. Probably the single greatest contribution of the Citizens' Association to the city and the reform tradition was its sustained crusade to clean up the air and water pollution spawned by rapid growth and industrialization. This was a challenge, unprecedented in scope and magnitude, that confronted many American cities of the late nineteenth century. Industrialization was having increasingly disastrous repercussions on public health and the quality of urban life. Through a persistent process of trial and error spanning twenty-five years, Chicago reformers became the nation's foremost experts in environmental engineering. The creation of a metropolitan sanitary district in 1889 represented the successful culmination of the Citizens' Association's reform efforts as well as the opening of a new era of comprehensive city building and planning on a regional scale.

In Chicago, the Union Stock Yards became not only the city's pride and the epitome of its industrial progress but its most obnoxious and inescapable nuisance as well. During the 1870s, sanitary reformers initially considered the problems of polluted air and water in traditional terms as isolated failures. From its founding in 1874, the Citizens' Association took an active role in helping city authorities to enforce the public health and license ordinances against individual polluters. The reform group paid the salaries of extra inspectors and applied its considerable talents to the subsequent legal battles over the city's police power to regulate private business practices. In spite of some notable triumphs over individual factory owners in the courts, however, the discharge of wastes in the south branch of the Chicago River by the fast-growing meat-packing industry became an embarrassing scandal that overshadowed these isolated victories. "The river stinks. The air stinks. People's clothing, permeated by the foul atmo-sphere, stinks," the *Chicago Times* exclaimed in 1880. "No other word expresses it so well as stink. A stench means something finite. Stink reaches the infinite and becomes sublime in the magnitude of odiousness."[37]

Gradually, the reformers began to supplant piecemeal attacks on indi-vidual polluters with more comprehensive approaches to improving the environment. In 1880, for example, a standing committee of the Citizens' Association issued a report that drew important links between the "drain-age problem" of the stockyards, the need to retrofit the city's housing with sewer hookups, and the necessity of protecting the purity of Chicago's water supply. By the middle of the decade, continuous study of these inter-related problems had helped city dwellers formulate more unified concepts of urban sanitation. Moreover, they broadened their perspectives on the geographical expanse that would have to be encompassed in any plan to engineer the environment. Anticipating continued growth, Chicago's spearheads of reform called for a plan "establishing a drainage district or municipality of an extent sufficient to take in all the territory and its popu-lation which may become urban in its character and a part of Chicago within [the next] century."

If the natural topography of the Chicago region encouraged reformers to draw plans encompassing a metropolitan area, the special-purpose tax district offered a ready-made institutional vehicle to finance and govern such a massive public works project. In 1887 the Citizens' Association introduced its plan into the state legislature as the "Hurd bill," but the scheme had such far-reaching consequences that it took the reform lobby another two years to win passage.[38] Chicago's sanitary district, which re-cently celebrated its centennial anniversary, continues to play an essential role in the environmental planning of the region.

In 1889 the members of the Citizens' Association could congratulate themselves on the triumph of their long crusade for sanitary reform. Over the previous fifteen years Chicago's mugwumps had accumulated an im-pressive record of civic achievement in the areas of public finance, election procedures, and environmental engineering. Locked out of city hall by a ward-centered system of politics, they had drawn upon the Civil War's legacy of constitutional adequacy to sustain the momentum of progressive innovation in a conservative age. By forming a permanent special interest group lobby devoted to municipal improvement, they contributed signifi-cantly to the search for practical solutions to the unprecedented problems of rapid urban growth and industrialization. The Citizens' Association's tactics of reform in the legislature and the courts also represented a creative approach to Chicago's fragmented and polarized political culture. It is ironic that the very success of these tactics helped to bring about the end of the business elite's extraordinary influence in the formation of public policy.

AT THE CROSSROADS OF PROGRESSIVISM:
ELITE REFORMERS AND THE TRANSFORMATION
OF URBAN POLITICS

From 1886 to 1893, Chicago politics entered a crossroads that led toward a new configuration of municipal reform and a realignment of partisan loyalties. During this transitional period, a dynamic interaction between the forces of continuity and change set the city on a new course marked by a proliferation of special interest group lobbies, coalition building around specific issues by these organized groups, and intense struggles at the ballot box for control of city hall by the two major parties. In the mid-1880s the accumulating success of the Citizens' Association's reform tactics spurred other groups to adopt similar techniques of lobbying special legislation through the statehouse and sponsoring test cases in the courts. The resulting competition between organized groups encouraged officeholders (and jurists) to assert a more active, independent role in the determination of public policy. The business elite, however, failed to adjust to the new politics of pluralism and coalition building. This inability to move through the crossroads of the 1890s brought about the decisive defeat of the businessmen's "home rule" charter at the polls in 1907, completing the transformation of urban politics.

The Haymarket tragedy of May 1886 represented a decisive event in Chicago's political history. In the aftermath of the anarchist bombing and police crackdown, responsible leaders of every class and interest began to seek a middle ground where debate and compromise rather than violence could decide public issues. The return to the battleground of the ballot box in the city triggered a basic redefinition of partisan loyalties that gradually spread throughout the state. The Panic of 1893 and the trauma of the great strike at Pullman by Eugene Debs's railroad workers further accelerated this process of partisan realignment. Old loyalties faded, and a new generation of ward-centered politicians in both parties engaged in a fierce rivalry to win the allegiance of the city's swelling number of ethnic and working-class voters.[39] After 1893, Chicago's elected officials could afford to pay less deference to its civic elite, forcing it back into the public arena of local politics to achieve approval for its unfinished reform agenda.

The origins of urban progressivism in Chicago can be traced to the legacy of reform established by the mugwumps during the Gilded Age. Perhaps the most important aspect of their achievement was simply to keep the post-Appomattox tradition of constitutional adequacy alive during a conservative era of laissez-faire. The Citizens' Association provided undeniable proof that positive use of government was effective in ameliorating urban problems and promoting the improvement of society. The following generation of progressives incorporated the best features of the Lincoln ideal and made original contributions of their own.[40]

The new breed of urban progressives also adopted the tactics of reform pioneered by the Citizens' Association. The group's campaign to purify the ballot box in the mid-1880s furnishes a good example of the evolution of this legacy from one period to the next. Drafted by the Citizens' Association, the election commission bill attracted the support of several other elite groups, including the Union League (Republican) and the Iroquois (Democratic), Union Veterans, Young Men's Republican, and Commercial clubs. Representing an early form of coalition building around a specific issue, the election reform campaign also produced a new umbrella organization devoted exclusively to a single cause, the Non-Partisan League. The formation in 1891 of a similar organization, the Ballot Reform League, and then two years later the far more influential Municipal Voters' League, were simply logical extensions of the mugwumps' lobbying techniques. Other organized groups soon adopted the same highly effective tactics of reform.[41] The organizational impulse meant that more and more special interest groups not only began to define their own reform agendas but also to sustain their lobbying efforts over extended periods.[42]

The Citizens' Association's unfinished agenda of reform issues was another important legacy of the Gilded Age that helped give direction to the course of urban progressivism. Although the association had accumulated an impressive record of achievement by the late 1880s, its success was neither complete nor final. In 1887, for example, the reformers uncovered a new source of corruption, public utility franchise seekers. The Citizens' Association sued the recently formed Gas Trust as an illegal monopoly. This dramatic move helped transform the issue of corruption and graft from a traditionally narrow concern of the taxpayers into a popular crusade against the utility barons and the "boodlers." The question of public utility franchises eventually became the first common cause in Chicago to unify a broad spectrum of the city's social, ethnic, and class groups behind a single issue. Heartened by the groundswell of support for its prosecution of the Gas Trust, the Citizens' Association assumed that it would have little trouble achieving a similar consensus in favor of other unfinished items on its agenda, especially a consolidated charter of metropolitan government.[43]

In many respects the period from 1889 to 1892 represents the high-water mark of influence for Chicago's elite reformers in the formation of public policy. During these pivotal years they scored major victories in the Gas Trust case, the creation of the metropolitan sanitary district, and the adoption of the secret ballot. In addition, the Citizens' Association lobby helped secure passage of an annexation law that expanded the size of the city from 35 to 178 square miles, added 220,000 mostly middle-class suburbanites to the electorate, and made Chicago the "Second City" in the 1890 national census. Riding the crest of these accomplishments, a united business community swept competitors aside in the race among American cities to win the prize as the site of a world's fair. In the 1891 city polls, the elevation of a Republican bluestocking, Hempstead Washburne, to the mayor's office over Carter Harrison seemed to cap the businessmen's long struggle to vindicate their brand of municipal reform. Now, the attainment of their last outstanding agenda item, a centralized charter of city government, also seemed within reach.[44]

But in a paradoxical fashion, the mounting success of the Citizens' Association lobby undermined any further advance toward this perennial goal of structural reform. The emergence of many other organized centers of power was creating a new politics of sharp competition among lobbyists in the legislature and the courts as well as at the polls. The rise of this "new citizenship," as David Thelen has called it, fueled a general political realignment, especially as partisan loyalties from the Civil War era waned in the late 1880s. During the transitional period of the 1890s, ward-centered politicians from the Republican party matched the efforts of their Democratic counterparts to capture the allegiance of the city's ethnic voters. In part, then, Washburne owed his victory to these ward heelers and their budding "machine." A year later, in 1892, a reinvigorated Democratic party scored an analogous victory by electing John Peter Altgeld, their first candidate since the Civil War to reach the governor's mansion. And in Chicago the party gave Carter Harrison the mayor's office the following year. It was a fitting last hurrah for the old master of ethnic accommodation during the celebration of the World Columbian Exposition. At the crossroads of the 1890s, party politics in the city became more competitive and inclusive, involving a broad cross-section of urban society in an intense public debate over specific issues.[45]

Chicago's civic elite appears to have failed to adapt to the changing course of urban politics. Perhaps its string of major victories during the predepression years created a false sense of confidence. Or perhaps the overwhelming success of the world's fair reinforced the illusion that Chicago's business leadership could impose a plan of government on the city's people in the same way that it had dictated the management of the fair—without inviting the participation of the city's politicians. Between 1889 and 1905 the reformers patiently scaled one state constitutional hurdle after the other in their pursuit of a "home rule" charter for Chicago.

But closer to home, the business elite stumbled when it badly misjudged the size and strength of the city's organized labor, ethnic, and women's groups. They correctly surmised that the proposed charter shifted power from the popularly elected council of thirty-five aldermen to a small number of administrators appointed by the mayor. Indeed, the elitist intent of the structural reform package to centralize power in the hands of the executive seemed confirmed by the virtual exclusion of labor, ethnic, and women's groups from the charter-writing convention. In addition to fears that the reform proposal would allow prohibition to be imposed by the state, they called for more, not less, direct democracy, including grassroots control over public education, utility franchises, and the extension of suffrage to women.[46]

Typical of the new politics, an organization called the United Societies for Local Self-Government arose to bring hundreds of ethnic and religious groups together under a banner of self-determination and personal liberty. Led by an astute and ambitious Bohemian immigrant, Anton Cermak, the United Societies proved to be a formidable political opposition. In 1907 Cermak and other leaders of the anticharter coalition handed the businessmen a stunning defeat when their proposal was rejected by more than a two-to-one margin in a crucial referendum vote.[47]

In defeating the businessmen's plan, Chicagoans expressed a preference for the traditional American values that enshrined ideals of a tolerant, pluralistic society. Chicago remained a "city on the make" with a vibrant political culture of anarchistic democracy. Although the Citizens' Association quickly became moribund after 1907, other businessmen's groups continued in its footsteps as nonpartisan special interest lobbies. Just two years later, in fact, the Commercial Club unveiled Daniel Burnham's Plan of

Chicago, a remarkable by-product of the mugwump legacy of environmental engineering. Yet neither the ward politicians nor their working-class constituencies would allow any single group to dominate the process of public policy formation. Chicago's unreformed, "hydra-headed system . . . of government" helped to ensure that political power would remain close to the grass roots. The question of who ruled and whose vision of the coming city ought to prevail remained hotly contested for another quarter century.[48]

NOTES

1. Hempstead Washburne, "Mayor's Annual Message," City of Chicago, *Municipal Report* (1892), xxx–xxxii, for the quotation; and Bessie Louise Pierce, *A History of Chicago,* 3 vols. (Chicago: University of Chicago Press, 1957), 3:360, for Washburne's background.

2. See Samuel Edwin Sparling, *Municipal History and Present Organization of the City of Chicago,* University of Wisconsin Series in Political Science and History, series 2, no. 2, bulletin 23 (Madison: University of Wisconsin, 1908); Charles Merriam, *Report of an Investigation of the Municipal Revenues of Chicago* (Chicago: City Club of Chicago, 1906); and Illinois, Legislative Reference Bureau, "Local Government in Chicago and Cook County," *Constitutional Convention Bulletin* 11 (Springfield: Legislative Reference Bureau, 1920), 933, 1014–15.

3. James Bryce, *The American Commonwealth,* 2d rev. ed., 2 vols. (London and New York: Macmillan, 1891), 1:608.

4. Geoffrey Bloggett, "The Mugwump Reputation, 1870 to the Present," *Journal of American History* 66 (March 1980):876, for the quotation.

5. Jon C. Teaford, *The Unheralded Triumph—City Government in America, 1870–1900* (Baltimore, Md.: Johns Hopkins University Press, 1984), 10, for the quotation.

6. In recent years the work of the "new" political history has made a major contribution to a better understanding of city politics during the Gilded Age. See the assessment by Richard Oestreicher, "Urban Working-Class Political Behavior and Theories of American Electoral Politics, 1870–1940," *Journal of American History* 74 (March 1988): 1257–86. In the case of Chicago, an able group of labor historians is revising more traditional interpretations. For an introduction to this important work see Richard Schneirov, "Class Conflict, Municipal Politics, and Governmental Reform in Gilded Age Chicago, 1871–1875," in *German Workers in Industrial Chicago, 1850–1910: A Comparative Perspective,* ed. Hartmut Keil and John B. Jentz (DeKalb: Northern Illinois University Press, 1983), 183–205; and John B. Jentz, "Class and Politics in Gilded Age Chicago, 1869–1875" (Paper presented to the annual meeting of the Social Science History Association, 1988).

7. Harold M. Hyman, *A More Perfect Union—The Impact of Civil War and Reconstruction on the Constitution* (New York: Alfred A. Knopf, 1973).

8. Ibid., 326–46.

9. Morton Keller, *Affairs of State—Public Life in Late Nineteenth Century America* (Cambridge, Mass.: Harvard University Press, 1977), 122–97. Also see Michael Les Benedict, "Preserving the Constitution: The Conservative Basis of Radical Reconstruction," *Journal of American History* 61 (June 1974): 65–90; Charles W. McCurdy, "Justice Field and the Jurisprudence of Government-Business Relations: Some Parameters of Laissez-Faire Constitutionalism, 1863–1897," *Journal of American History* 61 (March 1975): 970–1005; and Alan Jones, "Thomas M. Cooley and 'Laissez-Faire Constitutionalism': A Reconsideration," *Journal of American History* 53 (March 1967): 751–71.

10. Keller, *Affairs of State*, 330–38.

11. See Henry Binford, "The Civil War Experience and the Management of American Cities" (Paul Angle Lecture, Chicago Historical Society, February 1981). For a narrative history with statistical data, see Pierce, *History of Chicago*, vol. 3, passim.

12. Nelson Algren, *Chicago: City on the Make* (New York: Doubleday, 1951). Native-born city boosters had naturally assumed the early leadership during the 1830s and 1840s, but a vibrant form of city politics emerged in the 1850s that was characterized by ethnocultural conflict and sharp class struggles for control of city hall. The Lager Beer Riot of 1856, for example, went far beyond a protest by the Germans and Irish against a nativist ordinance and into the realm of class warfare. The pitched battle in front of the courthouse represented a revolt against a highly segmented structure of local government that favored downtown real estate developers at the expense of the residents of the neighborhoods. Virtually powerless to express their interests through legitimate channels, the immigrants took to the streets to demand a role in the formation of public policy. The coming of the Civil War led Chicagoans to resolve this particular conflict by drawing new ward boundaries along neighborhood lines, but ethnic and class tensions resurfaced almost immediately after the war ended. For a brilliant analysis of the beer riots see Robin Einhorn, "The Lager Beer Riot and Segmented Government: Chicago 1855" (paper presented to the annual meeting of the Social Science History Association, 1987). For a description of the riots see Richard Wilson Renner, "In a Perfect Ferment: Chicago, the Know-Nothings and the Riot for Lager Beer," *Chicago History* 5 (Fall 1976): 161–70. The influence of ethnicity and class in the formation of Chicago's political culture is explored in Bruce Levine, "Free Soil, Free Labor, and Freimanner: German Chicago in the Civil War Era," in Keil and Jentz, eds., *German Workers*, 163–82; and Michael F. Funchion, "Irish Chicago: Church, Homeland, Politics, and Class—The Shaping of an Ethnic Group, 1870–1900," in *Ethnic Chicago*, ed. Melvin C. Holli and Peter d'A. Jones (Grand Rapids, Mich.: Eerdmans, 1981), 8–39. The weak bonds of loyalty to the two major parties in contrast to

powerful ethnocultural and class allegiance is evaluated in Stephen L. Hansen, *The Making of the Third Party System—Voters and Parties in Illinois, 1850–1876* (Ann Arbor, Mich.: UMI Research, 1980). On the growth of the city and its social structure, see William J. Cronon, "To Be the Central City, Chicago, 1848–1858," *Chicago History* 10 (Fall 1981): 130–40; and Frederic Jaher, *The Urban Establishment: Upper Strata in Boston, New York, Charleston, Chicago, and Los Angeles* (Urbana: University of Illinois Press, 1982), 453–577. Cf. Kathleen Niels Conzen, *Immigrant Milwaukee 1836–1860: Accommodation and Community in a Frontier City* (Cambridge, Mass.: Harvard University Press, 1976).

13. Louise Carroll Wade, *Chicago's Pride: The Stockyards, Packingtown, and Environs in the Nineteenth Century* (Urbana: University of Illinois Press, 1987), 25–57.

14. Illinois, *Special Laws of Illinois* (1869), 4 vols. 1:342–79. Also see Glen E. Holt, "Private Plans for Public Spaces: The Origins of Chicago's Park System, 1850–1875," *Chicago History* 8 (Fall 1979): 173–84. For early models of special-purpose tax districts in Illinois see James E. Herget, "Taming the Environment: The Drainage District in Illinois," *Journal of the Illinois State Historical Society* 71 (May 1978): 107–18. For a historical compilation of Chicago park laws see William H. Beckman, comp., *Laws and Ordinances Concerning Lincoln Park: Annotated* (Chicago: Commissioners of Lincoln Park, 1928).

15. Holt, "Private Plans," 173–84; F. Garvin Davenport, "John Henry Rauch and Public Health in Illinois, 1877–1891," *Journal of the Illinois State Historical Society* 50 (Autumn 1957): 277–93; Wade, *Chicago's Pride*, 132–38; Pierce, *History of Chicago*, 3:314–22; and Michael P. McCarthy, "Businessmen and Professionals in Municipal Reform: The Chicago Experience, 1877–1920" (Ph.D. diss., Northwestern University, 1970), 82–99. Cf. George M. Fredrickson, *The Inner Civil War—Northern Intellectuals and the Crisis of the Union* (New York: Harper and Row, 1965), 98–112.

16. Illinois, *Special Laws*, passim; Illinois, Legislative Reference Bureau, "Municipal Home Rule," *Constitutional Convention Bulletin* 6 (Springfield, Legislative Reference Bureau, 1920), 377–78; and Janet Cornelius, *Constitution Making in Illinois, 1818–1970* (Urbana: University of Illinois Press, 1972), 56–60, for a review of the political origins of the 1870 state constitutional convention.

17. Jonathan Merriam (Tazwell County), quoted in Illinois, *Debates and Proceedings of the Constitutional Convention of the State of Illinois*, 2 vols. (Springfield: Merritt, 1870), 1:576. For broader perspectives see Morton Keller, "The Politics of State Constitutional Revision, 1820–1930," in *The Constitutional Convention as an Amending Device*, ed. Kermit Hall, Harold M. Hyman, and Leon V. Sigal (Washington, D.C.: American Historical Association and American Political Science Association, 1981), 74–83.

18. Illinois, *Debates and Proceedings*, 492–95; Illinois Constitution (1870), Art. 4, sec. 22. For a history of this section in the courts, see George D. Braden and

Rubin G. Cohn, *The Illinois Constitution: An Annotated and Comparative Analysis* (Urbana: University of Illinois Press, 1969), 203–15.

19. Illinois, *Debates and Proceedings*, 1:179, for the quotation. The question of public aid to railroads was indeed a troublesome problem in the postwar period. See George H. Miller, *Railroads and the Granger Laws* (Madison: University of Wisconsin Press, 1971); Charles Fairman, *Reconstruction and Reunion, 1864–1888*, 2 vols. (New York: Macmillan, 1971–87), 1:918–1116; U.S. Census Office, *Report on the Valuation, Taxation and Public Indebtedness in the United States, as Returned at the Tenth Census* (Washington, D.C.: Government Printing Office, 1884); and A. M. Hillhouse, *Municipal Bonds—A Century of Experience* (New York: Prentice-Hall, 1936).

20. John C. Haines (Cook County), as quoted in Illinois, *Debates and Proceedings*, 2:1672; Illinois Constitution (1870), Art. 9, sec. 12, and Art. 14, for provisions on local indebtedness and constitutional amendment procedures, respectively. Also see Braden, *Illinois Constitution*, 478–88.

21. Illinois, *Debates and Proceedings*, 2:1622–37, passim; and see note 19 above. Illinois does not fit the model of urban-rural conflict. Cf. Clifton K. Yearley, "The 'Provincial Party' and the Megalopolises: London, Paris, and New York, 1850–1910," *Comparative Studies in Society and History* 15 (January 1973): 51–88.

22. Henry Sherrill (Kendall County), as quoted in Illinois, *Debates and Proceedings*, 2:1624, 1622–37; Charles Fairman, "The So-Called Granger Cases, Lord Hale, and Justice Bradley," *Stanford Law Review* 5 (1953): 587–611.

23. See Illinois, *Debates and Proceedings*, 1:583–97, for the debate over classification systems for the city. For the special provisions, see Illinois Constitution (1870), Art. 6, secs. 13, 20, 23, 28, and Art. 10, sec. 7. Cook County approved the proposed constitution by a vote of 22,239 to 341. The voters also approved the regulatory commission by a margin of 21,236 to 1,122. See Illinois, *Debates and Proceedings*, 2:1894–95. On Medill, see David L. Protess, "Joseph Medill: Chicago's First Modern Mayor," in *The Mayors—The Chicago Political Tradition*, ed. Paul M. Green and Melvin G. Holli (Carbondale: Southern Illinois University Press, 1987), 1–15. For a review of the state courts' rulings on legislation incorporating a population classification scheme, see Albert Kales, "Special Legislation as Defined in the Illinois Cases," *Illinois Law Review* 1 (June 1906): 63–80.

24. *South Park Commissioners v. Cook County Clerk*, 51 Ill. 37 (1869), for the quotation; also see *Commissioners of Lincoln Park v. Mayor of Chicago*, 51 Ill. 17; Pierce, *History of Chicago*, 2:338–53, 3:314–39. The city government also employed an elaborate system of special assessment taxes to pay for street improvements. For insight on the links between municipal finance and city politics see Clifton K. Yearley, *The Money Machines: The Breakdown and Reform of Governmental and Party Finance in the North, 1860–1920* (Albany: State University of New York Press, 1970). For the operation of the special assessment system in Chicago in the 1870s see Christine Meisner Rosen, *The Limits of Power: Great Fires*

and the *Process of City Growth in America* (New York: Cambridge University Press, 1986), 125–27.

25. Rosen, *Limits of Power*, 147–218. Rosen's study of the rebuilding of Chicago after the fire is an ingenious and important contribution to the history of law and politics in American cities. For the viewpoint of the new labor history see Schneirov, "Class Conflict," 183–88; and Jentz, "Class and Politics." Also see Pierce, *History of Chicago*, 3:300–3; and Protess, "Medill," 1–5.

26. Illinois, *Laws of the State of Illinois* (1871–1874), passim; Protess, "Medill," 1–15; A[lfred] T[heodore] Andreas, *History of Chicago*, 3 vols. (1884–86; reprint, New York: Arno Press, 1975), 3:833–46, 854–63. The "Mayor's bill" was enacted as a temporary, emergency measure. In 1875 the city rejected a modified permanent version of this municipal charter in favor of the general incorporation act of 1872, which placed most policy-making power in the hands of the city council.

27. Jentz, "Class and Politics"; Rosen, *Limits of Power*, 95–109; and Christiane Harzig, "Chicago's German North Side, 1880–1900: The Structure of a Gilded Age Ethnic Neighborhood," in Keil and Jentz, eds., *German Workers*, 127–44. Cf. Einhorn, "Lager Beer Riot," as a precedent in Chicago for direct action when the normal channels of legitimate politics seemed closed.

28. Franklin MacVeagh, as quoted in Schneirov, "Class Conflict," 183; ibid., 183–205; and the sources listed in note 25 above.

29. For an early description of the association's reform methods see Citizens' Association, *Annual Report* (Chicago: Hazlett and Reed, 1877), 3–7. On the origins of this group, also consider Donald D. Marks, "Polishing the Gem of the Prairies: The Evolution of Civic Reform Consciousness in Chicago, 1874–1900" (Ph.D. diss., University of Wisconsin, 1974), 58–84. A more detailed description of the reform process follows.

30. On the evolution of radical politics in Chicago leading to the Haymarket event, see Paul Avrich, *The Haymarket Tragedy* (Princeton, N.J.: Princeton University Press, 1984); Christine Heiss, "German Radicals in Industrial America: The Lehr- und Wehr-Verein in Gilded Age Chicago," in Keil and Jentz, eds., *German Workers*, 206–33; Bruce C. Nelson, "Anarchism: The Movement behind the Martyrs," *Chicago History* 15 (Summer 1986): 4–19; Carl S. Smith, "Cataclysm and Cultural Consciousness: Chicago and the Haymarket Trail," *Chicago History* 15 (Summer 1986): 36–53. On Harrison see Willis John Abbot, *Carter Henry Harrison: A Memoir* (New York: Dodd, Mead, 1895), 93–154, 190–216; Claudius O. Johnson, *Carter Henry Harrison I: Political Leader* (Chicago: University of Chicago Press, 1928); Pierce, *History of Chicago*, 3:351–80; Michael L. Ahern, *The Political History of Chicago, 1837–1887* (Chicago: Donohue and Henneberry, 1886), 86, 99–101; and Edward R. Kantowicz, "Carter H. Harrison II: The Politics of Balance," in Green and Holli, eds., *The Mayors*, 16–21.

31. Citizens' Association, *Annual Report of 1879*, 10, for the quotation; ibid., (1876–99), passim. For a brilliant analysis of the Illinois legislature in the Gilded

Age see Ballard C. Campbell, *Representative Democracy: Public Policy and Mid-western Legislatures in the Late Nineteenth Century* (Cambridge, Mass.: Harvard University Press, 1980). Also consider Hansen, *Third Party System*, 157–99. See Teaford, *Unheralded Triumph*, 87, on the Cook County delegation's domination of the house's committee on the cities, and cf. 83–103, on legislative deference to large cities in other states.

32. A. M. Pence, "New Election Law" [letter], *Chicago Legal News* 18 (October 17, 1885): 50–51, for the quotation; *Chicago Legal News* 17 (January 3, 1885): 140, (January 10, 1885): 145; Citizens' Association, *Annual Report* (1884), 13, for the phrase "hideous vortex," also 13–14; Ahern, *Political History*, 41–68; Pierce, *History of Chicago*, 3:358–59.

33. Illinois, *Laws of the State of Illinois* (1885), 194, for the quotation, and 138–96, for the complete text of the three laws; "The New Election Law," *Chicago Legal News* 17 (July 18, 1885): 379; Pence, "New Election Law"; Citizens' Association, *Annual Report* (1885), 3–6. The Election Commission bill was enacted as an optional law for the cities. Chicagoans adopted the reform remedy by a vote of 32,000 to 15,000 in a referendum. On the referendum and subsequent court test of the law see Ahern, *Political History*, 41, and *State's Attorney v. Hoffman*, 116 Ill. 587 (1886), respectively.

34. *State's Attorney v. Hoffman; Chicago Tribune*, October 24, 1886, for the quotation; Citizens' Association, *Annual Report* (1885), 3–5. For the background to the test case see the *Chicago Legal News* 17 (July–September 1885): 379, 427; and 18 (October 1885–May 1886): 50–54, 187, 286. For the prosecution of vote fraud see *Chicago Legal News* 21 (April 13, 1889): 281; and Ahern, *Political History*, 47–68, which lists the names of the first group of poll watchers. Also see *Chicago Tribune*, December 5, 1885, January 6, 29, 1886, October 24, 1886.

35. Edwin Lee Brown, as quoted in Citizens' Association, *Annual Report* (1885), 31, also 3–6, 9–11.

36. "Reform the Election Laws," *Chicago Legal News* 23 (January 31, 1891): 185; Pierce, *History of Chicago*, 3:369. This reform initiative was led by Judge Tuley, who also organized the Chicago Ballot Reform League as an umbrella organization similar to the Non-Partisan League. Both groups were aimed at building winning political coalitions behind a single issue.

37. *Chicago Times*, June 22, 1880, as quoted in Pierce, *History of Chicago*, 3:311, also 311–13, 321–22; Citizens' Association, *Annual Report* (1876–1880), passim. Also see Wade, *Chicago's Pride*, 130–43, 313–21; and Louis P. Cain, "The Search for an Optimum Sanitation Jurisdiction: The Metropolitan Sanitary District of Greater Chicago, A Case Study," *Essays in Public Works History*, no. 10 (Chicago: Public Works Historical Society, 1980).

38. Citizens' Association, *Annual Report* (1885), 14, for the quotation; *Annual Report* (1880–1890), passim; Pierce, *History of Chicago*, 3:309–13; Louis P. Cain,

"The Creation of Chicago's Sanitary District and Construction of the Sanitary and Ship Canal," *Chicago History* 8 (Summer 1979): 98–111.

39. See Jane Addams, *Twenty Years at Hull House* (1910; New York: New American Library, 1961), 133–47; Ahern, *Political History*, 73–81, for the labor parties' platforms in 1886; Abbot, *Carter Harrison*, 140–52; and the sources listed in note 30 above for perspectives on the Haymarket tragedy. Also see Richard Jensen, *The Winning of the Midwest—Social and Political Conflict, 1886–1896* (Chicago: University of Chicago Press, 1971), chap. 6; and Campbell, *Representative Democracy*, chap. 1, on the process of partisan realignment.

40. On the origins of progressivism see the review essay by Daniel T. Rogers, "In Search of Progressivism," *Reviews in American History* 10 (December 1982): 113–32.

41. Pierce, *History of Chicago*, 3:360–70; Sidney Roberts, "The Municipal Voters' League and Chicago's Boodlers," *Journal of the Illinois State Historical Society* 53 (Summer 1960): 117–48; Ahern, *Political History*, 73–81. On the growth of diverse centers of power in the late nineteenth-century city see David C. Hammack, *Power and Society: Greater New York at the Turn of the Century* (New York: Russell Sage Foundation, 1982). On the transformation of the Republican party in Chicago see Joel A. Tarr, *A Study in Boss Politics: William A. Lorimer of Chicago* (Urbana: University of Illinois Press, 1971); and Maureen A. Flanagan, "Fred A. Busse: A Silent Mayor in Turbulent Times," in Green and Holli, eds., *The Mayors*, 50–60.

42. Samuel P. Hays, *The Response to Industrialism, 1885–1914* (Chicago: University of Chicago Press, 1957), 48–115; and Hays, "Introduction: The New Organizational Society," in *Building the Organizational Society—Essays on Associational Activities in Modern America*, ed. Jerry Israel (New York: Free Press, 1972), 1–15.

43. Citizens' Association, *Annual Report* (1886), 23–29; ibid. (1887), 43–47; ibid. (1888), 8–13; Pierce, *History of Chicago*, 3:221–28, 361–63. For the "confessions" of the first president of the Gas Trust see Norman C. Fay, "Plain Tales from Chicago," *Outlook* (March 1909): 547–52. For the most complete history of the trust see Illinois, Bureau of Labor Statistics, *Ninth Biennial Report—1896, Franchises and Taxation*, 239–320. For insight on the role of the public utility franchise issue in creating a new politics in Chicago, see Sidney I. Roberts, "Portrait of a Robber Baron: Charles T. Yerkes," *Business History Review* 35 (1961): 344–71; and David P. Nord, *Newspapers and New Politics: Midwestern Municipal Reform, 1890–1900* (Ann Arbor, Mich.: UMI Research, 1981).

44. On the political implications of the great annexation of 1889 see Michael P. McCarthy, "Chicago, the Annexation Movement, and Progressive Reform," in *The Age of Urban Reform: New Perspectives on the Progressive Age*, ed. Michael H. Ebner and Eugene M. Tobin (New York: Kennikat, 1977), 43–54. On the world's

fair see David F. Burg, *Chicago's White City of 1893* (Lexington: University Press of Kentucky, 1976); and Robert D. Parmet and Francis L. Lederer II, "Competition for the World's Columbian Exposition: The New York Campaign and the Chicago Campaign," *Journal of the Illinois State Historical Society* 65 (Winter 1972): 364–94.

45. David P. Thelen, *The New Citizenship: Origins of Progressivism in Wisconsin, 1885–1900* (Columbia: University of Missouri Press, 1972). On new directions in Chicago see Ray Ginger, *Altgeld's America: The Lincoln Ideal versus Changing Realities* (New York: Funk and Wagnalls, 1958); and Jensen, *Winning the Midwest.*

46. Maureen A. Flanagan, *Charter Reform in Chicago* (Carbondale: Southern Illinois University Press, 1987), 64–109.

47. Ibid., 110–60.

48. See John M. Allswang, *A House for All Peoples: Ethnic Politics in Chicago, 1890–1936* (Lexington: University Press of Kentucky, 1971); and Paul M. Green, "Anton J. Cermak: The Man and His Machine," in Green and Holli, eds., *The Mayors,* 99–110.

Contributors

NORMA BASCH is associate professor of history at Rutgers University. She is the author of *Women and the Law of Property in Nineteenth Century New York* (1982) and a study of nineteenth-century divorce law. Her articles have appeared in *The Journal of the Early Republic, Feminist Studies,* and *Law and History Review.* She has held fellowships from the National Endowment for the Humanities, the American Council of Learned Societies, and the American Antiquarian Society.

MICHAEL LES BENEDICT is professor of history at Ohio State University and author of *The Impeachment and Trial of Andrew Johnson* (1973), *A Compromise of Principle: Congressional Republicans and Reconstruction* (1974), *Civil Rights and Civil Liberties in American History* (1987), as well as articles in the *American Historical Review, Journal of American History, Political Science Quarterly, Supreme Court Review, Journal of Southern History,* and *Law and History Review.* He has held fellowships from the Institute for Advanced Studies at Princeton, the National Endowment for the Humanities, the Woodrow Wilson International Center for Scholars, the American Council of Learned Societies, and the John Simon Guggenheim

Foundation, and has been a Senior Fulbright Lecturer in Japan. During the 1990–91 academic year he was visiting professor of law at Yale University School of Law.

DAVID T. COURTWRIGHT is chair of the Department of History at the University of North Florida. He is the author of *Dark Paradise: Opiate Addiction in America before 1940* (1982), *American Addicts in the Classic Period of Narcotic Control* (1989), and articles in the *Journal of Southern History, Civil War History,* and the *Journal of Drug Issues.* He has held fellowships from the National Endowment for the Humanities and the Samuel Ziegler Education Fund, and has been a Mellon Fellow at Yale University.

PAUL FINKELMAN is visiting professor of law at the Brooklyn Law School. He is the author of *An Imperfect Union: Slavery, Federalism, and Comity* (1981), and has edited *Slavery in the Courtroom* (1985), *Slavery, Race, and the American Legal System* (1988), and *Law, the Constitution, and Slavery* (1989). His articles have appeared in *The Supreme Court Review, Civil War History, Journal of Southern History, Southern Studies,* and *Rutgers-Camden Law Journal.*

JOHN S. HUGHES is assistant professor of history at the University of Texas at Austin. He is the author of *In the Law's Darkness: Isaac Ray and the Jurisprudence of Insanity in Nineteenth Century America* (1986) and articles in the *International Journal of Law and Psychiatry, Missouri Historical Review,* and a collection of essays entitled *Masculinity Studies.* He has held a fellowship from the National Endowment for the Humanities and has been a Golieb Fellow at the New York University School of Law and a Bankhead Fellow in American History at the University of Alabama.

DONALD G. NIEMAN is professor of history at Clemson University. He is the author of *To Set the Law in Motion: The Freedmen's Bureau and the Legal Rights of Blacks* (1979) and *Promises to Keep: African-Americans and the Constitutional Order, 1776–1990* (1991). His articles have appeared in the *Journal of Southern History, Journal of Mississippi History, Encyclopedia of Southern History,* and a collection of essays entitled *An Uncertain Tradition: The South and the Constitution.* He has held fellowships from the American Bar Association, the American Association for State and Local History, and the American Historical Association, and has been a Senior Golieb Fellow at the New York University School of Law. During the 1990–91 academic year he served

as the Daniel M. Lyons Professor of American History at Brooklyn College, City University of New York.

PHILLIP SHAW PALUDAN is professor of history at the University of Kansas. He is the author of *A Covenant with Death: The Civil War and the Constitution* (1974), *Victims* (1980), and *A People's Contest: The North during the Civil War* (1989), in Harper and Row's New American Nation Series. His articles have appeared in the *American Journal of Legal History, American Historical Review, Journal of the History of Ideas,* and *Civil War History.* He has held fellowships from the American Council of Learned Societies and the John Simon Guggenheim Foundation.

HAROLD L. PLATT is professor of history at Loyola University, Chicago. He is the author of *City Building in the New South* (1983) and *The Electric City: Energy and the Growth of the Chicago Area, 1880–1930* (1991). He has published articles in *Journal of the West, Houston Review, Les annales de la recherche urbaine,* and two collections of essays: *The Age of Urban Reform* and *Proceedings of the International Conference on the City and Technology.* He has held fellowships from the Mellon Foundation, the American Historical Association, and the Southwest Center for Urban Research.

Index